Bitter Legacy

Contemporary Issues in the Middle East

PAUL SALEM

Bitter Legacy
Ideology and Politics in the Arab World

Syracuse University Press

Copyright © 1994 by Syracuse University Press, Syracuse, New
York 13244–5160

All Rights Reserved

First Edition 1994
94 95 96 97 98 99   6 5 4 3 2 1

The paper used in this publication meets the minimum
requirements of American National Standard for Information
Sciences—Permanence of Paper for Printed Library Materials,
ANSI Z39.48-1984. ∞™

Library of Congress Cataloging-in-Publication Data
Salem, Paul.
    Bitter legacy:ideology and politics in the Arab World/Paul
Salem.
        p. cm. — (Contemporary issues in the Middle East)
    Includes bibliographical references and index.
    ISBN 0-8156-2628-2. — ISBN 0-8156-2629-0 (pbk.)
    1. Arab countries—Politics and government—1945- 2. Ide-
ology—Arab countries. 3. Political science—Arab countries—
History—20th century. I. Title. II. Series.
DS63.1.S255 1994
320.917'4927—dc20   94-6775

Manufactured in the United States of America

Contents

Paul Salem teaches political studies at the
American University of Beirut.

Preface

I present here a critical and comparative analysis of the various ideological movements that arose in the Arab world after the collapse of the Ottoman Empire. I devote separate chapters to Arab nationalism, Islamic fundamentalism, Marxist movements, and regional nationalism and examine the nature of ideology, its relationship to sociological and psychological factors, and its influence on political life. Although many of these topics have been dealt with before, a comprehensive comparative approach has rarely been attempted.

The shortcoming of current scholarship on Arab ideology centers on several problem areas. First, scholars tend to treat each ideological movement separately; numerous studies exist that concentrate exclusively on Arab nationalism, the Islamic movements, or Marxism in the Arab world. Although this approach allows more focus and the inclusion of more detail, it loses sight of the larger arena in which ideologies operate and ignores the process by which "ideologies overlap, compete and clash, drown or reinforce each other" (Therborn 1980, vii). Indeed, it is exactly in this dialectical process that ideologies should be examined and can best be understood.

Second, most analyses of these ideological movements rely on only one methodological approach. Textual analysis or chronological political narrative are among the most common. To gain a fuller understanding of an ideological movement, however, it is important to examine simultaneously other variables such as the movement's class roots, its appeal to different generations, its satisfaction of basic psychological needs, and so forth. A multidisciplinary approach is necessary because ideology occupies an intermediate position between the spheres of politics, religion, culture, and psychology, and understanding the part is impossible before one understands the whole.

Finally, a proclivity exists among scholars to regard Arab ideological movements as somehow sui generis. It is the habit of Western orientalism, for example, to regard Arabs or Muslims as somehow different from other peoples. Ironically, both Arab governments and Arab intellectuals favor this view. Governments encourage the idea to avoid comparisons with Western political systems, whereas most Arab intellectuals are more comfortable thinking of their societies as profoundly different from those of the West, rather than contemplate that both societies are, perhaps, on the same civilizational trajectory but that Arab society has much catching up to do. This latter and rather sober view was that of the principal Arab and Islamic reformers around the turn of the twentieth century, but it was soon overtaken by a wave of apologetic literature. Indeed, Westerners need to demythologize the Arab world to understand it and interact with it more productively, and Arab intellectuals need to turn a solemn eye on the sorry condition of Arab political life without worrying about the taunts they may receive from what they perceive as a menacing West. The critical review and analysis of the main ideological movements of the post-Ottoman Arab world offered here, may be a small contribution in that direction.

In chapter 1, I provide a theoretical and historical framework within which to understand the rise of ideologies and ideological movements in the modern Arab world. In chapters 2–5, I address Arab nationalism, Islamic fundamentalism, Marxism, and regional nationalism. In each chapter I provide a history of the movement, a close look at its ideology based on the work of one or two of its principal ideologues, and an analysis of the sociological and psychological variables that help explain its rise or its decline. In addition, I end each chapter with an assessment of the political and intellectual legacy left by that particular movement to contemporary Arab political life and political culture. In the last chapter, I examine areas of crisis within contemporary Arab political culture in light of the preceding chapters and contemplate the future of ideology in the Arab world.

No book is written in a vacuum. I would especially like to thank Professors Stanley Hoffmann (Harvard), Lisa Anderson (Columbia), and Philip Khoury (MIT) whose comments and guidance have been invaluable. I also owe a great debt to numerous colleagues and friends at Harvard and in Lebanon and Egypt who read parts of the manuscript and gave me the benefit of their experience and insight. Needless to say, the views expressed in this book and any faults or shortcomings are solely my responsibility.

Beirut   PAUL SALEM
November 1993

List of Abbreviations

ANM	Arab Nationalist movement
ASU	Arab Socialist Union
CPE	Communist party of Egypt
CPI	Communist party of Iraq
CPI—CC	Communist party of Iraq—Central Command
CPJ	Communist party of Jordan
CPP	Communist party of Palestine
CPS	Communist party of Syria
CPSL	Communist party of Syria and Lebanon
CPSU	Communist party of the Soviet Union
CUP	Committee of Union and Progress
DPK	Democratic party of Kurdistan
ILO	Islamic Liberation Organization
KUTV	Communist University of the Toilers of the East
LNL	League for National Liberation
MDLN	Mouvement Democratique de Liberation Nationale
MELN	Mouvement Egyptien de Liberation Nationale
NFLP	National Front for the Liberation of Palestine
PDFLP	Popular Democratic Front for the Liberation of Palestine
PFLP	Popular Front for the Liberation of Palestine

PFLP—GC	Popular Front for the Liberation of Palestine—General Command
PLO	Palestine Liberation Organization
PRF	People's Resistance Force
RCC	Revolutionary Command Council
SAIRI	Supreme Assembly of the Islamic Revolution in Iraq
SSNP	Syrian Social Nationalist party
UAR	United Arab Republic

Bitter Legacy

CHAPTER ONE

An Arab "Age of Ideology"

The Concept of Ideology

The term *ideology* has a nearly two-hundred year history. Although many political thinkers as far back as the ancient Greeks had discussed the role of beliefs and attitudes in politics, the term was coined in the late eighteenth century by the French philosopher Antoine Destutt de Tracy. But it was Karl Marx who, drawing on the grand philosophy of Hegel, pushed the concept of ideology to the forefront of intellectual and political discourse. Marx explained ideology as that false consciousness generated by a social group's particular position vis à vis the relations of production. Weber, Gramsci, Sorel, and others modified Marx's materialistic, deterministic view, arguing that ideology possessed an autonomous dynamic and, to a degree, produced its own subjects. "Above all, man is mind," insisted Gramsci, and, therefore, his behavior is deeply influenced by the ideological and cultural patterns that inform that mind (Bennett 1981, 194). Sorel, for his part, emphasized the autonomous role of myth (e.g., the myth of the general strike) in reinforcing class solidarity and, thereby, providing a basis for a moral system. Karl Mannheim, however, is perhaps the only thinker to develop a full-blown theory of ideology. He developed a sociology of knowledge, fusing the traditions of German historicism and Marxism. "The thought of all parties in all epochs is of an ideological character," he argued (Mannheim 1968, 69). It was part of human functional adaptation to the environment and, thus, varied with environmental conditions. In his principal work, *Ideology and Utopia* (1968), Mannheim distinguishes between that thought which evolves to defend the interests of privileged groups, which he calls ideological, and that which evolves to promote the interests of underprivileged groups, which he calls utopian. Both are distinguished from "true" knowledge, which is based on scientific criteria, but they are, nevertheless, the predominant modes of thought and cognition throughout history.

Indeed, ideology has been one of the most popular topics of debate in political science; nevertheless, it remains a somewhat confused one. In the words of M. Seliger, "Despite the numerous studies that deal inter alia or directly with ideology in the varied fields of human activity, no generally accepted definition of the term exists" (Seliger 1976, 5). There are several reasons for this. First, the West's experience with fascism, nazism, and communism injected a strong political current into the debate that has hindered clear and calm scholarship on the matter. Second, many social scientists, eager for hard material data, have shied away from trying to grapple with such slippery variables as beliefs, attitudes, and emotions. Robert Lane and political culture theorists such as Gabriel Almond, Sidney Verba, and Lucian Pye, among others, are, of course, important exceptions to this generalization. Still, the concept of ideology is used to denote different things by different authors.

I use a definition of ideology here that draws on several strains in the debate surrounding the term. Borrowing a concept from Daniel Bell (1960) and other participants in the notorious "end of ideology" debate, I try to show that we have been passing through an "age of ideology" in the Arab world resulting from the breakdown of traditional social and cultural systems. I argue that this age of ideology began around World War I with the collapse of the Ottoman empire, reached its apex in the 1950s after the loss of Palestine and the breakthrough of a new middle class into power, and began to recede in the 1970s after the relative consolidation of political and economic systems. My particular understanding of the nature of ideology, however, is drawn both from Marx and Gramsci. With Marx, I agree that ideology may be a system of ideas generated, consciously or unconsciously, by a class or group to protect and promote its own interests; in that sense, ideology is a tool or a weapon used by one group against another. With Gramsci, however, I also consider that ideology in some cases may have its own dynamic simply as the particular way in which a group of people, dominant or dominated, view the world, regardless of their interests. In this sense, ideology is simply a cultural or psychological bias independent of interest. Both concepts of the function of ideology are necessary to understand the full scope of its influence.

In any case, in my analysis, I employ a rather streamlined definition of the term: "Ideology is a system of highly integrated ideas, principles, and aims that are related to sociopolitical action." An ideology, therefore, must be systematic, in the sense that it must provide a coherent and cohesive framework. A "highly integrated" ideology simplifies a complex sociopolitical reality by explaining that reality through a few central beliefs or theories. For example, Marxists may reduce all social phenomena to a struggle between economic classes, nationalists may explain the same situation by reference to the struggle of racial or cultural groups, whereas Islamists may offer an explanation based on religious principles. In this sense, ideology, in contrast to good social science, necessarily involves oversimplification. This, of course, is one of the strengths of ideology, for this reductionism is often welcomed in a rapidly changing society in which the tools for a full appreciation of the complexities of a new situation have not yet been developed. The last part of the definition emphasizes that ideology, unlike most social science or philosophy, is not just a system of ideas and principles but a system of sociopolitical action as well. Ideology, to recall Marx's observation about philosophy, seeks not only to explain the world but, more importantly, to change it. Ideology, therefore, is inextricably intertwined with political parties and political movements.

Sociocultural Strain and the Spread of Ideology in the Arab World

The concept of an age of ideology that intervenes between a supposedly traditional religious age and the modern rational, scientific age, was central to the end of ideology debate. It has roots in theories of psychology, sociology, and politics that show the process of modernization to introduce a set of individual and social strains of which ideology is a symptom and for which it is often a palliative as well. As has been stated often, modernization is a process that involves urbanization, industrialization, specialization, the spread of mass media, the growth of a national economy and power structure, and so forth. This process, however, is neither harmonious nor smooth but is characterized by tension and dysfunction. Ideologies arise as a means of expressing the stress and frustrations of these times as well as a means of treating and gaining relief from them. This approach, which emphasizes the relationship between ideology and social strain is referred to as "strain theory" and provides perhaps the clearest alternative to traditional Marxist understandings of the role of ideologies.

As Edward Shils, one of the leading analysts in this field, explains, "Ideologies arise in conditions of crisis and in sectors of society to whom the hitherto prevailing outlook has become unacceptable. . . . [They arise to satisfy] strongly felt needs . . . for an explanation of important experience, for the firm guidance of conduct, and for a fundamental vindication or legitimation of the value and dignity of the persons who feel these needs" (Shils 1968, 69). Clifford Geertz agrees with this train of thought, arguing that formal ideologies play a most crucial role when a society is moving away from received traditions, customs, moralities, and so forth. (Geertz 1964, 64).

Without a doubt, Arab society has been subject to the general set of social, economic, and cultural strains to which all developing societies are subject. As have most third world countries, it has undergone the trauma of colonial domination, had to come to terms with the formation of new nation-states, and has been faced with the task of searching for new sources of identity to integrate previously separate tribal, racial, linguistic, or religious groups. Other factors, however, intensified the appetite for ideology in the Arab world. Most importantly, the central role of Islam in organizing traditional political and social life gave a strong transcendental meaning to worldly affairs. Consequently, in the secularization and differentiation that characterize modernization, the need for political and social values with transcendental authority was felt especially strongly in the Arab world. This response, no doubt, contributed to the power and centrality of ideological political thought. As Fouad Ajami put it, "The mix between theory and practice in Arab political culture is susceptible to a recurring belief in grand schemes and ready-made doctrines" (Ajami 1981, 34). More to the point, Shils located a predisposition to ideological worldviews in all "high cultures" with "intellectualized religions." "An intellectualized religion provides the precondition for the emergence of ideology, since the former contains explicit propositions about the nature of the sacred and its cultivation, which is what ideologies are about. The fact that an ideology already exists serves both to form an ideological tradition and to provide a medium in which ideological dispositions can be precipitated by emulation and self-differentiation" (Shils 1968, 69).

This ideological receptivity was awakened by the rapid pace of social, economic, political, and cultural change, which began to introduce considerable strain within the structure of traditional belief-systems around the turn of the twentieth century. The decisive collapse of the old worldview came with the disintegration of the Ottoman empire, the abolition of the caliphate, European occupation, and the rise of Arab and other nationalist movements. These crises, along with the general hardships and dislocations that accompanied the war itself, ushered in a period of questioning in the Arab world. What was the basis of political community? What constituted a nation? Did one owe primary political allegiance to one's religious group or one's ethnic, or even regional, community? What was the historical significance of the collapse of the Islamic state? What was the place of religion in politics? What was the role of secular principles in social ethics? What should Arab society's attitude toward the West be?

Events around World War II only added fuel to the fire. The exhaustion of Britain and France in the war and the collapse of their mandates in the Middle East brought independence to many new states in the region and added urgency to questions of social, economic, political, and cultural organization. The loss of Palestine to the Zionists in 1948 was the single most traumatic event of modern Arab political life and sent shock waves throughout the Arab world. Within a few years, the political regimes of Egypt, Syria, and Iraq were toppled, and others were faltering. New groups were coming to power, and with them they brought new outlooks, new interests, new values—in short, new ideologies.

The 1950s represent the heyday of ideology in the Arab world, a time when new "ideas, principles, and aims" seemed to promise power, progress, and prosperity. The world was reduced to an idea, and the idea to a word, and the words arranged by inspired ideologues and orators to paint a dazzling portrait of an Arab utopia. The vision lost its lustre, however, after the disintegration of Egyptian-Syrian unity in 1961, the stunning defeat of Arab armies in 1967, and the death of Nasir in 1970. The limited victories of the 1973 war and the dramatic oil price rises that accompanied it set the stage for a new phase of more pragmatic, conservative, and less-ideological politics in the Arab world.

The above is a fairly conventional reading of the dynamics of ideological politics based primarily on particular political events and crises. It is impossible, however, to comprehend fully the reasons for the rise of ideological movements or the rise and decline of particular ideological movements at specific moments without a much more sweeping view of the nature of social, economic, political, and cultural change during this period and a working understanding of the dynamics of class, ethnic, and generational conflict at play there. What was the nature of social, economic, political, and cultural change that has wrought havoc within the modern Arab world? How did such rapid change impinge on the life and outlook of the individual? Finally, what was the relationship of ideology to all of this and to particular sociological variables, such as class, ethnic group, and generation?

Sources of Strain in the Arab World

Economic and social change. In the nineteenth century, the European-centered world economy finally and effectively penetrated the economic system of the Islamic Middle East, first in the more accessible cities and coastal regions but, eventually, deeper into the hinterlands. This process in its simplest form represented an influx of Western manufactured goods and a rise in the export of agricultural and mineral raw materials. It brought on a period of deindustrialization that ate away at the vast traditional urban manufacturing network that had supplied the needs of the Islamic world for many centuries. Tying in agricultural production with world markets rearranged agricultural patterns to benefit a small class of large landowners and made the domestic economy heavily dependent on the central industrial economies of Europe. The arrival of the steamship and the laying of railways also undermined the network of merchants, caravaneers, and sailors that had tied the realm together economically.

The Arab Marxist author, Samir Amin, traces the decline of Arab economic activity as a result of competition from Europe to as early as the sixteenth century when the Arab merchant class was defeated by a rising European merchant class that "had been able to extract commercial privileges from the Ottoman authorities. . . . The merchant-led growth of mercantile Europe had as its corollary the decrepitude of the Arab merchants' world. From then on the Arab cities decayed . . . With the rise of imperialism at the end of the [nineteenth] century, the whole Arab world was definitely brought into the capitalist system as a dominated periphery. The regions which had already been integrated were remodelled by the new form taken by imperialist domination" (Amin 1978, 24).

Responses from the governments of Istanbul and Cairo to Western penetration had their own disruptive effects. Secularizing reforms undermined the dominance of the religious class in education, the judicial system, and the economy. Modernization of the military did away with an old warrior class that had shared with the religious class the tasks of government. Profligate spending, gross mismanagement, and ignorance of the basic principles of modern economic dynamics led either to bankruptcy, as in Egypt, or gross indebtedness, as in the Ottoman state. While trying to transform their economies into something resembling those of the West, these Middle Eastern governments helped destroy the older economic forms and failed almost completely to arrive at the threshold of capitalist industrial development. The pronounced prostration of these economies contributed to an acutely uneven pattern of military and political relations with the West.

The penetration by international market forces and the nervous reforms of local governments also had an important effect on land tenure patterns in the Arab provinces of the Ottoman empire. Integration into the world market and rising world prices for agricultural production began to commercialize older agricultural patterns. These market forces, in addition to financial and legal incentives provided by modernizing governments, set in motion "economic differentiation, indebtedness, sale and alienation of land. The result all over the region was the development of a land tenure characterized by: large estates . . . a huge number of very small peasant proprietors . . . and a growing landless proletariat earning very low wages" (Issawi 1982, 138).

While the alienation of land was generally benefiting a Muslim elite—private landlords, tribal sheiks, *ulama,* or the state (except in Palestine where land purchase had been pursued vigorously by the Zionists)—the inequalities in other sectors of the economy were gathering to the benefit of foreigners and members of the religious minorities. By virtue of their capital and technical resources and the backing of their governments, Westerners had come to dominate the economies of the Ottoman provinces. Members of religious minorities had also risen to economic prominence by virtue of the immunity they derived from the capitulations system, the skills they learned from Western missionary schools, and the collateral benefit they derived from acting as middlemen and associates for the more successful Europeans. By World War I, "Europeans held all the commanding heights of the economy, except for landownership, in the Middle East, and the minority groups occupied the middle and some of the lower slopes" (Issawi 1982, 9). The dominance of foreigners and non-Muslim minorities was, of course, more offensive to Muslim sensibilities than the consolidation of a Muslim landed class.

Underlying these economic changes was a rapid population growth that introduced sharp strains within the system and drove many millions deeper into poverty. While Malthusian checks of famine and pestilence had, before the nineteenth century, kept the population of the Arab regions at more or less stagnant levels, improvements in health and government initiated both from Cairo and Istanbul in the nineteenth century contributed to growth levels of 3 percent annually, and in the nineteenth century alone, the population of the Arab regions grew an estimated 300 percent (Owen 1981, 287). With the deindustrialization and economic disruption of that same century, the problem of poverty grew unprecedentedly acute. As they looked for opportunity in urban areas, the influx of rural dwellers swelled cities to great proportions.

Finally, the Ottoman reformist regimes and, then, the colonial governments of the pre–World War II Middle East introduced bureaucracy and a modern legal code to the workings of economy and society. The revolutionary regimes of the 1950s and 1960s extended this bureaucratization and pursued a heavily interventionist policy in economic matters, nationalizing most large enterprises and establishing significant welfare programs. The interventionism of the modern secular state in the 1950s and 1960s completed the dismantling of the old institutional system. Whereas the colonial regimes trod softly in social issues and were concerned principally with maintaining central power rather than transforming society, the revolutionary regimes of the 1950s and 1960s launched a wholesale modernizing and secularizing campaign.

Running through all these developments was a gradual change in the pathways of economic life from, for example, the ways of the artisan, the peasant, the caravaneer, and the boatman, to those of the bureaucrat, the factory worker, the professional, and the technician. This socioeconomic transformation rearranged demographic patterns, displaced families, reorganized lines of communication, and forced the reorientation of most workers toward a centralized, urban-based, state-influenced national economy.

In socioeconomic terms, therefore, the Arab world of the twentieth century resembles in almost no respect that of the early nineteenth century. This vast transformation, of course, was bound to create strains and tensions as social and cultural norms that would otherwise prepare the individual for integration into society lagged confusedly behind the pace of material change. Ideologies arose in part to address the problems that resulted from that lag.

Political change. The political environment of the Arab world was transformed over the last one hundred years as profoundly as was the socioeconomic. To begin with, the expansionism of the colonial powers of the West led to the military defeat and subjugation of Arab Islamic countries to an extent further even than the experience of the Crusades. There were defeats in 1840 and 1882 for Egypt and in 1920 for the Arab East in addition to defeats in 1830 and 1870 for Algeria, 1882 for Tunisia, and 1911 for Morocco. The conquests of the colonial powers radically redefined the political environment not only in structural and institutional terms but also in terms of the symbols of political life and the popular attitudes and emotions associated with it. It was a disruptive break with the past and a development that helped establish a conflictual relationship between state and society.

In institutional terms, the twentieth century saw a steady centralization and bureaucratization of the functions of the state. Gaining in power and centrality, the state penetrated deep into hinterlands it had influenced only weakly before and involved itself in affairs that had previously been left to religious or private functionaries. In terms of political participation and political culture, the agitation for national independence that characterized the 1930s and 1940s and the revolutionary populism of the 1950s and 1960s expanded the horizons of political participation to large portions of the population. Although participation shrank again in the 1970s and 1980s, that experience of mass politics had an indelible effect on the societies that went through it. In short, the political environment of the Arab world in the twentieth century resembles only in very few respects the political environment of the previous century. Political attitudes, norms, and beliefs were not able to adjust quickly enough to the institutional and structural changes. As in the socioeconomic sphere, political beliefs and attitudes lagged far behind the rate of actual political change, leaving an opportunity for the growth of ideologies.

Cultural change. In *The Emergence of Modern Turkey* (1968), Bernard Lewis noted that "While western material culture transformed the structure and aspect of Islamic society, often for the worse, ideas from the West were affecting the very basis of group cohesion, creating new patterns of identity and loyalty and providing both the objectives and the formulation of new aspirations" (Lewis 1968, 54). The task now is to review the nature of this cultural change, which is, after all, central to the question of ideology for ideology functions mainly in the cultural sphere.

The secularizing impulse exhibited in post-Renaissance Europe proved to be more radical than it at first appeared. Beginning with the

Protestant Reformation as an insurrection against the authority of the church in religious matters, it evolved over time into a rebellion against the authority of religion in politics and economics and a veritable revolution against its authority even in matters of ethics and justice. The revolution against religion, part of the general liberal ethos of emerging Western culture, was taken by some to its logical extreme: the denial of the very existence of God announced by Marx on the Left, Nietzsche on the Right, and various humanists in between. Although the West was able to gradually adapt to its largely secular worldview, this adaptation did not always take place smoothly nor has it reached a point of equilibrium. Given that the challenge to the intellectual foundations of religion in the Arab world took place very rapidly and from a foreign source, it is not surprising that this challenge generated intense anxiety and serious cultural imbalance.

Furthermore, although the Christian West was eventually able to find a modus vivendi with the secularization of vast spheres of its public life, Islam may be hard-pressed to do the same. The fundamentals of the Christian outlook allowed for a spiritualization of religious life that is much more difficult to justify within Islam. The religious message proclaimed by Christianity advocates a withdrawal from the dominant social and political order to an inner, private life. Islam is fundamentally different. As revealed to Muhammad, it was in its very essence a call not only to reform human private spiritual life but to restructure radically the dominant social and political order. Whereas Christianity restricted its area of interest as an early pillar of its worldview, mainly to accommodate the colossal political reality of the Roman empire, Islam quite frankly claimed total, all-encompassing authority. Hence, although the secularization of some spheres of social life could be accepted within the Christian context without a direct challenge to the first principles of Christian belief, within the Islamic context, secularization is more problematic.

The threat of secularism, however, not only restricted the authority of religion but also elevated entities other than the divine as objects of near-religious adoration and veneration. The isolation of religion from other spheres of life meant that new sources of value—new idols—were needed to dictate and organize social attitudes and action for, as Edward Shils noted, "Ideology, whether nominally religious or anti-religious, is concerned with the sacred" (Shils 1968, 68). The need was especially acute in the political sphere where a religious attitude toward the "Nation" was promoted to replace the metapolitical order once imposed on politics by religion itself.

The need to maintain religiosity in political life after the falling away of religion from politics, that is, after the secularization of politics, is not peculiar to the Islamic world, although Islam's political claims probably make this need even more acute. This need, for example, can be plainly read in the history of the French Revolution. There, at the birth of modern nationalism, the transference of religious attitudes in politics from God to the Nation was quite explicit. Altars were built not to God but to the Fatherland. Hymns, prayers, feasts, and holidays were dedicated to the new deity. The flag replaced the cross as the symbolic object of adoration with solemn rituals governing its lowering and raising and the mode of salute. National monuments replaced the religious as objects of pilgrimage, and national heroes replaced saints in the pantheon of lesser gods. Civic baptism, marriage, and excommunication were introduced. Finally, treason replaced blasphemy as the ultimate transgression deserving of death or worse (see Isaacs 1975, 180; and Hayes 1960, 166–168). Nietzsche referred critically to this sanctification of the state in his bitter attack on "The New Idol": "It would like to range heroes and honorable men about it, this new idol! It likes to sun itself in the sunshine of good consciences—this cold monster! It will give you everything if you worship it, this new idol: thus it buys for itself the lustre of your virtues and the glance of your proud eyes" (Nietzsche 1961, 76). Communism tried to infuse its ideology with a religiosity similar to that of state nationalism directed not toward the nation but toward less internalizable concepts such as the international proletariat, revolution, science, progress, and so forth. In most countries, however, Communism finally had to present itself essentially as a form of socialist nationalism in order to elicit this form of pseudoreligious devotion.

In effect, secularization has evolved toward a kind of pantheism in the sense that human religious "instinct" is presented with different objects of veneration in different spheres of life. This implicit pantheism is especially problematic in the Islamic world where God claims direct sovereignty in all spheres of private and public life. The modern nationalists of the Arab world, however, were quite aware of the spiritual elements of nationalism and worked hard to enhance them. Satiᶜ al-Husri, the father of modern Arab nationalist thought, began many of his addresses with the invocation, "In the name of God and in the name of Arabism." Michel Aflaq, the founder of the Arab Baᶜth party, boldly declared that "the call of the Baᶜth is a spiritual one"; "faith is the basis of our struggle" (Aflaq 1959, 207, 29). Antun Saᶜadeh, the charismatic founder of the Syrian Social Nationalist party, unequivocally claimed to have founded a new religion. The competing claims of Islam and nationalism for exclusivity in the sacred realm within the sphere of politics were a source of great disorder in Arab political culture.

A society's conception and veneration of its past can be as powerful as religion in providing that society with a sense of identity and community, a set of shared values, common goals, and a framework of social interaction. As Harold Isaacs noted, "A principal function of the past is to legitimize the present" (Isaacs 1975, 118). Arab society, from its pre-Islamic preoccupation with genealogy to the Islamic orientation back toward the era of the Prophet and the early Golden Age, has always relied heavily on tradition. Of course, Europe also relied heavily on the stabilizing weight of history and tradition. The Enlightenment, however, and rapid advances in science and technology introduced a more future-oriented outlook in which truth was to be discovered in the future, rather than in the past, through the steady progress of empirical and reflective investigation. The idea of progress redefined the past negatively as simply retarded or backward. The past thus lost its ability to organize or to guide except in a negative sense. In Ernest Gellner's words, "[B]ackwardness replaced evil as the generic characterization of that which is undesirable. To call something 'evil' has come to sound archaic and vaguely comic. But *backwardness* is a form of denigration which now makes sense. It is a usable moral category, because it fits in with the way in which we see the world functioning" (Gellner 1987, 47).

Furthermore, a new breed of explorers—historians—set out with all the romanticism of clinical anatomists to dissect and demystify the past (Plumb 1970, 15). This challenge to the past reverberated beyond the spheres of the natural sciences and inspired utilitarian, egalitarian, and other social and moral philosophies. A facet of this attitude was expressed in Marx's dictum: "The tradition of all the dead generations weighs like a nightmare on the brain of the living." A strong current of historicism, especially in Germany with Hegel and his disciples, resisted this antihistorical outlook and tried to find an accommodation between modernity and the past. In very many ways, however, this struggle to redefine the place of the past in the West is still going on today although not as intensely as it was even a half-century ago, for example, with the historical mythology of nazism and Italian fascism.

In any case, the antihistorical strain in modern culture weakened the bonds of tradition in the Arab world and introduced a hostile attitude toward the past. At the intellectual level, a radically new orientation toward historical time was introduced with emphasis shifted from the past to the future. At the sociological level, it loosened a whole set of traditional controls that had played a large role in the ordering of social consciousness and behavior. In the educational realm, time and energy previously devoted to the absorption of the past, its glory, wisdom, and literature, had to give way to the study of modern science, mathematics, and foreign languages. In the social realm, the wisdom and values of the old—the curators and caretakers of the past—became quaint at best, but more often the object of amusement and ridicule by a new generation educated in the modern sciences. In the economic realm, the industrial ethos that modernizers promoted reinforced this view. "Industrial society, unlike the commercial, craft, and agrarian society which it [sought to replace], [did] not need the past. Its intellectual and emotional orientation [was] towards change rather than conservatism, towards exploitation and consumption. . . .[Industrialization had] no sanction in the past and no roots in it. The past [was to become], therefore, a matter of curiosity, of nostalgia, a sentimentality" (Plumb 1970, 14).

This antipathy toward the past was, of course, taken up by many native modernizing reformers. Nasir, for example, in a 1956 speech declared, "Wherever we look behind, we do so to destroy the traces of the past, the traces of slavery, exploitation, and domination." Indeed, as the Moroccan writer Abdallah Laroui noted in *The Crisis of the Arab Intellectual* (1976), "The place that such a society accords to the past in the pattern of its present and its future" is of central importance. "It is not a question of philosophy of history, as with Hegel or Spengler, but of an understanding, an integration of history with collective life" (Laroui 1976, 14).

The assault on tradition and the past created particular problems regarding the conception of social and political community. Most especially, the theories of secular nationalism directly challenged older religious-based concepts of community. Under the Islamic empires such as those of the Umayyads, Abbasids, or Ottomans, religious affiliation topped the subject's social and personal identity ladder, followed, perhaps, by family or tribal status. Nationality, that is, language or racial group, trailed in third or fourth place. As Zeine Zeine observed, "[T]he line of demarcation was not along racial but along religious lines. The political identity of the Sultan's subjects was Ottoman (Osmanli) and his 'nationality' was the *religion* of the Community to which he belonged, i.e. his *millet*. The idea of nationality in the West European nineteenth century sense was almost non-existent in the Ottoman Empire" (Zeine 1973, 29). Modern nationalists sought to change this condition, however, elevating national affiliation to the position of first determinant of personal and communal identity. This attempt to radically transform communal identity from being a Muslim to being an Egyptian, an Arab, or a Turk was a necessarily wrenching process.

The Psychological Crisis

The vast transformations described here in the social, economic, political, and cultural spheres created a general condition of crisis in which inherited social norms, attitudes, and explanations were no longer adequate to organize and inform the life of the individual. The crisis was especially acute for those individuals who experienced considerable mobility either horizontally, by moving from village to city, or vertically, by moving from one socioeconomic stratum to another. For many such individuals, the lack of congruence between inherited orientations and the realities of the contemporary environment left them in a direct and unmediated confrontation with society, which engendered deep feelings of weakness, fear, and anxiety.

Individuals experience social anomie as intense personal alienation from the social environment accompanied by feelings of helplessness and fear. From the psychological perspective, this alienation is felt as the "loss of a relationship and of a sense of participation and control, with reference to prevailing social structures" (Yinger 1973, 178). On the emotional level, individuals feel lonely, unloved, fearful, and overwhelmed. Without a familiar emotional support system, they lose their sense of self-worth and seek to escape even from themselves. On the psychological level, they find the symbols and structures of the new society unfamiliar. They are alien and meaningless to them. They are unable to derive a clear identity and role structure for themselves. On the intellectual level, they come face-to-face with national or international institutions with which they are unfamiliar and which they are simply at a loss to understand.

Such lonely, alienated, and confused individuals are, of course, highly suggestible. They are inclined to overcome their loneliness and alienation by forming hyperattachments to symbols and mass movements that can provide them with an identity, a role, a sense of self-worth, power, and companionship. They are also ready to accept comprehensive dogmatic interpretations of the complex and confusing reality that they face. In this way, ideologies and ideological movements thrive on the psychological distress of individuals engendered by the process of modernization. In the words of Erich Fromm, "The influence of any doctrine or idea depends on the extent to which it appeals to psychic needs in the character structure of those to whom it is addressed. Only if the idea answers powerful psychological needs of certain social groups will it become a potent force in history" (Fromm 1941, 65). In the words of Clifford Geertz, "Ideology is a patterned reaction to the patterned strains of a social role. . . . [It] provides a 'symbolic outlet' for emotional disturbances generated by social disequilibrium. The model here is not military but medical: an ideology is a malady . . . and demands a diagnosis" (Geertz 1964, 54).

I expand on this understanding of Strain Theory by exploring the relationship between several particular categories of psychological strain and the spread of ideology. Of course, these categories do not strictly define the characteristics of psychological strain—they are not exact and comprehensive—but they are helpful in isolating some of the key areas of psychological strain that are most relevant to ideology in the Arab world.

1. Identity Crisis. One of the primary questions each individual must answer, or have answered for him or her, in a rapidly changing environment, is the fundamental question of identity (see Erikson 1968, 15ff). This is especially true in Arab society. As Anouar Abdel-Malek observed, "[T]he reality is that the distinctive feature of the Arab today is the drive to reconquer an identity" (Abdel-Malek 1983, 16). Part of the answer to the question of identity lies in developing a personal identity—a sense of familiarity with the self and its structure and function, or what David Apter calls a "role personality"; an important part of it, however, lies in finding a social identity that links one to other individuals or groups in the social environment and separates one from the "other." As Laroui put it in *L'ideologie Arabe Contemporaine,* the individual must find out "Who is the other and who am I?" (Laroui 1977, 18). Without a social identity, individuals are deeply alienated from their social environments, their cultural environments and, ultimately, themselves; without a clear definition of the "other," they cannot delimit their social identity.

Not surprisingly, most members of modernizing societies suffer from an acute confusion of identity. The individual who inherited the identity patterns of a rural peasant environment, for example, cannot easily adjust to the identity patterns suggested by a modern urban environment. The comforting corporate identities of village communities do not prepare the individual for the individualist identity patterns imposed by the tumultuous and fluid urban environment. Along the same lines, someone who received an early Islamic education with all it entails of forming a particular concept of the self and one's relation to others, cannot quickly accept the different self-images and relationships to others suggested by other forms of education in the modern social and natural sciences.

By marshaling powerful cultural and social resources, ideology can help the individual resolve or find temporary relief from this type of identity crisis. As Kornhauser argued, the "individual who lacks a firm conception of himself and confidence in himself does not possess the basis for strong control over himself, and therefore is highly *suggestible* to appeals from remote places" (Kornhauser 1959, 108). Ideology can do this in two ways. By putting together a large integrated belief system and developing a concept of personal and social identity that fits in neatly within this system, ideologues can do a lot of the work of identity formulation and identity integration for individuals. By thinking through the problems of individuals, ideologues can help individuals along in their struggle against identity confusion and dissonance. Furthermore, gifted ideologues and charismatic leaders can draw on the symbolic resources of the culture to render their ideology more subconsciously powerful and attractive. They can use the power of myth and ritual to give their belief systems a beauty and subtle seductiveness that dry unadorned belief systems may not have.

Although ideas and symbols can help individuals develop a positive identity, a vibrant ideological movement can itself provide individuals with relief from identity confusion or even help them establish a lasting positive identity. Unlike the first approach, here identity is provided through identification and association not with ideas or symbols but with other people. By submitting to a charismatic leader, individuals can absorb the identity patterns exhibited by that leader. The leader is a role model they can fashion themselves after as children look to parents for a sense of identity and a means of relating to themselves and to others. The charismatic leader is, then, in a sense, a surrogate parent who continues the process of development and maturation for individuals after their own parents or guardians have left them inadequately prepared for the contemporary environment. Aside from the role of the leader, individuals' fellows in the movement, who all more or less share in the individuals' identity crises influence them and can provide them with tangible examples of how others are dealing with similar problems. Interacting closely in a movement, individuals can learn from each other, and by participating in a collective enterprise, they can acquire a collective identity that can serve as the basis for their own personal and social identities.

2. Moral Crisis. Much of the comfort of childhood derives from the clear organization of "thou shalts" and "thou shalt nots" established and enforced by parents and other authority figures. In well-adjusted societies, this harmony carries on into adult life with the moral order

imbibed in childhood reflected and reinforced in the general life of adult political society and culture. In modernizing societies, the harmony of moral authority is destroyed by the competition of different moral systems for recognition and also by the confusion of authority patterns. This dissonance often leaves the individual without a recognized moral standard of authority. In the Arab world, the traditional Islamic moral system was challenged by a secular liberalism, which was challenged in its turn by Marxism on the left and a fundamentalist puritanical Islam on the right. In terms of moral authority, the venerable position of the parent was undermined by the rapid education of the young, who soon found themselves more knowledgeable than their parents in many spheres. Furthermore, the authority of religious figures was challenged by that of the school teacher, the university professor, the party ideologue, or the charismatic nationalist leader.

Ideology can help individuals with this crisis in two ways. At the ideational level, ideologues can construct out of the cluttered and confused moral environment a more coherent and integrated moral system that eliminates much of the dissonance and moral chaos. Furthermore, by artfully drawing on their cultural heritage of myths and symbols, they can render their proposed moral system sublime and inspiring. Beyond the ideational level, individuals can respond to their moral crises by submitting to the moral authority of the leader of an ideological movement. For a while they can avoid the problem of moral choice altogether by surrendering their will to the group and its leader; over time the coherent moral system of the group will be absorbed by them, and they can then use it in resuming new and harmonious moral lives of their own.

In *Civilization and Its Discontents,* Freud pointed to an additional relationship between socioeconomic distress and moral crisis, arguing that when individuals encounter acute difficulties they are likely to interpret them within moral categories. "As long as things go well with a man, his conscience is lenient and lets the ego do all sorts of things; but when misfortune befalls him, he searches his soul, acknowledges his sinfulness, heightens the demands of his conscience, imposes abstinences on himself and punishes himself with penances," (Freud, 1973, 15). This relationship may help explain the heavy moralistic character of many ideologies and the particularly harsh, but popular, moral strictness of, for example, the later Islamic fundamentalist movements.

3. Intellectual Crisis. The gargantuan growth of the urban environment, changes in the institutional structure of society, new modes of education, exposure to the mass media, encounters with the international environment, and other concomitants of modernization that involve a transformation and expansion of individuals' environments, all generate significant confusion at the intellectual level. Individuals often find it difficult even to understand their new environments let alone adjust to or enjoy them, given that the worldview provided to them by their families and society no longer prove adequate to the task. Unable to understand, they are often unable to function; they drift into anxiety and crisis.

Ideology can answer this intellectual need. As Shils asserted, "[A]n ideology is the product of man's need for imposing intellectual order on the world" (Shils 1968, 69), and by training their intellectual powers on the confusion of the contemporary environment, able ideologues can construct a more coherent description and explanation of reality and individuals' places in it. By abstracting from a confusing reality, ideologues can provide individuals with usefully simplified accounts of the world that they can then employ in making choices and finding their ways in that world. Furthermore, by joining an ideological movement, individuals can have this simplified worldview reinforced to the exclusion of all others by the authority of a charismatic leader, the influence of a party or movement hierarchy, and the consensus of their peers.

4. Crisis of Aggression. All the crises described previously generate in individuals deep wells of frustration and bitterness. To keep this resentment from drowning individuals and shattering their modest stability and self-esteems, they must be presented with suitable targets for aggression on which to unload their hostility freely and healthily. As Eric Hoffer (1951, 79) observed, "Mass movements can rise and spread without a belief in God, but never without a belief in a devil." Lenin hinted at this dynamic of ideology in his remark that "hatred is the basis of Communism." Indeed, all desperate people need enemies. Ideologues and ideological movements can play a

helpful role here in identifying some person, group, class, nation, civilization, and so forth, as the source of evil against which all can vent their aggression. By situating the source of failure or defeat outside oneself or one's immediate society, one can maintain a reasonably positive self-image even in the worst and most desperate circumstances. The traditional Islamic worldview encouraged such an externalization of evil in its dichotomous worldview that pitted the forces of good in *dar al-Islam* against the forces of evil in *dar al-harb*. Marxism could echo this dichotomy by positing a world struggle of exploiters and exploited, nationalists pitted the nation against the evil oppressors, and so on.

The categories of psychological strain experienced by individuals in rapidly changing societies and how ideologies relate to these strains, taken together, form the backdrop for an understanding of the existence of an age of ideology in the Arab world. This age corresponds to a time of rapid social, economic, political, and cultural change which generates psychological strain, which, in turn, creates a need for ideological movements and worldviews. Psychological strain and ideology constitute a complex topic, but even a brief analysis reflects the appeal and power of ideology in the modern Arab world.

The Social Dynamics of Ideology

If one accepts the existence of a general age of ideology during periods of rapid social, economic, political, and cultural change, what explains the rise and fall of particular ideologies within that age of ideology? Socioeconomic class, minorities, youth, and crises are important variables.

Class and Ideology

The relationship between socioeconomic class and ideology is, of course, part of traditional Marxist theory that holds that ideology is merely an expression of the material interests of the dominant class. Borrowing a little from the sociopsychological analyses of Gramsci, Fromm, Gellner, and others, however, a more complete understanding of the relationship between class and ideology requires adding on to the "interest" theory of ideology approaches that take into account the different intellectual, emotional, and psychological biases of different classes.

As Marx argued, a class will generally adopt and promote an ideology that expresses its material interests. Thus, for example, the wealthy often promote liberal capitalism, the economically insecure frequently promote limited socialism, and the destitute may espouse communism. The ideology of a class, however, is also partially a politically neutral reflection of the educational, cultural, and social background of its members. Ideologies become especially active and important in times of class change when a dominated class is toppling a dominating class or when a dominating class is desperately resisting such a challenge. During such periods, ideology serves as a battering ram for the challenging class or as a shield for the dominating class. Ideology also serves, however, as a politically neutral means of explaining and understanding reality for classes that are newly formed or that are moving into new and unfamiliar social environments. Finally, the dialectical opposition between classes applies also to the content of their ideologies. A challenging class that seeks to replace or topple a dominant class naturally adopts an ideology dialectically opposed to the ideology of the dominant class; hence, the ideological outlook of any class is largely determined negatively by the ideology of the class it is struggling against.

In the crudest of terms, and by doing not insignificant violence to the historical record, the correlation between class and ideology in the Arab Middle East has been approximately according to the following progression: the landowning and merchant upper class that dominated politics in the Arab Middle East in the 1920s and 1930s espoused a secular, liberal, parliamentarian, regional form of nationalism. The new middle class of bureaucrats, technocrats, intellectuals, small businesspeople, and junior officers that broke into power in the 1950s and 1960s gravitated mainly toward a socialist, authoritarian, romanticized pan-Arab nationalism. Others among this class were attracted also to other revolutionary ideologies such as communism on the Left and the Islamism of the Muslim Brotherhood on the Right. (c) The membership for the radical Islamic movements of the 1970s and 1980s came from different classes in different countries: in Egypt,

Iraq, and Lebanon, it has come from members of the newly urbanized lower or lower-middle class, whereas in Syria it came from the urban middle and upper classes of the northern towns. I indicate here only the possible connections.

Minorities and Ideology

Not unlike economic classes, minority groups also use ideology in their struggle to break into positions of political dominance. This is especially true in the modern Middle East where the ideological activism of members of minority groups is quite apparent. Christians, Alawis, Shiʿites, Druzes, Kurds, and others were all overrepresented in one or another of the non-Islamic ideological movements. Zaki Arsouzi and Michel Aflaq, for example, founders of the Baʿth movement, were Alawi and Christian, respectively. The early Communist movement was founded largely by Jews, Christians, Armenians, and Kurds. Kurds and Shiʿites were overrepresented in the Communist movement in Iraq. The Baʿth in Syria is dominated by an Alawi minority. The Syrian Social Nationalist party was established by a Christian and drew its following mainly from the Greek Orthodox and other minority communities. Among the New Left parties that emerged after the 1967 war, Christians and other minority members were also overrepresented (e.g., George Habash, Nayef Hawatmeh, Wadiʿ Haddad).

The involvement of minority groups in ideological movements has been noted frequently by students of Arab intellectual history. As Hourani argued, the new ideologies offered minorities "a chance of escaping from their position as a minority" and an opportunity to "identify themselves with the majority" (Hourani 1970, 276–77). In any case, the overrepresentation of minorities in the non-Islamic ideological movements occurred for several reasons: first, because many members of these minorities, especially among Christians and Jews, had been exposed earlier and more directly to the civilization of Europe, they more quickly adopted European political ideas and ideals and sought to promote them in their political surroundings. Second, these minority groups saw in the decline of the Sunni-dominated Ottoman political system an opportunity to break out of the isolation and weakness imposed on them as religious or ethnic minorities;

they saw in the ideals and slogans of the West a means to secure a measure of acceptance in the wider political community and a measure of political influence that would be commensurate with their rising power in the economic sphere. Furthermore, these minorities had been less attached to the ideas and ideals of the Ottoman empire and, thus, found it easier to adopt new and different political worldviews. Except for the Islamic movements themselves, almost all the ideological movements in the Arab world were basically incorporationist at the sectarian level. As one notes the effect of incorporating different classes into the political system, so one must note here the effect of the incorporation of different religious and ethnic minorities into the political system: as they moved into politics, members of the minorities needed an overarching ideological umbrella that would cover them and members of other communities and include them all in one common political community.

Generations and Ideology

In the process of identity and role formation that characterizes youth, young individuals are almost always in some attitude of rebelliousness toward the dominant order of their parents and society. Entering the adult social and political system on the lowest rung in terms of economic and social power, they are naturally threatened by and hostile to the dominant order. Still coming to terms with the world, they also are at a high level of strain in most of the psychological strain categories outlined here. Not surprisingly, then, one finds youth very centrally placed in almost all the ideological movements of the modern Arab world. They support bold challenges to the status quo and are open to ideological formulations of the world and their place in it. In ideological orientation, however, they function more as followers than leaders. With as yet no definite position in the social system and no clear set of material or moral interests to protect, they are highly suggestible but have little original ideological preference of their own. Above all, they are opposed to the status quo and support almost any serious challenge from below (a direction they can identify with) to that status quo. In the modern Arab world, for example, they supported the upper class against the colonial powers, the new middle class against the upper class, and now support (e.g., in Egypt) the newly urbanized lower-middle class against the dominant middle class. Although the youth of any period comprises individuals with many class backgrounds, they tend to behave more as an autonomous rebellious peer group than as a collectivity with particular class affiliations.

The challenge of youth is great in modern Arab society as it is in most developing countries because the economic and social frustrations of embarking on an adult existence are high: the urban environment is large and confusing, unemployment is widespread, and the ideals of political participation far outdistance the practice. Furthermore, youth today, unlike in earlier times, are able to develop a stronger sense of community and self-awareness because they share a common existence, somewhat separate from other social groups, in the large school and university systems that have become a fixture of modernity.

What all this means for the course of ideological change is that cohesive and frustrated youth are almost always a rockbed of support for challenges to the dominant status quo and its ideology. As Apter put it, "Resentful of the anxieties that result from role search, youth in new nations characteristically seeks its identity through revolt against the system" (Apter 1964, 28). This implies that the direction of ideological development is somewhat endogenously determined by the automatic emergence of an antithesis to the dominant ideological thesis with support among the youth. In an environment as strained and problematic as the modern Arab environment, the intensified rebelliousness of youth will naturally contribute to a periodic rejection of the status quo, a continuous ideological to-ing and fro-ing. Again, according to Apter, "This anti-authority reflex can be demarcated generationally" (Apter 1964, 28). This process need not be pendular or cyclical in the sense that generations will go back and forth between two antithetical worldviews. Indeed, given the facts of an ever-changing social environment and the relevance of past ideological formulations, the process is more liable to be dialectical with each generation rejecting the status quo for a new formulation that draws many elements from past and present experience. In other words, ideological history will not exactly repeat itself but instead trace a jagged zig-zag pattern.

The problem of defining exactly what constitutes a distinct "generation" and determining whether that generation will, indeed, adopt a new ideological orientation or not is a problem that Mannheim (1952), Heberle (1951), and others have grappled with and found difficult to resolve. Mannheim pointed out that a biological generation may experience the same historical circumstances but that different "generational units" may "work up the material of their common experiences in different specific ways" (Mannheim 1952, 304). Furthermore, not every generation "creates new collective impulses and formative principles original to itself. . . . Largely static or very slowly changing communities like the peasantry display no such phenomenon" (309). In the end, Mannheim links the likelihood of a particular generation producing its own ideological outlook to "the tempo of social and cultural change" (310): the quicker and more significant the change, the greater the need of a generation for a particular ideology adequate to its particular situation.

This phenomenon, of course, runs parallel to a general association of an age of ideology with a period of considerable material and cultural change. Mannheim declined to give a particular autonomous period to generational change, arguing that "whether a new *generation style* emerges every year, every thirty years, every hundred years, or whether it emerges rhythmically at all, depends entirely on the trigger action of the social and cultural process" (Mannheim 1952, 310). Other, perhaps less-cautious, students of the problem have posited a "time span of a political generation in twentieth-century Western society" of about "ten to fifteen years" (Rintala 1968, 93). Looking at the succession of liberal conservative, authoritarian radical, and Islamic fundamentalist ideological movements in the Arab Middle East, one could possibly suggest a generational time span of about twenty-five years (liberal regional nationalism ca.1920–ca.1945; revolutionary pan-Arab nationalism ca.1945–ca.1970; Islamic revivalism ca.1970–?).

In any case, the tension between youth and the dominant order is relevant to understanding part of the "anti" nature of ideological choices. To be successful among youth, ideologues must show how their ideology is hostile to the dominant ideological order. Thus, successful ideologies must be at least as clear about what they are against as about what they are for. Thus, the content of a potentially successful ideology is largely influenced by the dominant ideology that came before it. The "anti" aspect of ideological change can shed some light on the sources of the content of the ideologies that emerged in the Arab world.

In the 1940s and 1950s, revolutionary pan-Arab nationalism arose in opposition to the rather conservative nationalism of the 1920s and 1930s: authoritarianism was offered in opposition to political liberalism and parliamentarianism; socialism was offered in opposition to a laissez-faire economic outlook; pan-Arab nationalism was offered in opposition to regional nationalism; profound hostility to the West was offered in opposition to weak accommodationist attitudes; and so on. In the late 1960s and 1970s, religion was offered in opposition to secularism; deep hostility to both East and West was offered in opposition to friendliness toward the East and renewed accommodation to the West; puritanism was offered in opposition to moral liberalism; Islamic nationalism was offered in opposition to Arab nationalism; and so on. Ajami hints at such a dialectical relationship between successive ideological orientations when he emphasizes, for example, the importance of "disillusionment with pan-Arab doctrines" and "disillusionment with secularism"—two negatives—in the positive "turn toward Islamic fundamentalism" (Ajami 1981, 13).

Ideological choices, of course, were not rigidly determined by a negation of the ideologies that came before them, for as Shils noted, "Mere rejection of the existing society and the prevailing outlook of the elites of that society is not sufficient. For an ideology to exist, there must also be an attendant vision of a positive alternative to the existing pattern of society and its culture and an intellectual capacity to articulate that vision as part of the cosmic order" (Shils 1968, 69).

There is no one antithesis to any thesis, and some elements of an ideology may be carried through from one ideological period to another. Nevertheless, the point here is that the content of an ideology challenging the status quo is not uninfluenced by the content of the ideology that it is challenging.

Once a generation has made its ideological choice in youth it is likely to hold roughly to that worldview through its remaining years. Although new challenges will emerge from a succeeding generation, the old generation is not likely to be converted at an age median of forty or fifty. Its conviction and enthusiasm may ebb, but it is unlikely to follow the new generation in a radical swing of outlook (Rintala 1968, 93). Young people are quite flexible; people in their forties or fifties are not. Youth is the age at which one establishes one's basic social and political worldview. The dominant ideology of one's generation plays a central role in organizing one's worldview. Once it is established, it is likely to serve for the rest of one's life with only minor modifications and alterations. So the experience of each generation in its period of youth is seminal in understanding its behavior and outlook later on in life. The young Arab nationalists of the 1950s and 1960s are still generally Arab nationalists today. They are older and their convictions are less enthusiastic and optimistic, but their secularist, mildly socialist, Arab nationalist outlook is still the fundamental framework through which they view their world. Similarly one can expect the young Islamists of today to remain Islamists, perhaps less fervently so, well into the 2010s and 2020s.

Crises and Ideology

As mentioned earlier, the effect of political crises on ideological movements is a conventional way in which students of the Middle East have analyzed the rise and fall of such movements. It is argued that the defeat of 1948 discredited the dominant liberal ideology of the time and triggered a turn toward a more revolutionary authoritarian Arab nationalism, while the defeat of 1967 discredited revolutionary pan-Arab nationalism and triggered a turn toward Islamism on the one hand and Marxism on the other. Fouad Ajami, for example, writes in *The Arab Predicament* (1981) that "Two great events dominate the period that concerns us: the Six Day War of June, 1967, and the October War of 1973. Men fought, worked, and reflected in the shadow of these events" (Ajami 1981, 5), and again that "The world *brought about by October 1973* blew away the cobwebs of Arab society. Buffeted by mighty winds and propelled by temptations and possibilities unknown before, its cultural container erupted. It strutted on the world stage for a brief moment, then the breakdown came" (Ajami 1981, 6; emphasis mine).

We encounter an emphasis on the paramount importance of the defeats of 1948 and 1967 also, for example, in the writings of Samir

Amin. "Little by little, the Palestinian problem became the pivot of the Arab question, the test of the ability of the various social classes which had pretensions to lead the national anti-imperialist movement. This was the test which broke first the comprador bourgeois and latifundist generation (1948), then the socialist petty bourgeoisie (1967)" (Amin 1978, 34).

Undoubtedly, these great events were of great significance to the course of ideological development. But to examine the effect of crises on ideological movements from a more general theoretical perspective, the ability of a dominant class to project its ideology on other classes as a source of political legitimacy is very vulnerable to crises. Crises undercut the authority of an ideology in at least two ways. On the political level, any serious defeat brings into question the performance of the ruling class and the suitability of its ideology. Convinced that the present political arrangement is partially to blame for a crisis or defeat, people begin to look for alternative arrangements of power and alternative ideologies to accompany it. On the psychological level, the historical association of any ideology with a painful defeat saps that ideology of its ability to evoke sentiments of optimism, power, and confidence for its people. It becomes itself a symbol of weakness and defeat. But the feelings of weakness and defeat and similar emotions are the very ones from which people generally seek to escape when they look to an ideology. Seeking to ease their frustrations, people not of the dominant class abandon the discredited dominant ideology and seek symbolic attachment and satisfaction elsewhere. As Shils put it, "In conditions of crisis, when hitherto prevailing elites fail and are discredited and when the central institutions and culture within which they associate themselves seem unable to find the right course of action, ideological propensities are heightened" (Shils 1968, 75). The dominant class (the upper class of 1948 and the middle class of 1967), however, appears to cling to its ideology even after defeat and even if its own conviction and creativity about its ideology diminishes to a low ebb. The dominant class, it seems, institutionalizes its outlook and cannot transform it without its own political position and dominance being transformed; other classes, meanwhile, are free to abandon the dominant ideology and adopt new ideological outlooks.

In this chapter I have argued that the modern Arab world has been passing through an age of ideology due to the depth and breadth of social, economic, political, and cultural change. I have also tried to show how psychological strain can provide an appetite for ideological formulations. Finally, I discussed a number of variables that could help us in understanding the rise and fall of ideologies. In the chapters that follow I will draw on the various arguments presented here as well as the historical record to try to provide a more meaningful understanding of the different ideologies and ideological movements of the Arab Middle East than can be provided by only one approach or one mode of explanation. I do not claim to have provided a model for predicting ideological change but only a framework within which to search for questions and answers having to do with the content and appeal of different ideologies.

CHAPTER TWO

Arab Nationalism

The History of Arab Nationalism

Early Origins

Before the nineteenth century, politics in Arab-Islamic society was largely a matter of religion and dynasties. The political system "made political rather than cultural claims on the subjects. Loyalty to the Sultan, payment of the tribute, and respect for peace and order were the main demands of the state, any infringement of which would incur its anger and rectification by force" (Harik 1972, 305). Increasingly intimidated by and impressed with the West, however, several Western-influenced Arab and Turkish writers became convinced that national patriotism was the secret of Europe's success. They sought to convince their audiences that national patriotism was the crucial missing ingredient in the political attitudes of the Islamic world.

Rifaʿa Rafiʿ al-Tahtawi, for example, was among the first group of students sent to France by the progressive Egyptian Khedive, Muhammad Ali, and after spending the years 1826–1831 in Paris, he returned enamored of the civilizational advances of Europe and dismayed at the relative backwardness of Muslim lands. In a collection of reflections on Europe published in 1834, he insisted that Muslims had much to learn from the Europeans even though Muslims still had the upper hand in matters of religion because they followed the true religion of God's final Prophet. He sought to spread the sentiment of national patriotism that he felt underlay the vigor and dynamism of European societies and directed this patriotism toward Egypt as a nation. He was one of the first to refer consistently to an Egyptian fatherland (*watan*) and an Egyptian nation (*ummah*). Loyalty to one's people and love of one's birthplace were relatively well-established virtues in Muslim society, but Tahtawi was one of the first to give them primary political significance and fix them as cardinal principles of political association and motivation. "Let the motherland be the site of our common happiness," he said, "which we shall build by freedom, thought and factory" (in Abdel-Malek 1983, 28). This type of patriotic-nationalist thought, exemplified in the writings of Tahtawi, came to represent the dominant strand of thinking among the Egyptian elite of the nineteenth century. Furthermore, the period of Egyptian occupation of Syria between 1831 and 1840 had an important effect on the emergence of nationalism in Syria as the Egyptians set up state schools, encouraged the activity of the foreign educational missions, granted equal rights to non-Muslims and Muslims alike, and hinted at the idea of a possible Arab state under Egyptian leadership.

About the same time, many of the young Ottoman reformers of the Tanzimat period (e.g., Reshid, Ali, Fuad) had also grown enamored of the advances of the West and were convinced that the evocation of a sentiment of patriotism or nationalism—in this case, Ottoman—was essential for the modernization of the empire and for its success in facing the challenges of the West. The Tanzimat period, which extended roughly between 1839 and 1878, had a great influence in laying the groundwork for the emergence of nationalism as it secularized large portions of public life, established a state school system that spread Western ideas, and arranged for the new Ottoman officer corps to be trained largely by Europeans. Moreover, the key slogans of the Tanzimat period—reason, science, progress—were incorporated into reformist Islamic thought at the turn of the twentieth century.

In addition to the Egyptian and Ottoman sources of the idea of nationalism in the Arab world was the direct influence of the American, French, and Russian missions. The French had an interest in introducing the idea of an Arab nation in order to help weaken the Ottoman empire and challenge Britain's trade route to India through the Suez Canal. The Russians fanned Arabist sentiment among local clergy to challenge Greek domination of the Syrian Orthodox religious community. The Americans had few colonial ambitions at the time but showed a genuine interest in spreading their Christian Protestant message in the vernacular Arabic of the native population. Thus, they contributed indirectly to a revitalization of the Arabic language and Arabic culture that was the first step toward Arabs awakening to their nationality and the subsequent politicization of that nationality in the ideology of nationalism. Indeed, all the missions contributed to the spread of the idea of nationalism by generally spreading the learning of the West and its social and political ideas and ideals.

The revival of Arabic literature and philology that would help promote Arab cultural self-awareness and serve as a pillar of Arab nationalism was carried out mainly by a group of Lebanese Christian writers and thinkers in close contact with the American Protestant mission. Nasif al-Yaziji (1800–1871) could be regarded as the father of this Arab literary renaissance. He wrote works of philology and poetry and essays on logic, medicine, history, and other matters. He mastered the Arabic language, and most later Arab writers of the century were in one sense or another his disciples. Faris al-Shidyaq (1805–1887), a Lebanese Christian convert to Protestantism, shared Yaziji's interest in Arabic language and literature. Butrus al-Bustani (1819–1883), however, was the first among these writers to express clear political Arab nationalist sentiments in his writing. He was particularly concerned about the exacerbation of confessional tensions in the Lebanese Mountain between 1840 and 1860 that had led to clashes and massacres in 1860 in the Mountain as well as in Damascus. He feared confessional fragmentation and regarded the encouragement of Arab national awareness in Syria as the best means to overcome these sectarian tensions. He believed this could be achieved through a revival of Arabic cultural life and a dissemination of modern patriotic ideals. He published the first Arab nationalist journal, *nafir suriyya* (Appeal to Syria), in the troubled atmosphere of 1860 and established *al-Madrasah al-Wataniyyah* (The National School), which taught in Arabic and admitted students from all communities. He also started the journal *al-Jinan* in 1870, whose motto, borrowed from a *hadith* of the Prophet and reminiscent of Tahtawi, proclaimed, "Love of one's country is an article of faith" (Abu-Manneh 1980, 294). Throughout, he promoted the idea of *'usba wataniyya* (national solidarity) over

ʿusba diniyya (religious solidarity) and warned against religious fanaticism. He argued that an Arab cultural revival would guard against European cultural domination and prevent the fragmentation of Syrian society. He maintained, however, a positive orientation toward the Ottoman state, believing that it had a helpful role to play in protecting Syria against European political domination and preventing confessional war within Syria. He regarded Syria's basic identity as Arab, based on the cultural heritage carried by Syria's common Arabic language. He published an Arabic dictionary, *Muhit al-Muhit* (The Breadth of the Ocean), and started work on an Arabic encyclopedia that was completed by his family after his death.

Others, however, took Bustani's Syrian Arab nationalism to further extremes. Ibrahim al-Yaziji (1847–1905), the son of Nasif al-Yaziji, called for an immediate Arab political upheaval. In a poem composed in 1878, which gained renown in some circles, he called on his fellow Arabs to rise in revolt and stake their claim to nationhood. A handful of secret Arab nationalist societies emerged in the 1870s among some students of the mission schools and colleges, calling for an independent Arab national state. The Arab nationalist effervescence among mostly Christian Lebanese and Syrians in the mid-nineteenth century, however, did not spread widely to the Muslim population, whose loyalties were still firmly invested in the Islamic state. As secularism spread among certain classes in Muslim society in the nineteenth century, especially among graduates of the new nonreligious state schools established after the Tanzimat period, political loyalties were rearticulated in an Ottoman protonationalism rather than in an Arab nationalism that would split the Muslim community. Even among Lebanese Christians, the idea of Arab nationalism was generally overshadowed by the idea of Lebanese nationalism that was gaining momentum throughout the nineteenth century. Meanwhile, in Egypt, the nationalist idea was being articulated as Egyptian, not Arab, nationalism.

It is important, however, in addition to the ideas described, to understand the roots of the Arab nationalist idea in the thought of several Islamic modernists around the turn of the twentieth century who developed an Arabist version of Islam that provided the door through which secular Arab nationalism later stepped into the Arab world. As

Zeine Zeine argues, "Arab nationalism in its genesis and growth has been inseparable from Islam" (Zeine 1973, vii); hence, the thought of some of the leading Islamists of the era—such as Afghani, Abduh, Rida, Kawakibi, Qasimi, and al-Jaza'iri—is of central importance.

Jamal al-Din al-Afghani, whose life and works I return to in chapter three, was one of the first of a succession of Muslim thinkers and publicists who shaped an Islamist response both to the challenges of the West and the secularizing reforms of Muslim leaders. He preached a revitalization and reform of Islam that would render it a viable engine for progress and success in the modern world of industrial production, mass politics, and intellectual achievement. He disseminated a nationalist version of Islam in which religious allegiances were to be recast as patriotic political loyalty to the Islamic *umma* and to the Ottoman government that led and defended it. Afghani also romanticized the period of the Prophet and the Rightly Guided Caliphs as the Golden Era of the Islamic *umma* when Muslims supposedly enjoyed religious excellence, intellectual enlightenment, political democracy, martial glory, and so on. Indeed, Afghani's thought and example gave rise to a wider reformist movement among Arab Islamic thinkers and scholars. The movement was described as *salafi* because its members claimed to follow the example of *as-salaf as-salih* (the worthy predecessors, the Prophet and the early caliphs) who taught "true" Islam and showed that religious men should be leaders, teachers, and reformers, not passive participants in a stagnant status quo. The *salafis* were mainly "middle ulama" distinct from the dominant Shaykhs who held high government and religious posts (Commins 1986, 408). Consequently, they had a smaller a stake in the traditional religious order and sought a role for themselves within a changing concept of Islam.

Afghani's Egyptian disciple, Muhammad Abduh, explored the harmony of reason and revelation in Islam, elaborated on the excellence of the early Muslim community, and emphasized the centrality of the Arabic language and the Arabs themselves in the history of Islam. Abduh, of course, was an Arab, whereas Afghani was of Persian origins. Abduh's Syrian disciple, Rashid Rida, editor of the widely read *al-Manar* journal, carried this train of thought further, insisting on the need for an Arab revival as the foundation for a general Muslim revival (Dawn 1973, 38). He joined the Ottoman Decentralization Society in Cairo and inveighed against the Turkification policies of the ruling Committee of Union and Progress (CUP). Another Syrian, Abd al-Rahman al-Kawakibi, who had come to Cairo in 1898 and joined the circle of Abduh and Rida, elaborated the most explicit Arabist Islamist position in a book he published serially in Rida's *al-Manar,* called *Umm al-Qura* (The Mother of Towns, Mecca). Kawakibi railed against the failings and inadequacies of the Turks and blamed them for the sorry state of the Muslim world. He demanded administrative autonomy for the Arabs within the empire and called for the establishment of a largely spiritual caliphate that would be in Arab hands. Not only in his committed Arabism but also in his proposal for a depoliticization of the caliphate—a kind of separation between church and state—Kawakibi, as Sylvia Haim points out, came quite close to articulating the secular Arab nationalist viewpoint of later decades (Haim 1964, 23).

In Damascus, Jamal al-Din al-Qasimi and Tahir al-Jazaʾiri elaborated reformist Islamic views similar to those being spread by Abduh, Rida, and Kawakibi in Egypt. Like Abduh, Qasimi endeavored to reconcile reason and revelation in Islam. He argued that "Islam was a rational religion: Islam calls on man to use reason; and whoever employs reason to study the natural world will grow stronger in faith" (quoted in Commins 1986, 406). Moreover, he respected the Comte-inspired positivism of the young Turks and was well aware that his society re-quired an able class of scientists and scholars to move it forward. He advocated the spread of modern schools that would teach in Arabic and the establishment of a liberal constitutional government within which this elite could find its natural place. Together with Jazaʾiri who held similar views, Qasimi served as teacher and mentor for many of the early Syrian Arab nationalists of World War I and the interwar period.

The secularizing reforms of the Egyptian and Ottoman states, the literary revival of the mid-nineteenth century, and the Arabist ver-sion of Islam developed by the Islamic modernists of the turn of the twentieth century, provided the main historical roots for the later emergence of the idea of Arab nationalism. The actual political history of the Arab nationalist movement as it emerged in Syria in the early twentieth century is somewhat more complex.

Arab Nationalism before World War II: The Conservative Ideology of the Syrian Upper Classes

The idea of Arab nationalism began to manifest itself in earnest in Syria in the early twentieth century after the Young Turk coup d'état in 1908 that brought the CUP to power. A number of conditions helped promote this nationalist movement. First, a set of Turkification programs promoted by the CUP leadership, such as replacing Arabic with Turkish in some schools and insisting that all official proceedings in the Arab territories be conducted in Turkish, aroused resentment among the local Arab ruling class, the *ulama*, and the nascent professional class. Second, a liberalization of printing restrictions allowed the rapid growth of an Arabic press in Syria and Lebanon, which, following the literary revival of the previous century, spread pride in Arabic culture and opposed the Turkification policies of the CUP government. Third, a revival of parliamentary life and electioneering also provided a forum for the articulation of Arabist points of view in contrast to the still dominant Ottomanism of most politicians. Fourth, the string of defeats suffered by the Ottomans in the Balkans began to raise the possibility of the collapse and dismemberment of the empire and, thus, gave more credibility to the idea of a potential Arab state.

The rising Arabist sentiment of the pre-1914 period was expressed in the emergence of a number of organizations that sought, in various ways, to defend and promote Arab interests. In Constantinople, a Society for Ottoman-Arab Brotherhood was constituted in 1908 of prominent Arabs and Turks and replaced in 1909 by the Arab Club of Constantinople. Several reform societies were founded in Beirut, Basra, and other cities in 1912 and 1913 (Dawn 1973, 149). Among the most serious groups were the Ottoman Decentralization Society based in Cairo with branches in Syria and two clandestine organizations, *al-Fatat* and *al-ʿAhd*, composed mostly of students and army officers, respectively. Among all these groups, only a small minority of Arabs were working for actual Arab independence; the majority simply called for decentralization and better political and cultural conditions for the Arabs in the context of the Ottoman empire. The majority view was expressed in the final resolutions of the 1913 Arab Congress

organized by *al-Fatat* in Paris, which called for decentralized administration, Arab national cultural autonomy, and a multinational constitutional monarchy (Tibi 1981, 83). A small number of Christian Arabs,
such as Negib Azouri and K. T. Khairallah, called openly for total Arab
independence from the Ottomans, although most Christian delegates
to the congress expressed the more moderate mainstream view.

In any case, the Arabist position, in general, was still a minority position in Syria before the outbreak of World War I. The mass of the
population maintained its Islamic Ottoman loyalties as did the majority of the *ulama* and the ruling upper class. This position left disgruntled members of the ruling class and the *ulama* and the majority
of the small, new, and younger intelligentsia of Arab writers and
schoolteachers promoting the Arabist point of view. As Dawn argues,
pre-1914 Arabism seems to have been promoted mainly by those
members of the upper class and *ulama* who were out of office in alliance with members of the new and younger intelligentsia. Together
they engaged in an intra-elite struggle with members of the upper
class and *ulama* who were enjoying high government office at the
time (Dawn 1973, 170). Such intra-elite conflict, Dawn argues, "was
traditional in Near Eastern society. The new element was the ideological definition of the conflict. Before the 19th century such conflicts were either left undefined or defined in terms of rival interpretations of Islam" (Dawn 1973, 173). Now, however, the conflict was
being defined in terms of Turkism versus Arabism.

Events between 1914 and 1918 had a seminal influence on the triumph of Arab nationalism in Syria. First, the outbreak of the war precipitated the establishment of direct Ottoman military rule in Arab
lands, which only aggravated Arabist grievances. Jamal Pasha, the
governor of Syria and commander of the Ottoman Fifth Army there,
proved especially harsh and unpopular. Among other things, he arrested and executed important leaders of the Arab nationalist movement and generally frightened and alienated the Syrian ruling class.
More importantly, however, a triple alliance between the British,
Sharif Husayn of Mecca, and civilian and military members of the
Arab nationalist movement carried out the Sharifian-led Arab revolt
of 1916, which, with British help, drove the Ottomans out of the
Syrian hinterland and established Arab rule in Syria. In 1918, the

Syrian Arab kingdom was proclaimed under the rule of Husayn's son, Prince Faysal. British promises of support for Arab independence and American support for principles of national self-determination only helped lend further credence to Arabist victories. By 1919, the overwhelming majority of the Syrian political class had been won over to Arab nationalism, which was the official ideology of the Arab government of King Faysal.

This government, however, was short-lived. In accordance with the secret Sykes-Picot agreement drawn up between France and Britain during the war, the British ended up supporting French demands for a mandate over all of Lebanon and Syria. The Arab government refused the European decision, but French troops forced their way into Damascus and toppled the Faysal government in 1920. Greater Lebanon was proclaimed, and Syria was dismembered into four ministates, isolating Damascus from other Syrian territories.

There had been internal sources of tension, of course, within the Arab government between Palestinian and Iraqi Arab nationalist officers and politicians, on the one hand, and members of the traditional Syrian ruling class, on the other, who resented having to make room for the Palestinian and Iraqi "outsiders" and often conspired against them. These rivalries were expressed in the tensions among the predominantly Syrian *al-ʿAhd* composed largely of Iraqi military officers, and the Arab Club made up mostly of Palestinians (Khoury 1981, 442). But the blatant French disregard for Arab demands and the dismemberment of Syria only gave more credibility to the Arab nationalists, who argued that the Arabs could only be saved from domination and decline if they unified their efforts and banded together in a pan-Arab union that would be strong enough to throw off not just Turkish but also European domination. As Hourani noted, "had [Syria] become independent as an individual whole, Arab national feeling might have been focused upon that particular entity and a certain balance between Arab and Syrian feeling achieved, as in Egypt and Iraq. The division into small states of which only Lebanon was a natural unit, left national feeling with no existing state to focus upon, and turned it outward" (Hourani 1970, 317). All in all, the period around World War I was seminal for the genesis of the Arab nationalist movement (see Khalidi 1977, 208).

After the collapse of Faysal's Arab kingdom in 1920, many Arab nationalist leaders were driven into exile in Europe, Egypt, or Amman. A Syrian-Palestinian Congress was established in 1921 to keep the Arabist project alive, but it soon disintegrated as the Palestinian representatives withdrew in 1922 and the Syrians split over ways to react to the Druze-led Great Revolt of 1925–27 (Khoury 1981, 444, 462). Even the relatively more pan-Arabist wing of the Syrian nationalist movement, represented by the Istiqlal party and such figures as Shakib Arslan, Rashid Rida, and Shukri Quwatli, was weakened by the eventual failure of the Great Revolt that engulfed much of Syria and south Lebanon between 1925 and 1927. The revolt represented, in a sense, the belated response to the dismantlement of Faysal's state; however, the French eventually crushed the uprising, and only those Syrian politicians who were willing to play by France's rules within the mandate system were allowed to return to Syria and resume political activity.

Nevertheless, Arab nationalist sentiment continued to find expression in other ways. In 1931, a general Arab conference was held as part of the General Islamic Conference called by Hajj Amin al-Husayni in Jerusalem. High-level representatives from a majority of the Arab countries, including Egypt and the North African countries, formed what they termed an "Arab National Pact," which asserted that the Arab countries were one indivisible entity and declared the participants' intention to establish a semipermanent Pan-Arab Congress (Coury 1982, 253). In 1932, a grouping of Syrian Arab nationalists (including Zaki Arsouzi, who would play a central role in founding the Baʿth movement in the early 1940s), formed the ʿUsbat al-ʿAmal al-Qawmi (League of National Action) which took the initiative from the dominant National bloc in resisting the French and in keeping the idea of Arab nationalism alive (Kaylani 1972, 3). With encouragement from Britain during World War II, the Arab nationalist idea eventually found institutional expression in the Arab League, established in March 1945.

The Arab nationalism of the period before 1948 was almost entirely conservatively oriented. Furthermore, it represented not so much an elaborate ideology but a simple pride in the Arab heritage and a preference for Arab self-rule over domination by Turks or Europeans. In class terms, it expressed the interests of the traditional Syrian landed and merchant upper class, which found Arabism an effective weapon against Turkish domination and hoped it would do the same against the French and British. As Samir Amin noted, it was a movement "bringing together all the great families of the Syrian towns" and as such represented vested social interests and proposed no radical change in social or political values (Amin 1978, 45). It had almost no social, economic, or political program beyond independence, Arab unity, and republican secular nationalism. Even its view of Arab unity rarely extended beyond the principal towns of Greater Syria so that the movement could also be described, as Hourani does, as a movement toward Syrian unity with Sharifian-inspired Arabism as its main banner and slogan.

Arab Nationalism after the Loss of Palestine: The Radical Reformulation

The radical revolutionary Arab nationalism of the post-1948 period is a profoundly different movement. Triggered by the upheavals of World War II and the humiliation of the loss of Palestine in 1948, this new Arab nationalism was led by middle-class elements and put forward an agenda of social revolution, immediate pan-Arab unity, and thoroughgoing secularism. Under the banner of this new radical nationalism, young party and army officer elites rose to power in several Arab countries. Under its umbrella, Gamal Abd al-Nasir and the Free Officers seized power in Egypt in 1952, the Ba'th rose to positions of power in Syria in 1955-58 and finally seized full control in 1963, and Abd al-Karim al-Qasim seized power in Iraq in 1958 followed by the Ba'th in 1963 and again in 1968. Rebel Arab nationalist movements nearly toppled the regimes of Lebanon and Jordan in 1958. Other traditional governments fell in Libya, Sudan, and Yemen. One can trace the history of this new Arab nationalism through the careers of its main promoters: the Arab Ba'th party, the Arab Nationalist movement, and Nasir himself, who became the main hero and demagogue of this new nationalism.

The Ba'th: crucible of the new radicalism. After the annexation of the Syrian province of Alexandretta by Turkey with French approval in 1939, Zaki al-Arsouzi, a thirty-eight-year old schoolteacher, a graduate of the Sorbonne, and an Alawi like most of the Arab inhabitants of

that province, moved into Syria proper and started the Arab Nationalist party as well as a more culturally oriented society called *al-Ba'th
al- 'Arabi* (The Arab Renaissance) (Batatu 1978, 722). Arsouzi, a former
member of the League of National Action established in 1932, succeeded in gathering a small band of followers, but his organization
soon lost ground to a similar movement in Damascus led by Michel
Aflaq and Salah al-Din al-Bitar. In 1940, Aflaq and Bitar, a Christian
and a Sunni Muslim, respectively, both born in Damascus and former students at the Sorbonne, had established a small political and
cultural study group that would become the nucleus of the Arab Ba'th
party. Both taught at the Tajhiz Dimashq high school, and most of the
early members of the group were older students at the school (Kaylani
1972, 4). Aflaq had been a member of the Syrian Communist party but
had left it in disillusionment over its subservience to Moscow and its
support of the 1936 Franco-Syrian Treaty negotiated by Quwatli's National Bloc government. The Ba'th party was officially established in
1946 with its own daily newspaper, *al-Ba'th*, and in 1947 it held its
first congress, which drew several hundred members "most of whom
were students, the others being teachers or lawyers or medical practi-
tioners or from other strata of the intelligentsia" (Batatu 1978, 727).

In these early years, the party was a loose association of young
writers and literati sharing an estrangement from the dominant
political and social order. They confined their activity to pamphleteering and speechmaking and scarcely seemed a serious political
force. In the words of one of its early members, "popular action was a
poem, and we composed it well" (Jundi 1969, 33). The party's fortunes improved as a result of the radicalization brought on by the
loss of Palestine in 1948. In 1952, it gained a more solid grass roots
organization and more credible party structure by merging with
Akram Hurani's popular Arab Socialist party that had strong organized support among peasants and army officers (Batatu 1978, 730).
Hurani had been a member of Antun Sa'adeh's Syrian Social Nationalist party but had left the SSNP to found his own organization. He
was a gifted orator and a master mobilizer who had gained overwhelming support among the rural population around Aleppo. He
also understood the value of party organization and the value of fos-
tering allies within the military. The party was now rechristened the

Arab Ba'th Socialist party and reemerged after the fall of the Shishakli regime in 1954 as a formidable political force in Syria. In Kaylani's words, "Hurani ultimately performed on the Ba'th what Lenin performed on Marxism: he changed it into a strategy of political action" (Kaylani 1972, 7).

Throughout most of the period between 1954 and 1958, the Ba'th party was represented in several key cabinet positions and shared power, off and on, with Khalid Bakdash's Syrian Communist party. In 1958, the Ba'th, with support from a number of key military officers and civilian politicians, took advantage of fears of Communist influence in Syria to send envoys to Cairo to convince Nasir to accept the unification of Egypt and Syria under his leadership. The Ba'th had been calling for unity with Egypt as a first step toward pan-Arab unity since early 1956. The actual experience of unity, however, was a bitter one for the Ba'th; the official dissolution of the party in Syria was one of Nasir's conditions for accepting the unity plan. Furthermore, the Ba'th soon found that it had significant disagreements with Nasir on matters of socialist policy, foreign policy, the nature of the unity arrangements, and the authoritarian and centralized nature of power under him. The Ba'th's reservations about the United Arab Republic (UAR) soon became public, and a number of leading Ba'thists, including Bitar and Hurani, supported the September 1961 conservative coup that withdrew Syria from the union.

Meanwhile, in February 1963, the Iraqi wing of the Ba'th, which had been locked in confrontation with the regime of Abd al-Karim al-Qasim since the latter's coup in 1958, seized power in Iraq and launched a vigorous campaign against their enemies in the government and the military, especially the Communists who had helped Qasim subdue the Ba'th and other Arab nationalist groups in 1958–59. But the Ba'th's reign in Iraq did not last the year. In March 1963, while the Ba'th moved into power in Iraq, the military wing of the Syrian Ba'th led the party in a coup that ousted the separatist regime of 1961 (Razzaz 1967, 90).

The disappointing experience of unity with Egypt, the collapse of the Ba'th in Iraq only months after acceding to power, and the general confusion attending the rise of the party to such high levels of political responsibility, all contributed to an atmosphere of crisis and division within the party in the mid-1960s. The main axes of disagreement were along the left-right issues of socialist policy; apportioning blame for the collapse of the UAR in 1961 and the collapse of the Iraqi Baʿth regime in July 1963; the leadership of the old guard of Aflaq, Bitar, and Hurani; and a basic struggle for power between the civilian party members and the better-placed military members. The conflict finally resulted in a polarization between the Syrian and Iraqi branches of the party. The military left wing seized control of the party in Syria in 1966 and expelled Aflaq and Bitar. Dissidents from the Syrian branch ended up in Iraq where they formed a core group of bitter opposition to the policies of the Syrian Baʿth branch and laid the foundations for bitter conflict between the two branches of the party that persists to this day. The Iraqi branch of the party seized power in Iraq in 1968 and, like its counterpart in Syria, stayed in power despite often serious domestic and regional challenges.

In the 1950s, the Baʿth developed branches in almost every Arab country. Its influence was strongest in Syria, Iraq, Jordan, and Lebanon and among the diaspora Palestinian community. Its membership was drawn mostly from the urban middle and lower middle-classes and appealed specially to professionals and other members of the intelligentsia. Although it attracted many Sunni Muslims, it was Alawis, Druzes, Shiʿa and Greek Orthodox Christians who were overrepresented in the party (Batatu 1978, 748). The Baʿth was from its inception a very vocal group and played a central role in spreading Aflaq's brand of romantic, spiritual Arab nationalism through speechmaking, pamphleteering, and organization, to a large section of the politically active generation of their time. Their line of thinking became the dominant one in Arab nationalist circles and underlay much of the rhetoric of Nasir and other nationalist leaders.

Gamal Abd al-Nasir: The Chimeric Arab Bismarck. The idea of Arab nationalism began to gain acceptance in Egypt in the 1930s as a result of the efforts of Husri and other spokesmen and with some encouragement from King Farouk who perceived a possible benefit in terms of regional authority if he were to lead such a movement. Farouk also was attracted by the possibility, which had also occurred to the earlier Khedive Ismaʿil, of being chosen as a new Arab caliph. The

British were encouraging their version of an Arab union that they hoped would help strengthen their monarchical allies in Egypt, Jordan, and Iraq. Moreover, Arabism in Egypt had always been closely linked with Islam among religious reformers such as Rida and Kawakibi who regarded a revived Arabism as part and parcel of a revived Islam. By the early 1940s, even the Wafd party, which had long been critical of Arab nationalist pretensions, negotiated Egypt's participation in the founding of the British-sponsored Arab League in 1945.

As Ralph Coury notes, the emergence of Arab nationalism in Egypt is distinct from its emergence in Syria and has different causes (Coury 1982, 459–61). First, as the Egyptian economy developed, Egyptian business leaders, especially the Misr group, began to realize the value of opening up Arab markets to Egyptian capital, products, and labor. Second, as the hold of European powers on the region loosened and as political movements in the Arab world, especially Syria, called for Egypt's political, financial, and moral support, Egypt began to discern a leadership role for itself in the Arab world. Finally, the issue of Palestine and the potential threat of a Zionist state there forced Egyptian elites to look beyond Egypt's borders and to consider common Arab interests.

The Free Officers coup of July 1952, which toppled the old regime and inaugurated Nasir's populist rule, soon confirmed Egypt's reorientation toward the Arab world. Although the Free Officers' early ideological proclivities were somewhat unclear beyond the stated goals of putting an end to "autocracy, imperialism, and feudalism," by 1956–57, Nasir had adopted a revolutionary Arab nationalism, in many ways similar to that of the Ba'th, as the guiding ideology of the new regime. Through his state socialist reforms of the 1960s, his establishment of a populist bureaucratic-authoritarian regime, and his leaning toward the Soviet Union while remaining within the Non-Aligned Movement, Nasir provided a concrete example for other Arab nationalist regimes that came to power in other parts of the Arab world. While the Ba'th provided the theory and poetry of revolutionary Arab nationalism, Nasir provided the policy and the practice. To be sure, he also provided the drama. Nasir's nationalization of the Suez Canal and his subsequent defiance of the combined Anglo, French, and Israeli invasion established him as the charismatic hero of Arab nationalism. Until his death in 1970, he remained, in popular perceptions, the nearly undisputed leader of the Arab nationalist movement and the central player in its evolution.

Nasir served a role similar to that of Lenin, Mao, Hitler, Castro, and Khomeini, among others, in helping the ideology of secular Arab nationalism come to dominate the thinking of most of the Arab new middle class in the 1950s and 1960s. His charisma derived not only from his personal qualities but also largely from the series of events (his prominence in the Bandung Conference, the nationalization of the Suez canal, the rapprochement with the Soviet Union, the Egyptian-Syrian union, the socialist reforms) which cast him in a particularly favorable light. As Nasir was accepted as a popular hero, the content of his declarations and speeches, which essentially reflected a secular, Arab nationalist, increasingly socialist outlook, was accepted by his receptive audience. Arab nationalism, it is true, developed considerably before the influence of Nasir made itself felt, but without him, the ideology would not have gained the wide prominence and legitimacy it enjoyed in the 1960s and still enjoys among the middle class that came to political awareness during his time.

Nasir, however, also helped elaborate a statist version of Arab nationalism. While espousing Arab nationalist slogans, he pursued forceful Egyptian statist policies, both domestically and regionally. He built up effective state institutions, especially in the security sphere, and expanded the public sector in the economic and educational spheres. He played a large role in defining the shape and function of the contemporary Arab state. The example set by Nasir was then emulated by numerous Arab nationalist military or one-party regimes in Syria, Iraq, Libya, and elsewhere. By forging a middle ground between Arab nationalist ideology and statist politics, he pointed the way for other Arab nationalist regimes stuck between the dreams of pan-Arabism and the demands of *realpolitik.*

The Arab Nationalist Movement: The Swing from the Authoritarian Right to the Marxist Left

The Arab National Movement (ANM), the second most influential Arab nationalist party after the Baʿth, was founded by a handful of students at the American University of Beirut in the aftermath of the 1948 defeat. They all had been students of Constantine Zurayq, a

Syrian Christian professor at the university with strong Arab nationalist convictions, and were inspired by his appeal to Arab youth to take the lead in promoting the nationalist cause. In his two main works, al-Wa'y al-Qawmi (National Awakening, 1939) and Ma'na an-Nakba (The Meaning of the Catastrophe, 1948), Zurayq called for revolution in the Arab world to create the material and spiritual conditions necessary for resisting European and Zionist domination and forging a new, bright future for Arab society.

The ANM was formed under the collective leadership of George Habash (Palestinian), Wadi' Haddad (Palestinian), Hani al-Hindi (Syrian), and Ahmad al-Khatib (Kuwaiti). It developed branches in Syria, Jordan, Iraq, Egypt, and the Gaza strip and focused more than any other Arab nationalist group on the problem of Palestine and the need to regain the lost homeland through the organization and unification of the Arab world's material and military potential. The movement was dominated by Palestinians and was attracted to the powerful figure of Nasir, who seemed to provide a shining example of the promise of discipline, organization, and bold action. It borrowed the nationalist arguments of Husri but injected them with the anger and bitterness of the Palestinian experience as expressed in their slogan: Unity, Liberation, and Vengeance (Kazziha 1975, 50). The ANM was criticized for its glorification of military virtues and was labeled the "Fire and Iron Group" by its critics (ibid., 54). The movement published only one theoretical work, which outlines its guiding principles, namely, Ma' al-Qawmiyya al-'Arabiyya (With Arab Nationalism, 1960), by al-Hakam Darwazah and Hamid Jabburi.

Unlike the Ba'th, the ANM was in favor of union between Arab states regardless of the nature of the regimes involved. They backed the Syrian-Iraqi unity plan of 1954, the Syrian-Egyptian merger of 1958, and the Hashemite Federation of the same year. Unlike other Arab nationalists, they insisted that unity would lead to social and political progress and not vice versa. In the years roughly between 1958 and 1965, the movement paid almost absolute allegiance to Nasir's leadership, and was generally regarded as an instrument of his will outside of Egypt. The ANM had set itself against left-leaning nationalists who had posited internal class struggle as part of the process of national liberation. The ANM argued that internal conflict weakened the Arab nation, and that unity and solidarity were before all other concerns in the nationalist struggle. They modified this position after 1958, however, to fall closer in line with Nasir's newfound socialism.

From the early 1960s, the party began a drift to the left that brought with it new ideas and orientations and eventually led to the disintegration of the group. A number of younger party members, led by Nayef Hawatmeh and Muhsin Ibrahim, began to take exception with the traditional right-wing ideology of the party and to introduce Marxist categories into their analysis of the Arab condition. They advocated a more mass-based ANM membership and objected to the authoritarian leadership of Habash. Many of the old guard and most of the Palestinians rallied around Habash, whereas most of the non-Palestinians lined up alongside the party dissidents. After all, the ANM's activities in areas not directly adjacent to Palestine could not all be conditioned by the need to unify Arab ranks at any cost in the fight against Israel. That position proved untenable in a political arena that was already awash with socialist and revolutionary rhetoric. By 1965, the ANM, for all intents and purposes, had disintegrated, with different branches pursuing their own local policies. Habash and many of the Palestinian leaders of the movement moved to focus more closely on the Palestinian issue especially as Fateh, the Palestine Liberation Organization (PLO), and other Palestinian organizations were beginning to challenge the ANM's standing in the Palestinian refugee camps. As discussed in chapter 4, after 1967 the ANM adopted a revolutionary Marxist line and gave birth to the Popular Front for the Liberation of Palestine (PFLP), the Popular Democratic Front for the Liberation of Palestine (PDFLP), the Popular Front for the Liberation of Palestine—General Command (PFLP-GC), and other groups.

The importance of the ANM comes mainly from its widespread ideological influence. Because it did not enjoy a prominent position in government power like the Baʿth and Nasir (a branch of the ANM did, however, come to power in South Yemen), the ANM came to attract the more radical elements of the nationalist movement and eventually moved into a Leninist and, in some cases, Maoist ideological position.

The general movement of revolutionary Arab nationalism had reached its high point with the Egyptian-Syrian unity of 1958–61. The secession of Syria, however, the embroilment of Egypt in the Yemen war, and the humiliating blow dealt to Egypt and Syria by Israel in 1967 deflated the movement. It was superseded in the late 1960s and early 1970s by a more radical Marxism on the left, and a resurgent fundamentalist Islam on the right (see chaps. 3 and 4). The movement, however, left behind a number of Arab nationalist regimes, most notably the Baʿthist governments of Iraq and Syria, and a generalized sense of Arab community. This sense of community was expressed in a vague common ambition to improve economic, cultural, and political relations between the various Arab states and, possibly, to develop some form of Arab community that would help regularize such relations. Even such modest ambitions, however, seem still very far from realization.

The Ideology of Arab Nationalism: The Contributions of Satiᶜ al-Husri and Michel Aflaq

As mentioned earlier, the Arab nationalism of the 1950s and 1960s went well beyond the Arabism of the interwar period. The latter was understood as a simple pride in the Arab heritage and a preference for Arab self-rule over domination by Turks or Europeans. It proposed no radical change in social or political values. Arab nationalism as it emerged after World War II, however, proposed a deep transformation of political and cultural life based on secularism, state socialism, and devotion to the nation in the spirit of modern Western nationalism. Of the two central formulators of the ideology, Satiᶜ al-Husri and Michel Aflaq, the former laid the foundations for a culturally based secular nationalism and the latter grafted onto that nationalism, a philosophy of social, economic, and cultural renewal that gave it deeper intellectual and popular appeal. A more comprehensive study would examine the work of Constantine Zurayq, Zaki al-Arsouzi, Nadim al-Bitar, Abd al-Rahman al-Bazzaz, Edmond Rabbath, and others. Considerations of scope and space prevent me from doing so here.

Satiᶜ al-Husri: Laying the Foundations

Satiᶜ Khaldun al-Husri was born to a Syrian family in Yemen in 1882 where his father served as chief Ottoman *qadi* (religious judge). He received a largely secular education at a number of Ottoman institutions, majored in the natural sciences, and eventually visited France, Switzerland, and Belgium where he pursued studies in education (Tibi 1981, 92). Turkish was his first language, French his second, and Arabic only his third, although by his middle thirties he had developed it to fluency. He started his career in the Ottoman educational system and soon acquired a reputation as an ambitious modernizing reformer. He rose to prominence after the 1908 coup under the patronage of the Young Turk regime. His first fling with the nationalist idea found expression in his championing of Ottoman nationalism as the sole means of preserving the Ottoman empire and resisting the threat from the thoroughly nationalized European world. His sympathies for Arab nationalism grew, however, as the Istanbul regime began to pursue a highly centralized policy of Turkification that clashed harshly with Arab political and cultural aspirations. He also had contact with several of the public and secret Arab organizations that were forming in the fetid prewar atmosphere.

In 1919, after the collapse of the empire, Husri traveled to British-occupied, Arab-governed Syria where he began a long and vital career as a champion of Arab nationalism in the Arab world. The bulk of his career was spent in Iraq where between 1921 and 1941 he served in many high educational posts, among them, his six-year stint as director-general of Education. Troubles with the British in 1941 forced him to leave Iraq for Beirut where he stayed till he was called to Damascus by the newly independent government there in 1944. After engineering a number of important educational reforms, Syrian opposition groups forced his ouster from Syria, at which point he returned to Lebanon and then to Cairo where he served as senior advisor to the Cultural Committee of the Arab League. He retired in 1957 after a long and vigorous career, returned to Beirut and eventually to Baghdad where he died in 1968.

Husri's thought was influenced most strongly by that of the German nationalist philosopher Johann Gottlieb Fichte who insisted on the central role of education in disseminating the nationalist spirit and bringing about the ultimate political unity to which nationalism naturally yearned. What Fichte proposed was "a total change of the existing system of education . . . as the sole means of preserving the existence of the German nation" (Fichte 1922, 13). What Husri undertook was to transform radically the educational programs in Arab countries in order to inculcate into the young that sense of national identity, pride, and allegiance that would provide the motive force for national unification at a later date. He sought to do this by educational reforms, the many lectures he gave, and articles he wrote, all of which were directed, as were those of Fichte, to "the educated classes" (Fichte 1922, 17). Husri summed up his emphasis on education in the nationalist struggle in the following terms: Assure me of unity of education, and I will guarantee all other aspects of unity.

The strength of Husri's influence on subsequent generations of Arab nationalists derives from the simplicity and clarity of his message and the singleminded tirelessness with which he pursued its dissemination. He marshaled reasonable arguments to show that the Arabs comprised one national unit shaped by language and history and that they, therefore, should and could form one political entity as had the Germans and Italians. He was convinced that the nationalist imperatives that had transformed Europe would similarly and inexorably culminate in the national unification of the Arab people, and he saw his role as that of the precursor and the herald who would help plant the nationalist idea and foster its transformation of Arab society in preparation for the final nationalist act of fusion.

I have opted to devote considerable space to an exposition of the views of Husri and Aflaq, and those of other central ideologues in succeeding chapters, in order to present the content of their thought within the complete structure of their worldviews. A brief paraphrasing would sum up their views, but, in the process, it would mask the complexity, power, and attractiveness of their ideologies.

Following the lead of another German thinker on nationalism, Johann G. von Herder, Husri assumed a cultural approach to politics that contrasted sharply with the social contract and natural law tradition developed in England and France. For Husri, as for Herder, "the proper foundation for a sense of collective political identity is not the acceptance of a common sovereign power (e.g., Hobbes, Locke, Rousseau), but the sharing of a common culture" (Barnard 1969, 7). This understanding of political identity fit nicely with the predicament of Arab political society in which a culture was widely shared but political sovereignty was deeply fragmented. This philosophy, therefore, could assert the existence of an Arab nation despite the absence of a unified Arab state—an assertion that could not have been made under the contractarian philosophies of the French and the English. It was in establishing the reality of the Arab nation in this way that Husri made his most seminal contribution to Arab nationalist thought.

As he considered culture the foundation of nationhood, so Husri understood language to be the principal source of culture. Hence, his definition of nationhood, as with many German thinkers that followed Herder, was based first and foremost on the dominance and dissemination of a common language. Indeed, for Husri, language was the living soul of a nation: "If a nation loses its language, and comes to use another language, that nation has lost its life, and has become totally dissolved in the nation from which it adopted its new language" (Husri 1944, 27). To document his convictions, Husri cited the example of the Germans and Italians whose linguistic heritage overcame their political fragmentation in defining and realizing their nationhood. He cited also the national revolutions of the Greeks, Slavs, and other Balkan linguistic groups. Understandably, Husri's emphasis on the importance of language dictated a dedication to the development and use of the Arabic language to the exclusion of all foreign languages at all levels of education and in all domains— journalistic, literary, and scientific. Although some earlier Arab nationalists had occasionally expressed their nationalist sentiments in French (e.g., Negib Azoury, *Le reveil de la nation Arabe*, 1906), with Husri, the Arab Nationalist message became inextricably bound up with the use of the Arabic language itself. Concomitantly, it became infused with Arabic's own stock of emotion and evocative power.

In Husri's understanding of nationalism, history followed language as a source of political identity and community. Whereas language was the soul and life of a nation, history was the source of its sentiment and self-consciousness. "Every nation gains a sense of itself and develops its personality through its own peculiar past" (Husri 1944, 28). This commonly held past "generates a commonality of emotions and outlooks; it leads to a homogeneity in the remembrance of past glories and past calamities and a similarity in attitudes toward the present and hopes for the future" (ibid., 28). Husri was quick to point out, however, that what was most important about history in this respect was not those facts and figures recorded in books and buried between the yellowed pages of aging manuscripts, but that living past, that imperfect but powerful remembrance of things past, that abides in the minds of people and quietly shapes their personality and behavior. He would not discount the importance of actual historical events in delimiting the boundaries of community and giving rise to a common language and a shared identity, but in his reference to history as the second source of national political identity, Husri was highlighting its subjective psychological side—the image of the past reflected in the present. As such, Husri's insistence on the importance of history was not a call to dispassionate historiographers but an appeal to gifted mythmakers who could construct from the debris of the past a grand and glittering edifice to serve as a source of confidence and inspiration for the entire nation.

In his less than scientific attitude toward history—especially the teaching of history—Husri echoed the thinking of the French philosopher Ernest Renan who argued that "forgetting, and I would even say historical error, are essential factors in the formation of any nation" (Renan 1882, 7). Husri defended his position by arguing that history was filled with an infinite array of events and processes; to teach it, one must perforce summarize and omit. Husri only asked that such summarization and omission be carried out in accordance with the interests of strengthening national consciousness (Husri 1944, 21). Although he himself shrank from the task of elaborating a monumental account of Arab history, the principle that such a history was needed and the conviction that, in some sense, it *must* exist was taken seriously by later historians in the Arab nationalist movement. Although Husri had warned that a nation that loses its language ceases to exist, he warned that a nation that has forgotten its past, although still alive, is inert and unconscious. Although the loss of language ended finally in death, the incapacitation brought about by the loss of one's history could be repaired through a resuscitation and reconstruction of that past. He opposed the use of foreign history textbooks in Arab classrooms and called on Arab historians to provide the nation with its own nationalist history as the European nations had each provided for their young.

Throughout his career, Husri would hold to the view that language and history, in that order of importance, were the two primary factors in the constitution of nations. This conviction was very much in the German nationalist tradition and went on to characterize the mainstream of Arab nationalist thought in later decades. Husri, however, did not deny the influence of other secondary factors, for example, religion. Similarly to language and history, religion tended to generate a commonality of feeling and belief that might serve as a potent social adhesive. Husri warned, however, that the effects of religion in the realm of politics were not all of one pattern. First, different religions had different political tendencies. Second, religion played different political roles in different political epochs. Among religions, Husri distinguished between national and universal religions. The former was confined to a nation as determined linguistically and historically; it was closed to other nations and, hence, joined language and history as a reinforcing pillar of national identity and nationalist esprit. Among such religions, he listed the Judaism of the Hebrews and the pagan, state, or tribal religions of ancient times. Universal religions, however, like Christianity, Islam, and Buddhism, overstepped national boundaries to reach people of all nations and to establish bonds higher and more comprehensive than those of language and history. In so doing, universal religions undermined national distinctions and undercut the value and belief systems on which nationalism rested. In this struggle between nationalism and universal religions for the organization of societies, Husri argued that nationalism had emerged triumphant. For even though Christianity and Islam both succeeded in temporarily maintaining multinational religious empires, neither was able, despite their utmost efforts, to replace language and history as the fundamental bases for political community. Both religious empires eventually broke down into their national components.

Although language would always overcome religion in the long run as the basis of community, the influence of geography, Husri pointed out, might not be so surmountable. Geography could play a potent and permanent disintegrative role, for if a nation, a people sharing a common language and history, came to be spread across a formidable geophysical obstacle, an ocean or a high mountain range, the language and history they initially shared in common might evolve in divergent directions and eventuate in the articulation of two distinct nationalities. Such was the effect of the Atlantic Ocean on the English who developed an American nation in North America or the Spaniards and Portuguese who developed distinct nationalities in South America. Unlike some other nationalist thinkers, Husri downplayed all but such extreme influences of geography in the formation of nations. Except where geography physically separated a people for centuries, its influence was subordinate to that of language and history. The physical was subordinate to the phenomenal; nature, subordinate to culture. Such a view was essential to the reinforcement of an Arab nationalist perspective because, unlike France, England, or Germany, the Arab nation inhabited lands as diverse as the dry deserts of Nejd, the fertile basins of the Nile and Euphrates, and the high mountaintops of Lebanon.

The alternative principles of nationality that Husri sought most ardently to refute, however, even more than religion or geography, were those based on race and individual will. The former would fragment the racially heterogeneous Arab nation; the latter would deny that such a nation existed on the simple evidence that people said so. The idea of race, descent from a common ancestry, has never been too far from any popular concept of nationality because people naturally yearn to recreate the familiar biological bonds of family in the larger political community. German nationalist thought, however, beginning in the racial romanticism of Fichte and Arndt and culminating in the grand distortions of Nazism, had elevated the notion of race to Olympian heights. Because Arab sentiment was quite favorable toward the Germans after the duplicity of the French and British in World War I, the racial theories of the German neonationalists were given widespread exposure. Most importantly, they were being championed quite forcefully in the ideology of the Syrian Social Nationalist party that Antun Saʿadeh had founded in the mid-1930s. Husri, however, rejected these theories, arguing simply that none of the European nations, Germany included, were racially pure, but that, quite to the contrary, they were composed of several different racial strains. Husri's criticism of racial theories was made easier by the antiracial ideological attitude impressed upon society by Islam.

The principles of contract, consent, and free will that had woven themselves into the fabric of French, English, and American nationalism could be accepted only equivocally by the early Arab nationalists. Because Husri's role was that of a preacher among skeptics, he had to prove the soundness of his message from sources other than the disposition of his audience. Husri's antipathy toward the free will and contractarian approaches to nationalism mirrored the German position in which, before 1870, evidence had to be provided for the existence of a German nation without a clear manifestation of comprehensive collective will in that direction. In the Arab world, Husri also had to combat divergent nationalisms, such as Egyptian, Lebanese, and Syrian nationalisms, and alternative forms of political community, such as the confessional sectarianism of the Levant and the tribalism of the Arabian Peninsula.

In arguing against the primacy of free will in the determination of nationality, Husri was responding to the view popularized by Renan in his *Qu'est-ce qu'une nation?* "L'existence d'une nation est (pardonnez-moi cette metaphore) un plebiscite de tous les jours" (Renan 1882, 27). Husri raised a number of objections to this view. The collective or general will could not be ascertained except through voting, but voting was vulnerable to outside influence and propaganda and was, hence, very changeable. Was the nation then little different from a political party whose fortunes ebbed and flowed with the tide of popular sentiment? "If we accept the proposition that 'the nation is a group of people who want to live together and want to constitute an independent nation' we must also ask: what are the reasons and factors that generate such a desire among certain groups?" (Husri 1944, 41), which brings one back to original causes—unity of language and history. Husri also marshaled historical evidence to bolster his view: Does one consider the United States two nations because the South wanted to secede from the Union? (ibid.,41) Does one have to be sure of an Egyptian's views before ascertaining that he is an Egyptian? (Husri 1951a, 45)

No, Husri concluded. Arabs were Arabs for linguistic and historical reasons beyond their control. Every person whose native tongue was Arabic was an Arab. If anyone denied or was unaware of his or her Arab identity, one must search for the cause of this peculiar self-deception: "If it stems from ignorance, we must enlighten him; if it stems from a sluggish sensibility, we must awaken him; if it stems from excessive selfishness, we must discipline him . . . [but] he is an Arab, whether we will it or not, whether he admits it or not" (ibid., 45). Like the Germans, Husri had established the existence of the nation in categories detached from contemporary political conditions. Even if it could not be seen on the surface of things, the nation was immanent and would gradually manifest itself in a natural inexorable unfolding.

Husri never questioned the assumption that a nation naturally yearned to express itself in the establishment of an independent self-governing national state. He pointed out that the French, having lived for so long in a unified national state, had lost the distinction between nation and state, referring to membership in either or both with the word *nationalité*. The Germans, on the other hand, had grown painfully aware of the difference, labeling membership in a state, *Nationalität;* and in a nation, *Volkstum*. The path from nation to national state, Husri was well aware, was a long and difficult one. The Arab nation was still taking its very first steps in a long march. What was needed for the journey, Husri believed, was a healthy store of faith and confidence to get it through its long formative years—conviction in the existence of the Arab nation, pride in its past, and faith in its ultimate triumph. He likened the nationalist struggle to a military campaign in which troop morale is a critical element of victory. A dispirited nation would easily falter and fail; a proud nation would refuse defeat and continue the struggle till the end was secured. To inculcate this pride into the population was a task for educational institutions and would be aimed at society's most malleable stratum—youth.

Of the feeble esprit of the young generation of Arab nationalists, Husri often spoke disparagingly. They expected quick and easy victories, he charged, and when such victories were not gained, they surrendered to pessimism and despair (Husri 1944, 51). Husri concluded that this weakness derived from an ill-conceived approach to Arab history and an unfamiliarity with the history of other national awakenings (ibid., 52). Belief in a triumphant future, Husri argued, was derived principally from an immersion in the glories of the past, which naturally fostered the conviction that such glories could come to the nation once again. But a student who was ceaselessly exposed to the seamier sides of Arab history—the epochs of decline, the dynastic

wars, the corruption—would come away with little pride in his nation and scant conviction that it could ever rise from its sorry state.
Similarly, youth with little understanding of the victorious eruptions
of other nations would have little concept of what a national
awakening meant and where it might lead. In pedagogical terms, to
foment the awakening of the Arab nation Husri urged the intensive
immersion of students in a selective glorified account of the Arab
past along with a more objective account of other nationalist movements, especially the German and Italian, but also the French and
several of the Balkan movements.

Husri forwarded this call for the teaching of selective Arab history boldly and without apologies. What was desirable in science, he
argued, the unfettered search for truth, might not be desirable in
education where the prime business was the molding of children into
adults with the character, values, and self-confidence to serve as leading
members of society. In the midst of a nationalist struggle, the need to
direct education was especially acute, and to overlook the early
sources of defiance or despair—in the school classroom—would be to
compromise the interests of the nation and its members, both born
and unborn. True to his word, Husri devoted the bulk of his career to
reforming educational curricula along these lines first in Iraq, then in
Syria, and soon more generally through his affiliation with the agen-
cies of the Arab League.

Husri was not unaware that actual political unification would
require political and, perhaps, military initiatives beyond his educational purview, but what was essential to him was that the idea of
nationalism be disseminated in Arab society so that a future Arab Bismarck or Gandhi would find a ready and responsive nation. Indeed,
Husri rarely spoke of how he thought Arab unity would eventually
come about or what political form it would take once it did. He felt it
distracting and divisive to so prematurely debate such complex issues.
For him, the task at hand was simply to prepare the community for
the idea of national unity. How unity would ultimately come about
and what form it would assume were still distant issues. On the one
hand, the vagueness of the programmatic aspects of Husri's nationalism helped protect it from criticism and political conflict and went a
long way in allowing the nationalist idea to thrive in polities where,

had programmatics been declared, bitter dispute would likely have arisen. On the other hand, this vagueness drove nationalist thinking into a romanticism that was emotionally very attractive but which provided little political guidance once Arab nationalist groups came to political power in the 1950s and 1960s. Beyond his strategy for education, Husri did not provide a strategy for securing unified statehood once the populace had been won over to nationalism, nor did he specify how Arab nationalists should proceed if and when they came to power.

Sati⁽ al-Husri, philosopher and educator, was the first major thinker of modern Arab nationalism. Drawing on the German nationalist tradition, he established the existence of the Arab nation on facts of language, culture, and history. His goal was to convince the Arab intelligentsia of the reality of the Arab nation and to spread faith in its ultimate triumph. He clung to a minimalist understanding of nationalism, describing it simply as a movement toward political unity. He avoided outlining a strategy for the establishment of a unified Arab state or a blueprint for its internal organization. Similarly, he avoided delineating the role of Islam within a unified Arab state. His was a pure and simple nationalism. It could be accepted by many, but it left many questions unanswered. His importance in the Arab nationalist movement itself was immense. In the words of Bassam Tibi,

the significance of Sati⁽ al-Husri's work lies first of all in the fact that it faithfully reflects an important phase in modern Arab history and the political thought which accompanied it, and secondly in that his writings themselves had a considerable impact on political developments in the Middle East. al-Husri's ideas became part of an obligatory political ideology in those Arab states which were formed out of the process of decolonization after the Second World War. They were also taken as the guiding principles of the nationalist parties and organizations which represented the Arab national movement in their period. (Tibi 1981, 173)

Michel Aflaq: Arabism as a Radical Sociopolitical Program

To work its effect on society, ideology must go through a sentimental and emotive process by which a group of ideas becomes a highly charged and motivating set of beliefs, slogans, and symbols. As Daniel Bell noted, "Ideology . . . is a secular religion" (Bell 1960,

394), and religion is first and foremost, faith and passion. In a role similar to that of the architect in construction, an artist must come along to breathe life and beauty into the cold lines and angles of intellectual constructions. For the idea of nationalism, "the outcome of the process is that a nationalist theology of intellectuals becomes a nationalist mythology for the masses" (Hayes 1960,168). Foremost among his contemporaries, the young Syrian historian Michel Aflaq helped transform the dry nationalist concepts first developed by Husri into a vibrant and compelling ideology. It was in the ringing slogans and romantic symbols that Aflaq and his colleagues draped over the nakedness of the nationalist idea that Arab nationalism found its way into the hearts of an entire generation and provoked intense ideological upheaval in the Arab world. The spiritual and romantic aspects of nationalism deemed so necessary by Husri, yet handled so clumsily by him for whom Arabic was only a third language, were highlighted by Aflaq and the Baʿth party. Although the contribution of Arsouzi, Bitar, and others was significant, Aflaq's thought dominated the Baʿth party from its establishment until the mid-1950s in Syria and the early 1960s in Iraq; in that period, the ideology of the Baʿth was essentially "Michel Aflaq writ large" (Batatu 1978, 730).

Poetic vision was by no means Aflaq's only contribution to the nationalist movement. In intellectual terms, he recast the Arab nationalist idea to reflect a strong, progressive revolutionary attitude consonant with the rising intranational class tensions of the postcolonial Arab Middle East, insisting on the overthrow of the ruling class and socialism as pillars of the new nationalism. He also more boldly delineated the separation of Islam from politics and the equidistance of Arab nationalism from both East and West. More than Husri, he gave meaning to Arab authenticity and insisted that the Arab nation had a unique spiritual mission to fulfill after its first contribution of Islam in the seventh century. Some of these ideas were not original to Aflaq but were adopted and arranged by him into a compelling and attractive tableau. Finally, Aflaq was a dedicated cabalist whose efforts gave birth to a political party whose explosive growth pushed it to the forefront of Arab politics and carried it to power in the central Arab lands of Syria and Iraq.

Michel Aflaq was born in 1910 to a middle-class Christian family in Damascus. A strong high school record took him to the Sorbonne from which he returned in 1933 to teach history in Syrian government schools. His association with French Leftists and his disaffection with the Syrian government and ruling class led him into the Syrian Communist party. Disgruntled with the party's support of the stillborn Franco-Syrian Treaty of 1936 and disappointed with the colonial policies of the ostensibly leftist Leon Blum government of France, Aflaq left the Communist party disillusioned but not uninfluenced by its ideology and organization, much of which would find its way into the Ba'th party. He was also impressed by the ideology and organization of the Syrian Social Nationalist party of Antun Sa'adeh which had just been established and was quickly becoming very powerful. As mentioned earlier, Aflaq cofounded the Arab Ba'th party in the early 1940s and led it to positions of political prominence in Syria and Iraq. Aflaq was forced out of Syria in the mid-1960s by the new Alawi-dominated military wing of the party there, which staged a coup against the party's old guard and embarked on a more leftist policy course. Aflaq spent most of his remaining years in Baghdad under the protection of the Ba'th regime that had reclaimed power in 1968. He remained the titular head of the party but had lost any real influence over party or political affairs. Upon his death in the summer of 1989, the Iraqi government announced that he had converted to Islam before his passing. Whether this was actually true, or whether the regime merely declared it to shore up its sagging legitimacy in a period of Islamic revivalism, is not yet clear. Nevertheless, this small, mild-mannered school teacher died a national hero, the spiritual godfather of two Arab states and a much wider pan-Arab movement.

Aflaq insisted that "thought in itself is an immeasurable revolutionary force in history" (Aflaq 1959, 109). If one is to gauge by the meteoric rise of his small band of unprepossessing intellectuals, Aflaq could not be too far wrong. What then were the ideas that were found so appealing by a generation of Arabs?

The existence of the Arab nation, a proposition that Husri struggled hard to establish, could be taken for granted by Aflaq. "In itself, Arab nationalism for us Ba'thists is a self-evident reality not in need of special investigation or affirmation, but the meaning and content of this nationalism are in dire need of clarification, elaboration, and struggle . . . in other words, it is not our business to debate whether we are or are not Arabs—for it is evident that we are—but rather to discern and delineate the content of our Arabness at this historical juncture of our Arab nation." (ibid., 102)

Following Husri's definition of nationhood, Aflaq affirmed that language was the principal unifying factor in the Arab nation in that unity of language promoted with it unity of thought, norms, and ideals (ibid., 103). Like Husri also, history, for Aflaq, followed language in the determination of nationhood as the "fertile ground in which our consciousness took shape" (ibid., 103).

Aflaq's nationalist ideology, however, was couched primarily in the philosophic concept of national cultural *inbiʿath,* or *baʿth,* i.e., renaissance, or flowering. Aflaq considered the heart of his message to be a call for a general Arab renaissance that would transform Arab civilization in all its aspects—political, economic, intellectual, and moral—and which would provide a unique and historic contribution to humanity and world civilization. This renaissance would be a reiteration inasmuch as it would resemble the spiritual and moral upheaval that accompanied the forging of Islam in the seventh century, but it would also be innovative in that it would express itself freely in a unique unprecedented system of values, beliefs, attitudes, and symbols inspired by the Arab nation's contemporaneous economic, political, cultural, moral, and religious conditions. Islam had been the Arab nation's seventh-century contribution to humanity; the Arab nation of the twentieth century in the crucible of its acute contemporaneous suffering would forge the elements of a new message for humanity. This philosophy was summarized by Aflaq in the Baʿth party's primary slogan and rallying cry: One Nation, Bearing an Eternal Message.

The means for promoting this renaissance get closer to the heart of his nationalist program. The groundwork for the Arab renaissance would be laid by the revolutionary transformation of Arab society toward the goals of unity, liberty, and socialism.

For Aflaq, all nations were either in a state of growth or in a state of decline. There was no middle course. Strong nations were like healthy bodies in that their natural progress was toward continued health. Nations in a state of decline, such as the Arab nation, were like ill bodies in that their natural progress was toward a progressive worsening of the illness (ibid.,78). The maledictions of the Arab nation, "feudalism, sectarianism, regionalism, intellectual reactionism," could not be eased without a revolutionary reversal (Aflaq 1958, 10). Any compromising reformism would only cloud the issues and allow further decline and deterioration.

The success of the revolution depended on the intensity and purity of the struggle between two minorities, a reactionary minority that clung to the Arab status quo claiming that the Arabs could achieve no more and a progressive minority that believed the status quo veiled the true potential of the Arab nation and choked its vitality. The former was in league with the colonial powers and enemies of the Arab nation and supported corruption, tyranny, and backwardness, whereas the latter had the interests of the nation at heart (ibid., 26). To succeed, the progressives, represented by the Baʿth party, had to hold religiously to their uncompromising revolutionary path (Aflaq 1959, 175). They could brook no compromise with the reactionaries lest the purity of their message be contaminated by the voracious corruption of their opponents (ibid., 166). Ideological stability and coherence were essential for the success of the struggle. In the end, change would come about as a dialectical result of the intensifying tension between progressives and reactionaries.

As in the Communist example, the success of the nationalist revolution depended on the creation of a vanguard party to spearhead the struggle, for the nationalist revolution was not a predetermined inevitable outcome. It was a goal that required great commitment and prolonged struggle. The Baʿth party was the vanguard party. Its first aim would be to create within itself the New Arab—one born of the contemporary deterioration but representing its absolute antithesis (ibid., 72). The task was to bring about the Arab of tomorrow to defeat the Arab of yesterday. Aflaq found the most fertile ground among youth. Unlike the old, youth had the most vital appetite and capacity for virtue and heroism and possessed a pure and necessary innocence unsullied by politics, private interest, and old outlooks (ibid., 37, 21). The young generation of Aflaq's contemporary Arab environment was especially ripe for enlightenment because "it had been driven to considering and questioning by the mistakes and hyperbole of the politicians" (ibid., 29).

The danger, however, was that the disillusionment of youth would promote an abandonment of civic and national virtues for an increasing obsession with individual gain and personal pleasure as Aflaq saw all around him. Such individualistic behavior made sense in healthy nations where individual and national interests had been brought into harmony by the nationalist revolution, but in regressive nations, like the Arab nation, individual and national interests were, for this prerevolutionary period, in deep conflict. Progress for the Arab nation, which meant revolution, required great sacrifice from the individual, and sacrifice required deep commitment and burning faith. Thus, the task of the party was to provide for the young generation a vivid image of the ideal society in which their true interests lay and for which they should struggle (ibid., 73). This vision must serve as a guide and a standard for action and commitment because the contemporary environment was too rife with corruption, compromise, and confusion to provide little short of dejection and despair. The party must bring forth a new self-confident generation of Arabs. And if the nation could produce this new Arab who had risen above the squalid reality, then surely the nation had the means to rise above itself (ibid., 74). The new generation's faith in the nation's potential would be derived from the very fact that the nation had created them.

As for the party itself, its organization must be determined by the general task of awakening more and more members of the nation to the new nationalist philosophy and challenging the elements of reaction and backwardness in the society (ibid., 186–91). In essence, the party was to constitute the nucleus of the future society. It expressed what was best and most essential in the Arab nation, and it served as the picture and model of its future (ibid., 154). In the beginning, the masses were left out of the party's domain of proselytization. Like the German nationalists of the early nineteenth century, Aflaq felt that the message must first be addressed to and absorbed by the educated elite and, preferably, the young among them. As the moment of confrontation with the status quo forces approached, however, the need for the gathering of sufficient political and economic influence loomed large. At that point, popular support was crucial. Furthermore, the success of the revolution depended on the vanguard's ability to unseat the old classes from their positions of political control. What was a general political, social, economic, moral, and spiritual movement would be narrowed down at the moment of decision to a political revolution; hence, the party, although allegedly concerned with social and cultural renaissance, was first and foremost a "political" party. As Aflaq explained, although politics was only "a means . . . [it] is the most serious of matters at this present stage" (ibid., 302).

In Communist revolutionary thought, the purpose of seizing power was to bring about the political and material conditions that would provide the basis for the emergence of Communist people and Communist society; in Baʿthist thought, the purpose of seizing power was to bring about the political and material conditions that would provide the basis for the emergence of new Arabs and the expression of the Arab spirit in an exuberant renaissance that would enlighten all of humanity. The conditions for this renaissance, which, taken together, represented the essential characteristics of the Baʿthist vision of the politico-economic future, were: unity, liberty, and socialism.

By the late 1930s and early 1940s the idea of Arab unity had accumulated a definite history in Aflaq's Syria from its beginnings in the 1916 Arab revolt through the agitation of the dominant Syrian elite against the French. Aflaq's main task, therefore, was to reinterpret the notion of Arab unity, strip it of its ruling class affiliations, and cast it in a progressive and revolutionary mold. He railed against the "illusions of kings and feudal lords who understood unity as gathering of backwardness to backwardness, exploitation to exploitation and numbers to numbers like sheep" (Aflaq 1958, 175). Indeed, it was the reactionary understanding of Arab unity, argued Aflaq, which had left the "struggle for unity without blood and nerve" (ibid., 175). Aflaq even went so far as to disparage the German example of national unification that had been central to much of Arab nationalist thought in the Germanophile interwar years pointing out that Bismarck had united Germany under the control of the reactionary and feudal classes, which only intensified the subjugation of the German people and gave rise to the harshest tyranny and oppression the modern age had seen. Were the Arab nation to follow that example, the dominance of the reactionary classes would only be enhanced and the slavery of the Arab mind and spirit further deepened (ibid., 41).

The vital potential of the nation, argued Aflaq, lay in *progressive* revolution; unity and the struggle for unity were integral parts of this revolution. To separate the struggle for unity from the social revolution was to weaken both movements. Arab unity and social revolution could only be fulfilled together, for the reactionary Arab ruling class, interested as it was in the status quo, would be hostile to the politico-economic transformation that true Arab unity would bring about, and the social revolution could not achieve its furthest stages unless the entire Arab nation was participating in it. Regional revolutions in one or another Arab state could secure some revolutionary headway but would be constrained by small populations, meager resources, and a hostile environment in which they were surrounded by enemies of progress across every border. To achieve its fullest potential, the Arab nation must live and breathe as a unitary organic whole. In a sense, Arab unity would be both a cause and an effect of the progressive nationalist revolution (Aflaq 1959, 231).

This radical understanding of Arab unity was evinced in Aflaq's critical attitude toward the Arab League, established in 1945, an institution which, Aflaq charged, consolidated regional interests and the influence of the reactionary ruling classes, thus, intensifying the problems of the Arab nation (Aflaq 1958, 20). In an Arab world populated in the majority by reactionary regimes, Aflaq was forced to sanction a piecemeal approach to Arab unity. Those Arab regions that had overthrown their reactionary classes would unite; as other regions shook free of reactionary control, they, too, would join the progressive unified state. All the while the liberated regions would be helping the other regions toward liberation knowing full well that true progress could not be realized until all populations were free and the Arab nation could seek out its future with the health and vitality of an organic whole.

The notion of liberty was close to the heart of Aflaq's nationalist philosophy. The realization and articulation of the nation's spiritual potential could only be realized through the unfettered development and interaction of individuals. Culture and values could not be dictated from above but could only grow in a climate of liberty and freedom. Political domination in the form of imperialism or local tyranny was an enemy of progress as was the moral or spiritual domination of religion and outdated value systems. The goal of the party was to interpose itself not only between the nation and its foreign oppressors, but also between the people and their tyrants, and between the individual and the oppressive rule of religion, custom, and tradition. The purpose was to salvage the spirit from coercion as "a means to release our high talents and creative forces, so we can realize our purpose, and the purpose of every human being, complete humanity" (Aflaq 1959, 206). "Liberty is not a luxury in the life of the nation but its basis and its essence and its meaning" (ibid., 319).

Aflaq, however, hesitated to clarify what arrangement of political institutions would best ensure this individual liberty. He was committed to an activist revolutionary party of the Leninist type which would spearhead the revolutionary struggle and seize political power to continue the revolutionary transformation of society by transforming the socio-economic and cultural foundations of society from above. The party had a vanguard activist role to play; hence, until such time as society had developed sufficiently, the party, although comprising only a numerical minority, would have to act on its own authority even if its policies met with opposition from the majority. As in the Communist model, the party supposedly knew the "true" interests of the people and had them deepest at heart, whereas the people, manipulated by oppressors and deluded by falsehoods and ignorance, often were the unwitting agents of their own misery. Liberty, it was assumed, would not be secured by institutional means vulnerable to the pernicious influence of reactionaries and exploiters but by the preeminence of the party for which liberty would be a deliberate positive policy. In a sense, liberty would not come about, it would be established by fiat of the party.

In short, Aflaq's concept of liberty under Baʿthist rule was not the common liberal concept of a set of established rights and duties under a democratic political system but an authoritarian form of political rule in which liberties of thought, expression, press, and so forth, would, presumably, be vigilantly protected by the government, but the liberty to contest political power would be conspicuously absent. The vulnerability of liberty in such an authoritarian political system is quite obvious; Aflaq never adequately addressed this risk.

Aflaq had been deeply impressed by the Marxist message. At the philosophic level, he regarded the Marxist insistence on the importance of material economic conditions in political life to be one of the great discoveries of the modern age (ibid., 8). At the practical political level he had seen the headway that the Communists and Socialists had made in the political arena by siding with the lower classes. Tomorrow belonged not to the ruling upper class but to the rising lower classes; therefore, for nationalism to succeed, it would have to tie itself into that unfolding dialectic. Aflaq admits as much, saying, "We did not adopt socialism out of books, abstractions, humanism, or pity, but rather out of need," for "the Arab working class . . . is the mover of history in this period" (ibid., 116). Aflaq conceded that Marx was right in arguing that classes were a central force in history (ibid., 222), but he diverged from the Marxist line toward a nationalist formulation by arguing that in the Arab world it was virtually the entire nation with all its classes that was struggling for advancement against the capitalist domination of foreign powers. Local capitalist industry was almost nonexistent, and the whole nation was held in economic subjection to the industrialized West. What in Europe was a struggle of classes was for the Arab world a struggle of an entire nation for economic and political independence. For the Arab, therefore, socialist and nationalist revolutions were one and the same (ibid., 203).

Aflaq's critique of Marxist socialism went further than that, however. While socialism justly emphasized the importance of material elements in political and moral life, Aflaq charged that Marx exaggerated his discovery by heralding it as the first and last truth of social life. To be heard, Marxism reduced life to only one of its dimensions—it announced a philosophy of materialism (ibid., 87). In doing so, it ignored the spiritual elements of human existence, and it failed to acknowledge the most potent, social spiritual force of the modern age, nationalism. Like all spiritual forces, true nationalism was a positive and uplifting force; by ignoring it, Marxism sank into a hateful, vengeful, and negative spiritual outlook. Aflaq accepted the possibility that lesser nations with weak national identities or less-vivid histories might follow the Marxist line because they had little to lose in the way of national spirit, but the Arabs had too grand a heritage for them to abandon it and follow a materialist internationalist philosophy (ibid., 197).

Like unity and liberty, socialism in Aflaq's philosophy was first and foremost a means to promote the ultimate *inbi'ath*, or renaissance. While unity provided organic wholeness to the nation and liberty provided the freedom necessary for renaissance, socialism provided the economic conditions that made political and cultural liberty meaningful. As Aflaq saw in Syria, constitutional democracy meant little in a country where pseudo-feudalism was the dominant form of economic organization. The peasant's economic bondage overshadowed and nullified his supposed political liberty. Liberty meant little for a population shackled by poverty and ignorance. Hence, socialism became a means to free the individual and to unleash the enslaved vitality of the nation. "What I seek through socialism is not to augment the bounty of factories but the bounty of life. It is not my ultimate goal that food is distributed equally but that every individual may be able to unleash his talents and powers" (ibid., 25). Socialism was "a means to satisfy the animal needs of man so he can be free to pursue his duties as a human being" (ibid., 26). By establishing economic equality it would "eliminate all privilege, exploitation, and domination by one group over another" (ibid., 95). Socialism, therefore, was the material precondition for liberty. It was not opposed to nationalism but an integral part of it.

Aflaq was by no means an economic thinker. His understanding of socialism was rudimentary. Essentially, it was a system within which state intervention would guarantee a fair and equitable distribution of wealth as a basis for equality and justice. Large enterprises would be under state control as would be prices and wages. Small-scale private ownership would be preserved as would be private inheritance. Unlike in Communist thought, the state played a principally distributive role in the economy and did not necessarily represent the working class or any other class. It was a progressive force that simply mediated and ensured economic justice.

Aflaq's use of the label "Arab socialism" had several significant elements. It signified that this socialism was in harmony with and subordinate to a certain nationalism, in this case, Arab nationalism. More importantly, however, Aflaq argued that this socialism was an original expression of the reformist egalitarian Arab spirit. The same spirit that had carried Muhammad to reform the social and economic institutions of his day carried the modern Baʿthists to transform their contemporary environment. Socialism was an expression of economic justice immanent in the Arab spirit and original to it. Therefore, in a very deep sense, this socialism was an authentic Arab expression.

It is not hard to discern that the interlocking of these three popular political themes of unity, liberty, and socialism was an intelligent move on the level of political strategy. By appealing to all three principles, Aflaq could place the Baʿth in the mainstream of progressive political life. We may recall that Husri was similarly concerned with broadening the appeal of his message, but whereas Husri was satisfied to show that his nationalist message was not in conflict with positions from the religious Right to the Communist Left, Aflaq took a more fruitful approach, eliminating the two extremes of religious Right and Communist Left and forging out of the divergent tendencies of the broad center a philosophy that insisted that nationalism contained all their objectives and was essential to the realization of each one of them. Aflaq was able, thus, to group all the progressive tendencies of the Arab center together and to multiply the power of the nationalist movement through diversification and consolidation of its sources of support. Outside of the Arab nationalist mainstream he left the Communists, the religious establishment, and the Islamic revivalists; within the arena he had gathered Arab nationalists, liberals, socialists and nearly all non-Communist, non-religious opponents of the status quo. This central alliance would prove a powerful and explosive force in the 1950s and 1960s.

It is difficult, in this detached analysis of Aflaq's thought to convey the music and emotion redolent in his work—the ringing phrases, the happy metaphors, the pithy epigrams. The strength of Aflaq's contribution to Arab nationalism lies as much in the ideas he elaborated as in the style in which he presented them. As George Sorel noted, "The idolatry of words plays a large part in the history of all ideologies" (Sorel 1950, 53). Aflaq was an especially gifted weaver of words. His awareness of the political power of the Arabic language would become a central pillar of Arab nationalism's hold on large sections of the population. In the words of Fouad Ajami, "The gripping language had been one of the principal weapons of the pan-Arabists in Cairo and Damascus: it intoxicated and created an impression of great power and accomplishment" (Ajami 1981, 26).

In intellectual terms, Aflaq's ideological contribution was seminal although not without its internal contradictions and omissions. He harnessed the appeal of Islam to the movement of Arab nationalism but did not resolve the obvious contradictions between his own secular outlook and the religious outlook of Islam. He also introduced socialism into the heart of the Arab nationalist message but failed to clarify what this "Arab socialism" meant in terms of workable and detailed social and economic guidelines. In Batatu's words,

The logical difficulties that, on examination, his ideology betrays, are not due merely to his romantic style, but also to his undisciplined eclecticism: his thoughts are a mixture of an essentially humanitarian nationalism and aspects of the individualism of the Enlightenment, the democratism of the Jacobins, the youth idealization of Mazzini, the class standpoint of Marx, the elitism of Lenin, and over and above that, a strong dose of Christian spirituality and a nationalistically interpreted Islam. (Batatu 1978, 730–31)

The Appeal and Social Dynamics of Arab Nationalism

The popularity of nationalist ideologies during the intermediate phases of modernization is not a phenomenon confined to the Arab world. Throughout the developing world, nationalism provides a way to adopt many of the patriotic, secular, and progressive outlooks of the West, recast them in nativist form, and then use them as a weapon against the domination of the West. It is a way to marry the ideas and principles of the West to the symbols and identity-structures of one's native culture. Arab nationalism was no exception. It was the door through which Western modernity entered the Arab world. As Kemal Karpat observed,

Ideology in the Middle East . . . performed an intellectual function within the general framework of modernization. It introduced new ideas by adapting them to indigenous forms of expression and values and eventually claimed to have created a new—albeit eclectic—national ideology. [This] facilitated further borrowing of ideas and values from other cultures without risking internal opposition. . . . It added new dimensions to thought by introducing to it economic, social, and political elements. (Karpat 1982, xxii)

Under Arab nationalist regimes, sweeping reforms of educational, economic, and social systems transformed most Arab societies beyond recognition. The success of Arab nationalism, however, rested on the fact that its ideologues succeeded in relating the progressive ideals and reforms that people desired with the romantic myths and symbols that they missed. It was a way of linking the future to the past; the West, to the East. Its ability to bridge that gap, to contain that contradiction, even if temporarily, was the key to its success as an ideology.

Conservative Arab nationalism. In chapter 1, I argued that ideologies owe much of their existence to the role they play in satisfying particular psychological needs of individuals experiencing acute social and cultural strain. I posited that in developing societies, ideologies can provide a sense of identity, a means of escape from intellectual and moral confusion, and a system for the healthy displacement of aggression. This may be referred to as the psychological appeal of an ideology to denote its somewhat subconscious and pathological nature. It should not be confused, however, with the more conscious interest-oriented appeal that a set of ideas may have to a particular group or class. The latter type of appeal is, of course, associated with Marx, whereas the former category is associated with the Strain Theory school as discussed in chapter 1.

Unlike radical Arab nationalism, the appeal of conservative Arab nationalism can best be understood with reference to considerations of interest rather than those of acute psychological strain. The reason for this is that the main protagonists of this Arab nationalism came from a class that was experiencing relatively moderate social, economic, and cultural flux and, hence, did not develop intense psychological needs. The class basis of this early Arab nationalism was mainly from among the Sunni landowning, bureaucratic, and merchant upper classes of the Syrian towns. This class had traditionally sat at the top of the social pyramid in the economic, political, and cultural spheres and was disturbed by the events of World War I only insofar as it had to adjust to a loss of Turkish-Ottoman suzerainty and adapt to the establishment of, first, an Arab state under Faysal, and later to a fragmented Syrian governmental system under French control. Its social, economic, and cultural position remained relatively unchanged although the identity and structure of the political system within which it was to hold power went through considerable transformation. Unlike the new middle class that formed the backbone for the radical Arab nationalism of the post-1948 period, members of this traditional Syrian upper class experienced little of the confusion and anomie that is a result of rapid role change and swift vertical and horizontal social mobility. Members of the Syrian upper class derived a fair measure of stability from the status of their families and their classes and their traditionally accustomed role in society, polity, and economy. There was no desperate search for identity or urgent quest for a role, but rather a redefinition of certain political principles and assumptions to adapt to the decline and collapse of the Ottoman state and the rise of alternative political frameworks. It is important to note, however, that among the nascent professional and intellectual class, most of which supported the Arab nationalism of the upper class before World War II, one begins to see in the 1920s and 1930s those elements of strain characteristic of the new middle class that rose to power in the 1950s and 1960s. This nascent professional class, however, played only a secondary political role during this period.

Conservative Arab nationalism reflected the interests of the upper classes that promoted it. First, members of the dominant landowning and merchant class had a stake in unifying under their control the Syrian towns and territories in which they had material and political interests; this course recommended to them an Arabism that resisted foreign influence and a program of Arab unity that expressed Syrian unity in the guise of a more rousing rhetoric of Arab unity. Second, their vested interests in the social status quo suggested a conservative social program that would preserve their dominance. Indeed, they "offered little in the way of concrete solutions to the social and economic problems affecting the Syrian people," and confined their political activism to "intermittent popular protest, diplomacy, and regional and international activity" rather than revolutionary armed struggle (Khoury 1987, 620–21). Third, the fact that this ruling class comprised a network of families distributed across several towns whose fortunes would more or less rise or fall together recommended to them a liberal constitutional parliamentary political system that would protect their political freedom and private property and provide them with a broad and legitimized hold on government. Fourth, the fact that members of this class "were educated in modern professional schools . . . had experience in the new branches of the Ottoman administration . . . and shared similar political experiences . . . in the political parties and secret societies of Damascus, Beirut, Cairo, and Paris before the First World War, and afterwards in Faysal's short-lived Arab kingdom" recommended to them a secular outlook free of the religious and tradition-bound influence of the *ulama* class (Khoury 1987, 620). Of course, none of these relationships are iron-clad laws of cause and effect, but they do highlight an important and effective symbiosis of interest and ideology.

To be sure, early Arab nationalism did have some of the psychological appeal that would become so crucial for the new middle class and the radical Arab nationalism of the 1950s and 1960s. Most importantly, it offered a secular Arab identity to respond to the identity confusion created by the collapse of the Ottoman state. It offered principles of cultural and racial community to supplant principles of religious community. Indeed, early Arab nationalism was quite successful in this sphere as this secular Arab nationalist identity survived the interwar period and was eventually adopted by radical Arab nationalists and confirmed as a basic element of modern Arab political thought until serious challenges in the 1970s and 1980s from Islamic revivalists. Unlike in the sphere of identity confusion, in the spheres of intellectual and moral confusion discussed in chapter 1, this early Arab nationalism had little to offer. In contrast to the Communists or radical Arab nationalists, these early Arab nationalists shied away from ideological dogma as they modeled themselves more after the liberal upper classes of the democratic West than after the upstart party activists that had come to dominate Russia and would rise to positions of dictatorship in Germany and Italy as well. Intellectual and moral truths were supposed to be the objects of private pursuit not the subjects of official decree. In this attitude, they also reflected their aversion to the role of determining official dogma traditionally held by the *ulama*. Finally, they offered little satisfaction in the category of aggression-displacement that would also become a prominent element of Arab ideological life later on. Theirs was an accommodationist attitude, and although they showed some hostility both to the Turks and to their French successors during and immediately after World War I, their traditional role was to accommodate these imperial powers not to ardently resist them. Their hostility, therefore, was sporadic and was used primarily as a lever in the political bargaining that necessarily accompanied such power sharing within an imperial system.

The variables of class, ethnic, or sectarian identity, intergenerational opposition, and political crises (see chap. 1) help explain the rise of early Arab nationalism around World War I and its decline in the late 1940s. It is fair to say that the rise of Arab nationalism cannot be understood in isolation from the deep crisis engendered by the collapse of the Ottoman state, the defeat of Faysal's Arab government, and the fragmentation of Syria under French rule. The orientation and outlook of interwar Arab nationalism were shaped by these traumatic events. The weakness and collapse of the Ottoman state discredited traditional Islamic models of government while the divide-and-rule policies of the French underlined the necessity of Arab unity. The victory of the French, however, also highlighted the strengths of the capitalist democratic systems of the West, which served as an example for emulation for many early Arab nationalists.

From the perspective of class, this early Arab nationalism, as mentioned, was an upper-class phenomenon. It began in the last years of the Ottoman empire as an opposition movement among those members of the landowning, bureaucratic, and merchant upper class who had lost political power as a result of the Turkification policies inaugurated after the 1908 CUP coup in Istanbul. These disgruntled members of the Arab Syrian upper class represented the second rung within the native ruling class and directed much of their hostility toward rival and more dominant members of the local ruling class who still held positions of power within the Ottoman system and still displayed strong pro-Ottoman sentiments. This discontented portion of the upper class could count on the support of large portions of the nascent professional and intellectual class who were attracted to many of the secular and nationalist ideals of Arab nationalism and had an important role to play in galvanizing popular support. In essence, however, early Arab nationalism emerged not as an expression of class struggle but as an expression of normal political tensions between rival branches of a dominant upper class. As Philip Khoury noted, "Class conflict was not the foundation of political rivalry in Damascus or for that matter in other Syrian towns. Rather conflict was mainly confined to the politically active elements in one particular class that rested at the top of the social hierarchy in Damascus," (Khoury 1983, 74). Surprisingly, the Syrian Arab upper class, which championed this early Arab nationalism, came to enjoy considerable prominence under the mandate system despite the hostility of the French authorities to the Arab nationalist cause. Admittedly, the upper class enjoyed this prominence only at the cost of toning down its Arab nationalist rhetoric, especially after the failure of the Great Revolt of 1925–27. Nevertheless, this liberal conservative form of Arab nationalism would remain the most widely accepted ideology in the Syrian political arena until the authority of the traditional upper class was challenged by the power of a rising new middle class and the legitimacy of conservative Arab nationalist ideology was challenged by a new revolutionary version of Arab nationalism.

From the perspective of intergenerational opposition, whereas the main beneficiaries of early Arab nationalism, especially during its rise in the wake of World War I, were of the same generation that had shared power with the Turks before the war, the liberal atmosphere of the 1908–14 period and the collapse of the Ottoman army and Ottoman bureaucratic institutions had freed a significant number of young intellectuals and military officers who sought empowerment in a new political order. The adoption by the traditional local ruling class of the new ideology of Arab nationalism served as a means to co-opt these younger elements and diffuse the threat they posed to the older generation. As education and modernization expanded the outlook and role of the younger generation, however, this subordination and co-optation would no longer be workable. The tension this created would engender a new ideological orientation, expressed in radical Arab nationalism, that would become the adopted worldview of the generation of the post–World War II period.

From the perspective of interconfessional or inter-ethnic competition, many Christian Arabs who had acquired education and economic power under European protection benefited from the redefinition of the basis of political community in terms of Arabism rather than Islam. Despite its avowed secularism, however, the Arab nationalism of this early phase was still perceived by many as closely associated with Islam, and its leadership was dominated by Sunni elites that had been formed under the Islamic government of the Ottoman state. Furthermore, many Christians as well as other non-Sunni Muslims (e.g., Alawis, Druzes, and Shiʿa) benefited directly from the European mandate itself, which checked Sunni power and provided opportunities for Christians in government and non-Sunni Muslims in the army. Indeed, the full effect of the push of minority groups into mainstream politics would not be felt until after World War II when it would be expressed through a far more secular Arab nationalist ideology in which members of minority groups would play a leading role.

This early conservative Arab nationalism owed its ascent to the decline and collapse of the Ottoman empire and the need of the Syrian upper class to devise a new ideological worldview that would ensure their material and political interests within the new political environment. It largely reflected the interests of that dominant upper class at a time when social and psychological strain had not yet reached the critical levels of later decades. Its rise can best be understood from the perspectives of political crisis and class conflict; the categories of inter-ethnic or intersectarian conflict and intergenerational competition are less relevant. Nevertheless, this form of Arab nationalism survived until the late 1940s when the power of the rising middle class and the shock of the loss of Palestine in 1948 fatally weakened the ruling upper class and irreparably discredited its ideological worldview.

Radical Arab nationalism. The new revolutionary Arab nationalist ideology that gained prominence in the 1950s and 1960s can also be analyzed—and with great profit—from the various perspectives of crises, classes, generations, and inter-ethnic or interconfessional competition. From the perspective of political crises, it is evident that the sudden rise of revolutionary Arab nationalism cannot be understood in isolation from the bankruptcy of the traditional ruling elites and their liberal conservative ideology after the collapse of British and French power in World War II and the loss of Palestine to the Zionists in 1948. These events marked a watershed between the decline of conservative Arab nationalism and the rise of its radical rival and set the stage for a new phase of ideological politics.

From the perspective of class, the socioeconomic class that adopted and disseminated this new revolutionary ideology has been described by most authors as the "new middle class," or, more technically, the "new petty bourgeoisie." As Erik Wright argues, "In the course of capitalist development the traditional petty bourgeoisie—independent artisans, small shopkeepers, etc.—has steadily dwindled. In its place there has arisen what Poulantzas calls the 'new petty bourgeoisie,' consisting of white-collar employees, technicians, supervisors, civil servants, etc." (Wright 1978, 34). Others, such as James Bill, have referred to this class as a "nonbourgeois" or "professional" middle class, pointing out that "the members of this class are engaged in professional, technical, cultural, intellectual, and administrative occupations and include teachers, professors, students, technocrats, engineers, physicians, writers, artists, journalists, bureaucrats, and middle-ranking army officers" (Bill 1972, 433). Strictly speaking, this group does not constitute a class in the Marxist sense but "may be negatively defined as what remains after one has positively defined the classical trio: landed aristocracy, bourgeoisie, proletariat" (Laroui 1976, 16, see also Halpern 1963; Binder 1978; Vatikiotis 1985; and Dekmejian 1971). Furthermore, the socioeconomic roots of members of this class are extremely diverse. Some are descendants of traditional urban petty bourgeois families, some are fallen members of the traditional upper class, whereas others have worked their way up from the large class of urban poor. A large portion, however, are individuals of rural origin who have come to the city to take advantage of the social and economic opportunities available there. Indeed, the mixed origins of this new middle class that arose to fulfill new bureaucratic and economic functions in rapidly developing societies helps explain this class's psychological confusion and its appetite for ideological politics.

In any case, this new middle class was "the first to 'make it' in the wake of the limited growth of capitalism after World War I," and it successfully challenged the political dominance of the big bourgeoisie in the 1940s and 1950s (Hussein 1973, 29). It succeeded in this ascent into power mainly through penetration into the Middle East's most rapidly expanding bureaucracy, namely, the military bureaucracy. Seizing power through coups d'état at the highest level of government, it came to dominate all areas of society. As Laroui observed, in all Arab countries "we find public administration, the technical services of public and private organizations, teaching and culture in the hands of the petite bourgeoisie" (Laroui 1976, 161). Furthermore, as Hussein points out, the politically volatile high-school and university student body of the 1940s and 1950s, which played a key role in revolutionary party politics, was also "largely petty bourgeois" (Hussein 1973, 34). Hussein goes so far as to say that "all the political parties and organizations which challenged the established system and the ruling class were led largely by individuals who came from this petty bourgeois section" (Hussein 1973, 36). Indeed, this new petty bourgeoisie provided the followers for the three principle ideological movements that challenged the conservative nationalist status quo after World War II: revolutionary pan-Arab nationalism, communism, and the activist Islamism of the Muslim Brotherhood. Eventually, the first of these three elbowed out the other two to become the dominant ideology of the new middle class.

To understand why the principles and symbols of revolutionary Arab nationalism were attractive to this rising middle class, one examines its psychological and material environment and first, the category of alienation and identity confusion. Halpern argues that the defining characteristic of the petty bourgeoisie is the isolation and separation of its members, which derives from the great variety of social and economic environments from which they come. "The new middle class is distinguishable from all other classes," he states, "by being the first to be composed of separate individuals. . . . Coming into being by influx from all social classes . . . the salaried new middle class is the first in Middle Eastern history for whom family connections can no longer help automatically to establish class membership" (Halpern 1963, 280). Hussein agrees that the petty bourgeoisie was most importantly "a fragmented class" (Hussein 1973, 28). Naturally, such a fragmented class suffered from considerable identity confusion. The highly romanticized Arab nationalism of Aflaq could directly address this crisis of identity.

Hussein adds to this sociopsychological portrait, however, the point that the nature of this class's work was essentially mental as opposed to manual: they were involved in the bureaucracy, the educational system, or the modern economy, not in the manual fields of agriculture or handicrafts. This means, Hussein argues, that this class had a marked intellectual orientation and a strong cultural sense derived from its literacy and its active immersion in the Arabic language. Taken together, these two factors—the fragmented and literate nature of this group—indicate that members of this class would normally exhibit symptoms of a rather acute identity confusion but would be open at the same time to intellectualized appeals to an Arab identity based primarily on language and culture. This approach may help explain the success of a highly intellectualized version of Arab nationalism, such as that of Michel Aflaq.

Second, in the category of intellectual confusion, revolutionary Arab nationalism could also be quite helpful. Although intellectually rather able, members of the new middle class were typically still quite confused by the vast economic and political arena that confronted them. Experiencing considerable mobility and unprepared by families or schools for the complexities of modern urban life and the politics of mass societies, they would be attracted to ideologies that simplified this mystifying reality and provided them with intellectual direction within it. Typically, also, members of this class had a positive orientation toward modernity because they had secured their current status through the modern job types of the bureaucrat, the officer, the professional, the university professor, the technician, and so forth. Generally, therefore, they were favorably disposed toward modernity with its attendant scientific and secularist principles. These two factors, taken together, suggest that members of this class would be especially attracted to fairly sophisticated and modern ideological theories of social and political affairs. Such theories were provided by revolutionary Arab nationalism through its adoption of most of the pseudoscientific socioeconomic and political philosophy of Marxism under the guise of "Arab socialism." This pseudoscientific ideology offered a simplified version of reality to the intellectually confused new middle-class individual, and it was a version in which modernity was regarded positively.

Along with identity and intellectual confusion, members of the new petty bourgeoisie also typically experienced deep moral crises. Exposed to both traditional Islamic and modern Western moral systems and presented with a liberal social framework, they were, naturally, morally confused. The need for moral guidance, however, seems to have evoked a not fully satisfactory response from nationalist ideologues. Aflaq, for example, drew eclectically from the moral systems presented by Western liberalism, Marxist socialism, and Islam, with liberalism given the central position. This approach left the individual in considerable moral confusion. Indeed, revolutionary Arab nationalism's inability to address the crisis of moral confusion may have been its Achilles's heel, for it left the door open for the rise of the heavily moralistic Islamic movement that began to gain ground in the 1970s. If Arab nationalism would not squarely address moral issues, other ideologies would.

Finally, the loneliness, vulnerability, and frustration of average members of this new petty bourgeois class, faced with the challenges and hardships of modern mass society, can help explain the growing emphasis on power, militarism, and hostility to the West with which revolutionary Arab nationalism became infused, for these themes could serve as a vicarious source for a sense of individual power and a direct target for relocating frustration and aggression.

In addition to considering how revolutionary Arab nationalism may have reflected the psychological and material condition of the new petty bourgeoisie, or new middle class, one must also consider how the ideology served the practical political interests of this class. Although this class began to emerge in the process of economic growth that followed World War I, it was not until the 1940s that it reached sufficient size and power to challenge the older landowning and merchant ruling class. In this class struggle, the rising class needed an ideology that would distinguish it from the ruling class, justify the overthrow of that class, and provide a new basis for legitimacy. Revolutionary socialist Arab nationalism provided an attractive set of ideological characteristics with which to oppose and overthrow the ruling upper class: (1) pan-Arabism was conveniently antithetical to the regionalism of the upper classes; (2) socialism was antithetical to the upper class's laissez-faire liberalism; (3) chauvinism was antithetical to the upper class's Europhilism; and (4) Marxism-Leninism could provide a justification for the revolutionary overthrow of the upper class whose members, it could now be proclaimed, were "exploiters of the masses" and "agents of international imperialism." From this perspective, revolutionary Arab nationalism was the means by which a rising middle class facilitated its move into a position of dominance.

In terms of generational dynamics, the dialectical movement from conservative to radical Arab nationalism is rather straightforward. The groups that conquered political, and with it, economic and cultural power, in the wake of World War II and 1948 were generally young officers or party activists, and they enlisted the help of members of their own generational group to serve in positions of influence throughout government and society. In this sense, the revolution of radical Arab nationalism was a revolt against the old generation and its political traditions as much as it was a positive vision of new options.

Finally, the role of minorities in promoting a radically secular Arab nationalism and smothering the role of traditional Sunni Muslim precepts cannot be underestimated. The founder of the Baʿth was a Christian as was the founder of the ANM. The ranks of non-Sunnis in army officer corps that had been swollen by French and British designs to circumscribe Sunni power also played an important role in bringing about the military putsches that did away with many of the traditional regimes. This is especially true of Syria, of course, where Alawi and Druze influence in the army eventually developed into an almost purely Alawi dictatorship.

Revolutionary Arab nationalism began to decline in the late 1960s and 1970s. On purely intellectual grounds, the ideology remained quite vague and eclectic. It never achieved much coherence and unity because of the dearth of able ideologues and the divisions within the movement of Arab nationalism itself. The fragmented nature of the ideology carried within it the seeds of its weakening and collapse. Splintered and divided, revolutionary Arab nationalism left itself wide open to criticism and attack. Furthermore, although the romantic side of Arab nationalism was quite developed, its concrete pragmatic side was not. Although it borrowed from socialism to try to provide a detailed and comprehensive worldview, that borrowing was always partial, inexact, and selective. As a result, Arab nationalism never provided a strong, coherent, and concrete worldview in light of which social and economic developments could be understood and reacted to. Although its romanticism made the ideology superficially attractive, its weakness at the concrete analytical level meant that it would not stand the test of time as a stable mental framework within which to interpret political, social, and economic processes over the decades. To survive, an ideology must have a strong intellectual foundation and continue to build actively on that foundation in light of new developments and events. No such attention was given to the serious elaboration of ideological positions within the movement of Arab nationalism. Ideology was a source for mobilizing popular support and a symbol of legitimacy for new regimes. Once in power, nationalist regimes tended to fall back on traditional means of maintaining power—especially coercion—largely ignoring the need to continue the elaboration and updating of ideology.

From the perspective of class, if revolutionary Arab nationalism is viewed as the cover under which the new middle class successfully challenged the power of the upper bourgeoisie, then its function once the new middle class had firmly established itself in power is questionable. When it was out of power, the new middle class needed ideology as a means to justify its overthrow of power and to galvanize widespread political support for that overthrow. Once in power, however, that class no longer needed ideology as badly. The conventional political power of the state was more or less sufficient to maintain a position of political dominance. No longer needed politically, the ideology of Arab nationalism lingered but languished; no longer a necessary source of political power, it lost its vitality and dynamism.

The same general comment can be made about the integration of members of the minorities into the social mainstream. Revolutionary Arab nationalism was, for them, a necessary vehicle for their acceptance into positions of political power after they had achieved economic, cultural, or military prominence. Once they were in positions of political power, however, they could maintain their position through the normal levers of institutionalized political power. They no longer needed ideology as an extraordinary source of power, for they now enjoyed the benefits of ordinary state power. With their fate no longer tied up in the success of the ideology, their dynamic absorption in it waned.

From the perspective of generational change, the decline of revolutionary Arab nationalism is quite normal. Faced with a confusing and frustrating social reality, every new generation, especially in developing societies, is driven to assemble some simplified ideological worldview through which to interpret and interact with reality. Because of their natural hostility to the status quo, which is presenting them with significant difficulties and obstacles, they are inclined to adopt a worldview in opposition to the worldview of their elders, who are in positions of social dominance. In societies experiencing rapid material and cultural change, unless the dominant class exerts a supreme effort to socialize and integrate youth both materially and mentally, new generations left largely to their own devices are likely to develop an outlook in deep hostility to the status quo and its legitimizing ideology. From this perspective, the emergence of an antithetical challenge to revolutionary Arab nationalism—as it happened, in the form of Islamic fundamentalism—was almost inevitable.

Finally, as for the rise of revolutionary Arab nationalism, the timing of the decline of that nationalism was closely linked to certain historical crises throughout the 1960s, most importantly, the collapse of the UAR in 1961, the breakup of the Baʿth party in the mid-1960s into competing factions, the defeat of 1967, and the death of Nasir in 1970. The ability of radical Arab nationalist ideology to evoke feelings of positive identity, self-esteem, security, and power was shattered. Its authority as a guide in directing socioeconomic and cultural change was also deeply shaken. The ideological arena was blown open to allow new ideological orientations to compete for popular allegiance, namely, a radical Marxist revolutionary nationalism rallying around the forces of the Palestinian leftist guerilla organizations and an equally radical, puritanical fundamentalist Islamic movement.

The Legacy of Arab Nationalism

Whereas early conservative Arab nationalism focused on Syria and the major Syrian towns, the revolutionary Arab nationalism of the postwar period addressed itself to the entire Arab world "From the [Atlantic] Ocean to the [Arabian] Gulf." It created a sense of shared identity and community among a group of societies that had been left isolated from one another after the collapse of the Ottoman empire. While the Ottomans had provided Islam as the macro-identity overarching tribal and regional identities, Arab nationalists offered Arabism to serve the same purpose. Arabism gave rise to a sense of community among Arab peoples whose effects, although far from decisive, cannot be ignored. This communal sense led to several attempts at unity between Arab states, most notably the Syrian-Egyptian unity experiment between 1958 and 1961. It also helps explain the fairly uniform early Arab response to the creation of Israel as well as Arab attitudes toward Palestinian rights and demands. Furthermore, although conflicts and rivalries between Arab states are often intense, this sense of shared community can also help explain why these tensions only rarely erupt into open warfare. Moreover, it helps reveal the hidden logic behind the Arab League and the practice of Arab summitry. Despite its failure to even come close to its proclaimed objective of Arab unity, Arab nationalism has succeeded in implanting the desire for inter-Arab cooperation and condominium, and it is not unlikely that this will become articulated in the form of increasing bureaucratization and institutionalization of inter-Arab economic, technological, and cultural relations.

But the legacy of Arab nationalism is deeper and more pervasive than a communal sense. First, as mentioned previously, Arab nationalism "performed an intellectual function within the general framework of modernization. It introduced new ideas by adapting them to indigenous forms of expression and values and . . . added new dimensions to thought by introducing to it economic, social, and political elements" (Karpat 1982, xxii). In a sense, Arab nationalism was the avenue through which Western modernity entered the Arab world.

The Arab nationalism of the 1950s and 1960s, for example, brought with it a wave of secularism that unseated Islam from its central position in political, social, and cultural life. Although early Arab nationalism, led by traditional Sunni elites, adopted secularism only half-heartedly, the new radical Arab nationalism introduced a thoroughly secular outlook. Although the secularization of Arab society is in no way complete, neither in scope nor in depth, nevertheless, in the countries that succumbed to the rule of Arab nationalist parties or military cliques, political, social, and economic life was transformed beyond recognition. The traditional religious classes were drastically weakened, and the secular state took control of the domains of education and justice that had been previously the preserve of religious classes.

Based on their adoption of socialist outlooks, Arab nationalists also succeeded in raising important issues of wealth distribution and economic justice. They introduced a theme of revolutionary egalitarianism that had been absent in early Arab nationalism and that contributed to the overthrow of the traditional social and economic systems. After their rise to power, radical Arab nationalist regimes constructed moderately socialist state-dominated economic systems, which, although they did not produce efficiently, did succeed in reducing foreign influence in local economies and in achieving more even levels of wealth distribution. This opposition to unfettered capitalism and attachment to principles of socioeconomic egalitarianism has become a mainstay of political culture in the countries that came under the control of Arab nationalist regimes.

Furthermore, unlike early Arab nationalism, revolutionary Arab nationalism had a strong understanding of the challenges of state-building in developing societies. It borrowed both from Marxist-Leninists and the Fascists of Germany and Italy the awareness of the need to construct a strong and stable state. Ironically, while Arab nationalists claimed that their objective was to dismantle the state system that had grown out of the collapse of the Ottoman empire, their vigorous state-building efforts within their own state boundaries greatly reinforced the political divisions that they claimed to oppose. While seeking to change the political map of the Arab world, they contributed unwittingly to its ossification.

Along with revolutionary Arab nationalism's emphasis on state-building, however, came an understanding of state organization borrowed from both extremes of the European Left and Right. This understanding, shared by both Bolsheviks and Fascists, was that state power is based on authoritarian one-party rule. Satiᶜ al-Husri was the first to reject French and British contractarian notions of nationalism in favor of more deterministic German notions. Aflaq confirmed this rejection of contractarian thought by borrowing notions of class struggle and one-party rule from the Marxists. In the end, Arab nationalists based their rule on a fervent faith in their mission and a heavy dose of coercion. This is as true of the Baᶜth, whose founders were greatly influenced both by the Arab Communist parties and the proto-fascist Syrian Social Nationalist party of Antun Saᶜadeh, as it is true of the ANM, which borrowed many of its attitudes from the popular expressions of European fascist and hypernationalist movements. Nasir's form of authoritarianism was more homegrown but still borrowed from the authoritarian and totalitarian tendencies present in revolutionary Arab nationalist ideology.

Furthermore, the idea of class struggle itself that Aflaq and others introduced into the mainstream of Arab nationalism had its own dangerous effects. By undermining ideas of social solidarity and social harmony, which were part and parcel of traditional Islamic political culture and part of the liberal democratic ideology introduced by the French and the British, the radical Arab nationalists dealt a serious blow to the political stability of their own societies. They encouraged intrasocial conflict as a necessary ingredient of progress. The politically alarming element of this position was that it posited a situation of social war in which the use of violence was normal and necessary. By denying the existence of a basic social consensus, it undermined the possibility of peaceful politics. This logic was convenient to the parties and army cliques that seized power in several Arab countries for it allowed them to use the instruments and propaganda of war to deny the legitimacy of any opposition and enforce their complete monopoly on political power. Acting in the name of oppressed classes, new ruling groups waged wars against large sections of their own populations.

Furthermore, although Arab nationalism was effective in subduing religious and confessional tensions for a number of decades, it had the reverse effect on inter-ethnic tensions. This rendered Arab nationalism flawed in the ethnically mixed Berber-Arab societies of the Arab *maghrib* and contributed, more perilously, to the exacerbation of Arab-Kurdish relations in Iraq. The latter resulted in open warfare between the Arab Baᶜthist Iraqi state and its large Kurdish minority.

Finally, one of the more subtly destablizing legacies of Arab nationalism is the ideological delegitimation of current state boundaries. Although, as argued here, Arab nationalist and other regimes have built state structures which, by their very existence, reinforce the current state system and generally act within its framework, Arab nationalism denies the state system complete legitimacy because the only fully legitimate state is the one unified Arab nation-state. By continuously undermining state legitimacy, Arab nationalism has introduced a mood of continuous crisis into Arab politics. Moreover, regimes that are not allowed sufficient legitimacy are forced, by the normal laws of politics, to shore up their stability through coercion, which may help explain the chaotic and coercive nature of contemporary Arab political life.

Furthermore, the myth of Arab unity has also allowed many Arab regimes to distract attention from pressing domestic political and economic issues. Because the state and the society it is ruling over are not considered complete and legitimate units, the responsibilities of the government toward its population are not clearly understood nor are the rights and duties of the population itself. With the dominant ideology concerned with a theoretical Arab nation and Arab state, actual Arab societies and Arab governments are left in an open, uninformed political confrontation. By focusing on issues beyond their borders Arab nationalist regimes help keep issues of domestic reform off the political agenda. In an important sense, by keeping the dream of Arab unity alive, they are suppressing awareness of the nightmare of Arab politics.

CHAPTER THREE

Islamic Fundamentalism

The fourteenth century of the Islamic calendar that ended in A.D. November 1979 was characterized by many defeats. The Christian powers of Europe had occupied vast regions of the Muslim world from Algeria, Tunisia, Libya, Egypt in Africa to Palestine, Syria, Iraq, and India in Asia. The Ottoman empire, a state that represented the continuity of Muslim governance in the office of the caliphate, had been destroyed. In the wake of the Christian colonial powers of Europe had come a wave of Western-influenced native reformers like Mustafa Kamal, Gamal Abd al-Nasir, and various Baʿthists and Marxists, who continued the assault on Islam through sweeping policies of secularization and Westernization. By the 1960s, Islam had become a thoroughly embattled faith, circumscribed in its influence to a few aspects of personal and family law and derided by a radical and self-confident intelligentsia as a quaint relic of an outdated past.

In the final decade of the Islamic century, however, Islam underwent a significant revitalization. In the Arab world, Islamic groups rose to champion their faith and emerged as the chief articulators of public unrest. In the wider Islamic world, governments moved to accommodate a resurgent Islam by bringing their constitutions and legal codes closer in harmony with Islamic law. Most importantly, the fourteenth century ended with the Islamic revolution in Iran, the greatest resurgence of Islam in recent history. The fifteenth century was rung in with an attempted revolution in Saudi Arabia led by a self-proclaimed *mahdi*, who, with a band of zealous followers, occupied the Grand Mosque at Mecca and called for the overthrow of the Saudi government.

Indeed, many Islamists hold that the fifteenth century will be one of successes for them. The victory of Islam, they contend, will be brought about, in part, by the decline of the two worldviews promoted by the capitalist West and the Communist East. They argue that defeats in Vietnam, Algeria, Cuba, and elsewhere point to the capitalist West's political decline; loose sexual practices, the debasement of women, and the collapse of the family point to a moral crisis while the spread of drug-abuse and crime indicate a deep social disintegration. Meanwhile, the Communist East has suffered political disintegration and economic collapse. In between lies the world of Islam, recently liberated from the shackles of Christian occupation and still in the process of pushing back the frontiers of domestic secularism that had weakened and poisoned the Islamic body politic. Indeed, to many, the Muslim community seems on the verge of recovering from the most devastating blow since the Crusades. Upon entering Jerusalem in 1917, General Allenby, at the head of victorious British troops, had declared, "Today, the Crusades have come to an end." With the triumphant revolution against the Shah in 1979, the assassination of Sadat in 1981, the uprising in Hama in 1982, the rise of Hizballah in Lebanon, the Islamic turn in the Sudan, the aborted victory of the Islamic Front in the Algerian elections of early 1992, among other indicators, some Islamists feel they are finally gathering a response to the Christian West and the corrupting secularizing influence that it left behind in the Muslim world.

The Early Muslim Reformers

The beginning of a conscious appraisal of the challenge posed by Christian Europe emerged in the early nineteenth century at the hands of Muslim intellectuals, such as al-Tahtawi and Khayr al-Din al-Tunisi, who endeavored to determine how the science and technology of Europe could be safely and successfully imported into the Islamic world without disturbing the moral and social foundations of Islamic society (Hourani 1970, 67ff). But in the early nineteenth century, the relationship between the Islamic and Christian worlds was still relatively relaxed and not yet obsessed with the threat of conquest and domination. By the end of the century, however, the relationship had become quite strained. In 1860, Western powers landed troops in Lebanon to impose a settlement there. In 1877, the Russo-Turkish war had threatened the very seat of the caliphate. In 1881, the French occupied Tunis. In 1882, the British occupied Egypt. The material, intellectual, and cultural challenge of the West had now turned into a direct military and political conflict. A Muslim activist of Iranian origin, Jamal al-Din al-Afghani formulated the principal Muslim reaction to the new European threat. His thought was elaborated upon by other Arab Muslim reformers such as Muhammad Abduh and Rashid Rida.

Jamal al-Din al-Afghani: The Father of Modern Islamic Activism

Al-Afghani was a complex figure whose biography has been ably and revealingly explored by Nikki Keddie, Elie Kedouri, and Albert Hourani, among others (Keddie 1983; Kedouri 1966; Hourani 1970). Born into a Shiʿite community in Asadabad, Iran, circa 1838, he received his formative education there and was greatly taken by the rationalist Greek-influenced Muslim philosophy preserved and respected in Twelver Shiʿite theology. He came to political consciousness in travels through India and Afghanistan at a time when those countries were rising against British rule. The intense nationalism and anticolonial sentiment that he imbibed there accompanied him throughout his life. Traveling to Istanbul as an itinerant teacher, he was deported by the authorities for allegedly spreading heretical theological teachings. Arriving in Egypt in 1871, he soon acquired a devoted coterie of young theology students who were attracted to his blend of unorthodox theology and rebellious patriotism. He rose to a position of public prominence in the unsettled atmosphere of 1878–79 in Egypt where he helped rouse public opinion against the British in a series of inflammatory speeches (Keddie 1983, 20). During his stay in Egypt, Afghani encouraged the establishment of newspapers and other vehicles for intellectual activism and contributed to the genesis of Egyptian nationalism. He was forced out of Egypt after British occupation and ended up in Europe from where his views continued to be influential, especially through the journal entitled *al-ʿUrwa al-Wuthqa*, which he founded and co-published in coöperation with his Egyptian disciple, Muhammad Abduh. Afghani returned to Istanbul in 1892 where he died five years later.

In content, Afghani's thought had two main branches. One represented his public position intended for the masses; the other represented his private reflections intended for his close associates and other Muslim intellectuals. He feared that his private critiques of traditional Sunni theology and culture, which he shared with his associates, would only engender apprehension and confusion among the masses. In his public utterances, he spoke in ringing phrases of Islamic history and Islamic tradition and exhorted his fellow Muslims to rise against foreign domination and work for the unification and rejuvenation of the entire Islamic *umma*. He addressed Muslims as members of an Islamic nation and endeavored to instill in them the enthusiasm and dedication to be found in European nationalism. He warned his coreligionists that the Muslim world had fallen behind and that Muslims had to take matters into their own hands to regain the initiative and prominence they once enjoyed among the civilizations of the world. "Verily," he quoted from the Qur'an, "God does not change the condition of a people until they change their own condition" (cited in Smith 1957, 50).

In his early exposure to the Indian nationalist opposition, he grew impressed with the force of nationalist sentiment. He had expressed his perception of the affinity between patriotic, nationalist, and religious zeal in an early article published in India. "The desire to protect the fatherland and nationality and the wish to defend religion and coreligionists, that is, patriotic zeal, national zeal, and religious zeal, [all] arouse men to compete in the arena of virtues and accomplishments" (quoted in Keddie 1983, 66). In this sense, Islam was to be considered first and foremost a communal identity—a basis for solidarity that distinguished the conquered from the conqueror and gave the conquered the cohesion and confidence necessary for rebellion and triumph. In this pan-Islamic nationalism of his, the loyalty and energies of the people should be directed to the Ottoman state because it was the strongest and most central Islamic institution and, hence, the most able to lead the Islamic world against the West.

Afghani, of course, was not the first to combine nationalist sentiment within a pan-Islamic framework, but he made out of Islamic nationalism a powerfully political sentiment more in harmony with the strong nationalist currents of the modern world. "He brought inspiration and a popular program to the pan-Islamic movement by restating the bases of the Islamic community in terms of nationalism" (Gibb 1947, 27). Furthermore, Afghani gave a concrete and practical orientation to this Islamic nationalism by emphasizing "loyalty to the Ottoman Caliph . . . [who] as the head of the most powerful Muslim state . . . [was] therefore the authority most fitted to direct and to coordinate the political forces of the Muslim people" (Gibb 1947, 111).

Afghani expressed this nationalism through a romanticized picture of the Age of the Prophet. He portrayed those early years as a Golden Age when Muslims enjoyed strength, enlightenment, and prosperity. If Muslims could recapture the faith and purity that they enjoyed in those early years, God would grant them victory over their oppressors and justice and prosperity among each other. What Afghani meant was that Muslims could find the resources for responding to the challenge of the West within themselves—within their history, their religion, their culture. He refuted the fear that all the keys to power and success resided with the West and their philosophies and traditions. For Afghani, this was a means of restoring the Muslims' faith in themselves and their past at a time when many Muslim intellectuals were beginning to be convinced that their culture was inferior to that of the then resplendent West.

In his private conversations and writings, however, Afghani was critical of the Muslim tradition and stressed the need to reform Islamic theology and culture. The Islamic world, he argued, was lagging far behind the Christian West in terms of basic civilizational variables such as technology, science, and philosophy. The fault lay in the hostile attitude to reason that Sunni theologians had adopted ever since the closing of the doors of *ijtihad* (interpretation) at the end of the ninth century (A.H. third century). Afghani argued that if reason ascertained truths that were in apparent contradiction to scripture, then the interpretation of scripture was at fault. The Qur'an's hidden meaning, he insisted, was infinite; therefore, it encompassed all advances in human knowledge. What Afghani proposed was nothing less than the reopening of the doors of *ijtihad* with a smaller role for *taqlid* (imitation), more emphasis on the Qur'an as opposed to later accretions in the Sunni tradition, and a more prominent role in interpretation for reason. He hoped for a reform of Islam from above carried out by an elite of Islamic thinkers and statesmen—a sort of Protestant Reformation in which he fancied himself, according to his own admission, a Muslim Luther (Keddie 1983, 82).

Afghani's intellectual legacy would reflect the division that existed in his own thinking. While Afghani held the two sides of his philosophy in controlled balance, many of his disciples took one or another aspect of his thought and carried it to extremes that he himself would never have encouraged. On the one hand, secular-minded Egyptian reformers such as Lutfi al-Sayyid, Taha Husayn, and others found in Afghani's rationalist ideas sanction to freely adopt rationalism as a basis for thought and practice in any and all spheres of life. For them Islam was no longer relevant as a source of philosophic, social, or political truth, and was relegated to the sphere of private piety and morality. On the other hand, more traditionally-minded thinkers like Rashid Rida and Hasan al-Banna interpreted Afghani's legacy to sanction a puritanical revivalist movement based on a strict literalist interpretation of the Qur'an and *hadith*.

Afghani's role in inaugurating a long period of ideological and intellectual effervescence in the Arab world is seminal. His charisma and political courage gave expression to a latent nationalist-patriotic energy that would continue to animate the Arab world for decades to come. And although he had opted for Islamic nationalism, his thought also flowered, in the hands of others, into Egyptian and Arab nationalism. The sentiment that he first set astir would be used by others not only to animate Islamic movements but also to galvanize secular nationalist movements of various stripes.

Muhammad Abduh and Rashid Rida: Moderate and Radical Interpretations

Afghani's most influential disciple was the Egyptian, Muhammad Abduh. Abduh was born in 1849 in a small village of the Egyptian delta. He received a religious education first in the town of Tanta and then at al-Azhar University, and became absorbed in the thought and practice of Sufism. In the 1870s, he joined the company of Afghani, himself a one-time Sufi. Under Afghani, Abduh was exposed to the rationalist theology of the Muslim philosophers and to the political activism that characterized Afghani's life. He was a close associate of Afghani both in Egypt and in Europe, and after the latter's death, he was his principal interpreter and biographer.

Unlike Afghani, Abduh gradually lost interest in political agitation and conspiratorial revolutionism. He preferred, instead, to introduce change into the Islamic world through more gradual methods. From his position as a religious instructor, Abduh became a judge in the Egyptian courts and rose to great prominence in 1899 when he was appointed Grand Mufti of Egypt. From that position, which he held till his death in 1905, he had a commanding influence in the fields of education, law, and theology; this influence was not left unused.

In the realm of education, Abduh emphasized the compatibility between Islam, properly understood, and much of the science and learning developed by the West. Revelation and reason, he argued, could not but illuminate God's self-same universal truths; hence, anything arrived at beyond doubt by reason was inevitably in harmony with revelation. This attitude allowed for a growth in Muslim higher education to include many of the new Western disciplines and also helped generate an intellectual renaissance of sorts among Muslim thinkers in Egypt who could now explore the learning of the West with the sanction of Islam and without the fear of being charged with heresy and unbelief (Gibb 1947, 43). In the realm of law and theology, Abduh endeavored to strip Islamic doctrine of the grafts and accretions it had accumulated over the centuries. These additions Abduh considered to have a corrupting influence on Islam and were the main cause of the faith's weakness and malaise. He sought to purify Islamic thought and take it back to a cleaner orthodoxy based on the Qur'an, the *sunnah* of the Prophet, and the enlightened commentary of the pre-Umayyad period. By uncovering the true foundations of Islam, Abduh insisted, the affinities between Islam and such contemporary ideals as democracy, science, liberalism, and so forth, would become apparent. Along these lines, Abduh was active in defending the reputation of Islam against attacks by Christians or Muslim secularists who charged that Islam stood in the way of progress in the modern world.

The different strands in Abduh's thought soon evolved in different directions. A group of his disciples, such as Lutfi al-Sayyid, Muhammad Haykal, and others, understood the compatibility of reason and revelation to allow an almost complete reliance on reason, and reason, of course, was often equated with the civilization of Christian Europe. These, therefore, soon adopted a thoroughly secularizing program based on Egyptian nationalism, liberal parliamentarian politics, and a thoroughly modern secular education. Some went so far as to consider Egypt part of Europe and to deny all ties with the Arab or Islamic worlds.

In counterbalance to this tendency emerged another group led by Rashid Rida, an associate of Abduh, and one of his closest disciples. This group grew increasingly alarmed at the Western secular drift of Arab Muslim thought and developed, in opposition to it, a quite conservative literalist position. In the pages of *al-Manar,* a journal that Rida had founded with Abduh, Rida increasingly emphasized the part of Afghani's and Abduh's thought that called for loyalty to Islam and adherence to its principles as revealed in the Qur'an and elaborated in the earliest sources. In the pages of *al-Manar,* the fairly liberal work of Abu Hamid al-Ghazali was gradually replaced by the more fundamentalist and conservative thought of Ibn Taymiyya. Rida's group found allies in this new fundamentalism in the resurgent Wahhabi movement in the Arabian Peninsula, which also set its lights with reference to the work of Ibn Taymiyya and other conservative theologians. Although the secularists took the rationalism of Afghani and Abduh beyond its intended limits, Rida's *salafiyyah* movement endowed the fundamentalism of these same thinkers with a centrality and literalism unforeseen by them. The former tendency lost all reference to Islam and eventually was stigmatized as alien to the faith; the latter loosened its relationship with rationalism and drifted into a romanticism that glorified early Islam but set little provision for interpreting and adapting Islam to meet the complex material and intellectual challenges of the modern world. The marriage of romanticism and rationalism that Afghani and Abduh had recognized as essential for the healthy emotional and intellectual evolution of the Muslim world was seriously compromised.

Alongside this split arose an engulfing wave of apologetic literature that labored to illustrate that Islam was a very valid faith for the modern world—that, correctly apprehended, it contained the kernel of truth in all realms of politics, ethics, science, and so forth. Unlike the Islamic nationalist propagandizing of Afghani aimed at stirring a nation of believing Muslims to action, this wave of apologetic literature was intended to shore up the faith of an increasingly nonreligious educated class (Gibb 1947, 95). Unlike Afghani's rousing message, which was based on the premise that all was not well in the Muslim world, the new apologetic literature sounded more like a call for calm and contentment: Islam already contained the advances of the West; there was no reason for anxiety or especially strenuous effort. The attempt was "to prove to oneself or others that Islam is sound . . . to champion rather than to understand, to buttress rather than to elucidate" (Smith 1957, 85). This self-congratulatory attitude was pleasing but scarcely a program for action and change.

The History of the Modern Islamic Movements

The defeat of the Ottoman empire by Christian European powers in World War I and the abolition of the caliphate by Mustafa Kamal in 1924 had a devastating impact on most Muslims, especially those that had previously lived under the shadow of the empire. The caliphate had been a symbol of Islamic dignity and historic continuity that had served as a linchpin of Muslim loyalty and self-esteem even in periods of Islamic decline such as those that preceded the Ottoman collapse. Its abolition was a harsh affront to Muslim sensibilities and triggered a crisis of doubt and questioning. Among modernist Muslim thinkers, there was a rough consensus that a caliphate was necessary, even if it were only a spiritual directory to help articulate *ijmaᶜ* and fight heterodoxy. Several conferences and discussions were held toward this end, and King Abdulaziz of Saudi Arabia and King Fuad of Egypt were mentioned among others as possible heirs to a revived caliphate.

Among the more secularist Muslim intelligentsia, however, the collapse of the Ottoman caliphate only accelerated their induction into nationalist movements whether Egyptian, Arab, or other. Indeed, the loss of the caliphate as the focus of loyalty and a source of communal identity was a shot in the arm to the nascent nationalist movements which could now put themselves forward as alternative repositories of loyalty, legitimacy, and identity.

The Egyptian Movements

The Society of Muslim Brothers: Champions of Islam in an increasingly secularized environment. It is in this turbulent atmosphere, and especially under the thoroughly secularizing shadow of Egyptian nationalism, that *Jama'at al-Ikhwan al-Muslimin* (the Society of Muslim Brothers) took shape. It was the first Islamic group in modern times to recognize the need for organized, sustained, and mass-based political action to face the challenge of secularism and Westernization. Indeed, it served as the spawning ground for most of the Islamic groups and activists that came to populate the Arab world in later years. The founder of the brotherhood, Hasan al-Banna, was born in 1906 in the town of Mahmudiyya northwest of Cairo. His father was a graduate of al-Azhar University and the *imam* of the local mosque (Ismael and Ismael 1985, 59). The young Banna received a religious schooling and as an adolescent joined several Islamic societies and, later, a Sufi order. He participated in the nationalist unrest of 1919, and in 1923 he left to Cairo where he enrolled in Dar al-'Ulum University to train as a school teacher. Banna was deeply disturbed by what he saw in Cairo: political division between the Wafd and the liberal constitutionalists, moral lassitude, a cultural assault on Islam and Arab tradition, and the pervasive influence of the British. While in Cairo, Banna came under the influence of Rashid Rida and organized a group of Dar-al-'Ulum and al-Azhar students into a proselytizing youth movement that offered religious guidance and services to the public at large not only in mosques but also in coffeehouses, market squares, and anywhere else people gathered.

In 1927, Banna graduated from Dar al-'Ulum and was appointed to teach in Isma'iliyya in the Suez Canal Zone. It was there in 1928 that he formally established the Society of Muslim Brothers. The society, composed of graduates of religious institutions and like-minded youths, defined itself as a movement dedicated to defending and re-asserting the place of Islam in society through educational and political means. By 1932, it had sprouted branches on the eastern edge of the Nile delta. In 1932, Banna moved to Cairo where the *Ikhwan* merged with the Society for Islamic Culture founded by a younger brother of his. The brotherhood grew rapidly in strength and influence to become by 1939 "one of the most important political contestants on the Egyptian scene" (Mitchell 1969, 13). Its following was drawn mainly from newly urbanized members of the middle- and lower-middle class of students, teachers, civil servants, shopkeepers, small businesspeople, and laborers who felt lost in the secular urban environment and found solace in the *Ikhwan*'s familiar message.

With prominence, however, came the first signs of stress within the movement. In 1939, a small dissident group, calling itself *Jamʿiyyat Shabab Sayyidna Muhammad* (Muhammad's Youth), left the society disgruntled with the brotherhood's cooperation with the monarchy and its conservative position with regard to the use of political violence and revolution. The alliance with the palace had been a key component of the brotherhood's meteoric rise to prominence, as both King Fuad and King Farouk after him backed the brotherhood to counterbalance the power of the Wafd. Banna, however, was a cautious politician and was intent on holding back some of his more eager followers from a premature and overhasty bid for power. The militant dissident group quoted the verse of *hadith* that exhorted, "He among you who sees an abomination must correct it with his hand; if he is unable, then with his tongue; if he is unable, then with his heart. The last of these is the weakest of faith." Banna preferred a more moderate Qur'anic verse: "Call unto the way of thy Lord with wisdom and fair exhortation, and reason with them in the better way. Lo, thy Lord is best aware of him who strayeth from His way and He is best aware of those who go aright" (Qur'an 16:25).

In any case, the unrest of the war years and the *Ikhwan*'s strong hostility toward the British presence in Egypt eventually brought the brotherhood into conflict with the monarchy. In October 1941, after a large anti-British demonstration in which the brotherhood participated, Banna and other brotherhood leaders and members were jailed. This was the first of many *mihnas* (crises, persecutions) that the brotherhood would suffer at the hands of the authorities, and the brotherhood responded by beginning to develop an underground apparatus. In 1942, the first military and secret arm of the Muslim brotherhood was established under the name of *al-Nizam al-Khass* (Private, or Secret, Branch). A network of *Jawwalah* (rovers, basically preachers and doers of good works) had been established in 1936 to help spread the *Ikhwan*'s message, and a network of so-called *Kataʿib* (battalions; in practice, educational and athletic groups) had been established in 1937 for the same purpose (Mitchell 1969, 31). The new Secret Branch, however, was a more serious affair concerned with the organization of tightly knit armed cells to carry out military operations. In this period as well, the *Ikhwan* began to develop its contacts in the army where many disgruntled officers were beginning to consider an overthrow of the regime.

As World War II drew to a close, political conditions in the country were reaching a fever pitch. The economic hardships of the war and its aftermath emboldened opposition to a weakened Britain, and growing alarm with regard to the situation in Palestine generated tensions that the authorities could scarcely contain. During the fight for Palestine in 1948, the *Ikhwan* led the way in acts of sabotage and political destabilization in Egypt and in blaming the government's corruption and collusion for the loss of Palestine. It also sent a group of brotherhood volunteers to fight alongside the Arabs in Palestine. The brotherhood was finally outlawed and officially dissolved in December 1948 as part of government efforts to cope with a situation that had slipped beyond their control (Ismael and Ismael 1985, 72). The final rupture came on December 28 when a Muslim Brother—a member of the Secret Branch, apparently acting without Banna's consent—shot and killed Nuqrashi Pasha, the Egyptian prime minister who had signed the order to dissolve the brotherhood. Banna, still not under arrest, worked desperately to ease the tension and head off the impending collision between the government and his organization. On February 12, however, Banna himself was gunned down by agents of the Egyptian political police.

With Banna's death, the movement gained a martyr but lost a brilliant and charismatic leader who had nursed the organization from its infancy and kept it together for its first two formative decades. Banna's fame and prestige had spread not only throughout Egypt but far and wide across the Arab world. Although he preferred to refer to himself only as a *murshid* (guide), he was regarded by many as a historic *mujaddid* (renewer of the faith) of whom the Prophet had spoken: "Allah will raise, at the head of each century, such people for this community as will revive its religion for it" (*hadith* quoted in Maudoodi 1963, 32). He commanded great loyalty and fervent devotion among his followers. The movement would never regain such leadership for itself.

In January 1950, the Wafd returned to power and adopted a friendly attitude toward the *Ikhwan* in hopes of using it as a buttress against the palace and the Sa'dists. Salih 'Ashmawi, Banna's deputy and the leader of the Secret Branch, assumed the temporary leadership of the *Ikhwan* and set about to heal its wounds (Ismael and Ismael 1985, 36). The issue of a permanent successor to Banna was resolved in October 1951 when Hasan al-Hudaybi, a judge of twenty-five years standing, was chosen as the new *murshid*. Hudaybi had not been a member of the *Ikhwan* and his selection was intended not only to placate the traditional *ulama* class and the palace (his brother-in-law was chief of the Royal Household) but also to avoid the divisive rivalries that would emerge from a power struggle among the more senior *Ikhwan* candidates. Hudaybi was regarded as a safe compromise candidate. Trained as a lawyer, Hudaybi had not led a particularly political life. He abhorred violence and had a marked distaste for most public political displays. His legitimacy within the *Ikhwan* rested on the fact that although he was not an official member, he had been a close friend and a reverent admirer of Banna ever since the two had met in 1944. The choice was not a particularly happy one. Hudaybi did not have an appetite for the militant course of action that the core of the brotherhood favored nor could the senior leadership easily accept the conservative leadership of this erstwhile judge. In any case, events soon overtook the movement.

On January 25, 1952, British forces clashed with Egyptian police in the Suez Canal Zone. The next day massive riots erupted in Cairo demanding war on Britain. In the anger of the moment, seething hostility toward the wealth of the Egyptian upper classes and the alien

Western modes in which it was flaunted resulted in the burning of most of downtown Cairo. The brotherhood was not officially involved in the riots and condemned some of its more reckless excesses, but many brotherhood members had enthusiastically taken part. Egypt was on the brink of revolution, and rumors abounded of an impending military takeover. Meanwhile, the brotherhood leadership was enhancing its ties with Gamal Abd al-Nasir's Free Officers group especially through the cooperation of the young Anwar Sadat. The Free Officers were quite advanced in their secret plans for a military coup, and it was agreed that at the time of the planned putsch the brotherhood would help maintain public order, organize supportive demonstrations for the Free Officers, help with intelligence and fighting if necessary, and, if the plan failed, help the Free Officers escape from Egypt (Mitchell 1969, 103).

On the date of the coup, July 23, 1952, most of these provisions were not needed and, hence, were not used. The majority of Egyptians welcomed the coup and complied willingly with its early directives. Nevertheless, the brotherhood took pride in its role in backing the coup and publicly referred to the overthrow as "our revolution." Relations between the new Free Officers regime and the brotherhood began on a good footing. The Revolutionary Command Council (RCC) dissolved the hated secret police of the Ministry of Interior and reopened the case of Banna's assassination. It even invited the brotherhood to propose three candidates, to be included in the new cabinet. Hudaybi, apparently without wide consultation, suggested three candidates of whom only one, Shaykh Hasan al-Baquri, was accepted by the RCC. The senior membership of the brotherhood, deliberating in the brotherhood's Guidance Council, rejected the RCC's offer to participate on such a small scale in the cabinet and dismissed al-Baquri from the brotherhood.

Relations between the brotherhood and the government would only worsen. In January 1953, the government outlawed all political parties; the brotherhood, however, technically classified as a religious society, remained legal. The new regime apparently did not want to aggravate religious sensibilities, but it made it quite clear that it expected the brotherhood to stay clear of political affairs: "Religion is for God," proclaimed one of the government's slogans, "the Fatherland is for Everyone." Things came to a head again in January 1954 when brotherhood and nationalist students clashed at a university rally. The government responded by redefining the brotherhood as a political party, dissolving it, arresting Hudaybi and hundreds of others, and launching a vigorous propaganda campaign to discredit it. Again afraid to trigger a religious backlash, the government soon went back on its actions. A final showdown, however, seemed inevitable. Later in 1954, brotherhood-government relations worsened again as the brotherhood openly opposed the government's position in the negotiations with Britain over the Suez Canal Zone. The conflict exploded fully on October 26 when a brotherhood assassin, acting according to a plan devised by the Secret Branch, attempted to assassinate Nasir during a public speech in Alexandria. Nasir reacted swiftly to this provocation. He banned the brotherhood, arrested 450 of its leaders and more than 4,000 of its members, and launched another propaganda campaign calling the *Ikhwan* an enemy of the revolution and the people. Hudaybi and six others were sentenced to death although Hudaybi's sentence was commuted to life imprisonment. From them on, official repression would be fierce and efficient. "The revolution shall not be crippled," Nasir warned in an October 29 speech, "if it is not able to proceed white, then we will make it red." In the excitement, General Neguib's name was also linked to the brotherhood and their plans. Nasir used this pretext to get the RCC to remove Neguib from the presidency, confine him to his residence, and, thus, finally remove the only remaining obstacle to his complete domination of the Egyptian state.

Without a strong leadership and under the heavy repression of the government's security apparatus, the brotherhood remained fairly weak throughout the decade after 1954. In the meantime, Nasir set out to eliminate the influence of Islamists and the religious classes from society. The *shari*ᶜa courts were incorporated into the civil legal system. al-Azhar university was brought under state control and expanded to include departments in all the modern sciences and to admit women, and the network of Friday preachers came under the centralized control of the state. Furthermore, although the Constitution of 1956 had declared Islam to be the state religion, the National Charter of 1962 proclaimed religious freedom and advocated

equal status for all faiths. Finally, to bathe the socialist and secular reforms of the state in the glow of Islamic legitimacy, the government
encouraged a flood of literature that showed how Islam was in agreement with socialism and revolutionary change. Conservative Muslims, of course, resented this manipulation of Islamic tradition and
referred to it bitterly as the "Bolshevication" of Islam.

The brotherhood resurfaced briefly in 1964 when Nasir freed some
of its leaders to help contain the increasingly powerful Communists.
The alleged discovery in mid-1965, however, of a plot among the
brotherhood to overthrow the government led to another wave of arrests and executions. It was in this wave that Sayyid Qutb, one of the
movement's more radical theologians and a charismatic leader in his
own right, (see below) was hanged.

The Muslim Brothers, like most Egyptians, were shocked by the defeat of 1967, but they gloated over the extent to which it discredited
and weakened the Nasir regime (see Sivan 1985, 17). They interpreted
the defeat as a divine indictment inflicted by God on a regime of unbelievers that had set out to exterminate Islam from society and that
had persecuted the Muslim Brothers and other committed Muslims.
The Qur'an abounds with verses promising defeat to those who stray
from God's path, and these were quoted with great satisfaction. "That
which befell you, on the day when the two armies met, was by permission of Allah; that He might know the true believers" (Qur'an
3:166). "O ye who believe! If ye obey those who disbelieve, they will
make you turn on your heels, and ye turn back as losers" (Qur'an
3:149). The defeat also had a shattering effect on public opinion, as
the promises of power and progress made by the regime, already cast
into doubt after the Syrian secession, the tribulations of the war in
Yemen, and near economic collapse, were more thoroughly dashed.
The secular, socialist Arab nationalist ideology on which Nasir had
based his legitimacy could no longer command the loyalty and faith
of a disillusioned nation.

The Islamic movement stood to benefit from the vacuum left by
the crisis of Arab nationalist ideology. Nasir himself was keenly aware
of the effect of the defeat on his legitimacy. He endeavored to por-
tray himself increasingly as a pious leader, and his government as le-
gitimately Islamic. For example, in a letter to the army in August

1969 during the War of Attrition, he wrote, "[Our soldiers] in their next battle are not the soldiers of the nation only, but the army of God, the protectors of His Religions, His Houses [a reference to Jerusalem], and His Holy Books" (Haddad 1982, 36). The enmity between Nasir and the Islamic movement, however, had become too painfully ingrained for such gestures to redeem him. It was up to Sadat to recapture—albeit temporarily—the favor of the resurgent Islamist wave.

In May 1971, a few months after his accession to power, Sadat carried out his so-called Rectification movement (*al-Harakah al-Tashihiyyah*). He weakened the socialist strongholds that had grown around Nasir in the institutions of the state and the army and reduced their influence over society. Abandoning the nationalist socialist formulations of the Nasir regime, he proclaimed that the nation was to be built on *iman* (faith) and *ʿilm* (both science in the modern sense and religious knowledge in the traditional sense)(Ibrahim 1980, 426). He released hundreds of Muslim Brothers from prison, relegalized their publications, and encouraged their resurgence to help him challenge the influence of the socialists and nationalists who had grown strong under Nasir. The new 1971 Constitution made Islam once again the state religion and established *shariʿa* as a source—although not the only source—of legislation.

The limited victory of 1973 was an especial boon to Sadat's Islamic legitimacy. The war launched on the 10th of Ramadan was referred to as the Ramadan War. The operation itself was code-named Badr, recalling Muhammad's first victorious battle against the unbelievers in A.H.1, or A.D. 623. Whereas the 1967 battle cry had been Land, Sea, Sky, expressing the modern reliance on the combined infantry, naval, and air forces, the 1973 battle cry was simply Allahu Akbar (God is great). The part played by Saudi Arabia, a religious Islamic state apparently favored by God with bounteous wealth, was also not overlooked.

The radical wing: Open rebellion against a secular state and society. Sadat's relationship with the Islamic mainstream, however, was strained after 1973 by his Open Door policy toward the West and his increasing dependence on the United States. The relationship finally snapped in 1977 after Sadat's visit to Jerusalem and his campaign for a peace treaty with Israel. Throughout, however, a radical wing that had

split away from the Muslim Brotherhood, and would come to dominate the Islamic movement, violently opposed the Sadat regime and
was only outraged by his attempts to drape the mantle of Islam over
the secular body of the Nasirist state. The ideology of these new radical
groups had crystallized in the 1960s, especially among the circles of
imprisoned Muslim Brothers. The main articulator of this new radical
outlook was Sayyid Qutb, a student of the thought of the radical
Indian Islamic thinker, Abu A'la al-Maudoodi, and a prison inmate
until his death in 1966. Qutb's ideology, adopted Maudoodi's central
thesis that both the governments and the societies of the contemporary Muslim world had slipped back into *jahiliyya* (unbelief). It was in-
cumbent on true Muslims, therefore, to revive the *jihad* of Muhammad
and his early followers who waged a holy war even against their own
families to drive out unbelief and establish the sovereignty of God.
This radical tendency gained many adherents especially after 1967.

The most prominent of these new radical groups, the Society of
Muslims, known also as *Jama'at al-Takfir wa al-Hijra* (The Society of
Excommunication and Holy Flight), was founded by Sheikh Shukri
Ahmad Mustafa who split with the brotherhood in 1967. This group's
first cells were formed in prison in 1967, but it gained a wider following after Mustafa was released from prison by Sadat in 1971. Mustafa,
a lay figure who held a B.S. in agriculture, was an autocratic and
charismatic man who was considered by many of his followers to
be a *mahdi*. His group regarded the entirety of Egyptian state and
society to have slipped from Islam into apostasy (*riddah*). True Muslims must withdraw from the society of the unbelievers, as Muhammad had withdrawn from Mecca, band together, and develop the
faith, discipline, and power necessary to wage and win a war of *jihad*
against the unbelievers. The name Excommunication and Holy Flight
refers to the charge of apostasy they directed against society and their
policy of withdrawal, or flight, from that society. The *Takfir* group's
strength lay among the youth mainly in the towns and surrounding
rural areas of upper Egypt.

The second most prominent group was the Islamic Liberation
Organization (ILO) established in the early 1970s and led by Salih
Siriyya, a Palestinian with a Ph.D. in education, who had been a
member of the brotherhood in Jordan (Dekmejian 1985, 95). Unlike

the *Takfir* group whose hostility was directed toward society as well as the state, the ILO focused its hostility exclusively on the state. It also had a more immediate activist program as evidenced by its attack on the Technical Military Academy in April 1974. It sought to overthrow the government by violent means and acted on those intentions well before other radical leaders felt the time for revolution was ripe. Predictably, the ILO brought heavy government repression not only on itself but also on other radical Islamic groups even as Sadat pursued warm relations with the now rather moderate brotherhood mainstream.

As mentioned, Sadat and the brotherhood had parted ways in 1977 after Sadat's trip to Jerusalem. The brotherhood expressed its opposition not only to this move but also to his Open Door policy toward the West, the cultural Westernization of Egyptian society, and his support of the Coptic Church. Tensions worsened in 1978 in the wake of Muslim-Coptic disturbances. The Islamic Revolution in Iran, of course, only emboldened the Islamic movement, radicals and moderates alike. Sadat scrambled to shore up his legitimacy by declaring *shari‘a* the primary source of legislation and depicting himself more consistently as the Believer President (*al-ra’is al-mu’min*). Islamic opposition to his rule and Muslim-Coptic disturbances continued to grow. In September 1981, in an effort to regain control of the situation, he ordered the arrest of more than three thousand religious leaders and seized control of the mosques. On October 6, 1981, in a military celebration marking the eighth anniversary of the 1973 Ramadan War, Sadat was assassinated by soldiers who were members of *Munazzamat al-Jihad* (The Holy War organization), a radical group that had first come to light in the Muslim-Coptic riots of 1978. Serious fighting erupted in Asyut and other localities as part of what the regime charged was an organized plan to overthrow the Egyptian government. Sadat's successor, former Air Force Chief Hosni Mubarak, responded with a wave of arrests and a tough and sustained security policy. Unlike Sadat, he kept a low profile and did his best not to offend the Islamic groups while keeping a close watch on them through the secret police network.

The founders of the *Takfir* group and the ILO, Shukri Mustafa and Salih Siriyya, were both executed in the late 1970s and were replaced by others. Hasan al-Hudaybi, the pacific nominal leader of the brother-hood died in 1974 and was succeeded by Sheikh Umar Talmasani, a more mainstream Muslim Brother, but one who had also been mel-lowed by long imprisonment to foreswear violence and advocate pros-elytization, *da'wa*, as the primary means of promoting Islamization.

At present, two currents exist within the Islamic movement in Egypt. The first, the older and larger of the two, is represented by the Muslim Brotherhood, which is still attached to Banna's gradual Is-lamization of state and society through education, demonstration, electioneering, lobbying, and so forth. The second branch comprises the radical offshoots of the brotherhood that emerged after 1967. These groups aim at a complete overthrow of the secular state and advocate the use of violence as a means to achieve that end. These radical groups are especially popular among the young and the newly urbanized members of the lower middle class.

The Islamic Movements in Syria: Sunni Resistance to Alawi Domination

The Syrian Muslim Brotherhood was established in Aleppo as a branch of the Egyptian Muslim Brotherhood by a group of Syrian theology students from al-Azhar University. In 1944, its headquarters moved to Damascus, and between 1945 and 1961 it was led by the legalistic-minded Sheikh Mustafa al-Siba'i of Homs (Dekmejian 1985, 112). In this period, it opposed Westernization and secularization and favored a series of socialistic political and economic reforms (Hinnebusch 1982, 151). It also succeeded in returning a number of candidates to parliament. Siba'i had been a friend of Banna's in Cairo while at al-Azhar and generally followed Banna's ideological line. The Syrian Muslim Brotherhood was suppressed by Shishakli in 1952 and again by various Ba'thist, Nasirist, and Communist coalitions between 1954 and 1961. The movement enjoyed a slight resurgence under the secessionist regime of 1961–63 but was again hit hard by the Ba'th in 1963. Siba'i was replaced in 1961 by 'Isam al-'Attar, an engineer by training and a moderate brotherhood leader who was against violent opposition to the government (Hinnebusch 1982, 151). 'Attar was forced into exile in 1963 and actual leadership fell to other figures on the scene.

Expressing resentment against the Baʿth's increasingly exclusive usurpation of power, the Syrian Muslim Brotherhood led an unsuccessful uprising in Hama in 1964 in which they were joined by a majority of *ulama*, Nasirists, merchants, urban notables, and other anti-Baʿth elements. As in Egypt, the 1967 war triggered a radicalization of the Islamic movement with groups of the northern towns favoring open *jihad* against the government and opposing the moderation of ʿAttar and his Damascene followers. Foremost among the new militant groups was *al-Mujahidun* (Holy Warriors) led by Marwan Hadid. Hadid had been influenced by Qutb while in prison in Egypt in 1965. He had also received guerilla training from Arafat's Fateh organization in 1968 (Dekmejian 1985, 113). Forging his followers into a tight militia organization called *Kata'ib Muhammad* (Muhammad's Battalions), Hadid led an assassination campaign against leaders of the Baʿth regime. Arrested in 1976, he was succeeded in leadership by Salim Muhammad, then ʿAdnan ʿUqla, who were, in turn, succeeded after their deaths by ʿAdnan Saʿd al-Din.

The new Syrian president, Hafiz al-Asad, had tried to ease opposition to the radical policies of the Baʿth in the early 1970s by stepping back from some of the nationalization and socialization policies imposed by the party in the middle to late 1960s. He improved relations with the conservative regimes of Saudi Arabia, Jordan, and Sadat's Egypt, oversaw a slight liberalization of political life, and eased economic pressures with an injection of oil money. These manuevers, however, could not resolve what was essentially a power struggle among various sectarian and socioeconomic groups. Both the Baʿth and the military, who in condominium came to rule Syria from the late 1960s, had carried out their early recruitment largely among non-Sunnis and the rural poor. Their socialist policies also held a strong attraction for large portions of the urban working class. The ʿAlawi community, which represented about 12 percent of the population, was especially strong in the Baʿth and the military. The bulk of the Sunni community, about 70 percent of the population, as well as the *ulama*, merchants, and artisans of the northern towns came to bitterly resent the authoritarianism of the ʿAlawi-dominated regime. The regime also favored rural interests over urban interests and lower-class interests over upper-class interests, none of which pleased the

Sunni notable families of the Syrian towns (see Batatu 1981b). The Islamic opposition to the Ba'th regime, therefore, evolved into primarily urban Sunni opposition to 'Alawi rule, with strong support from the middle and upper-middle classes, especially of the northern cities (see Hinnebusch 1982).

After initial calm, Islamic protests erupted in 1973 against a secular constitution promulgated by the Asad regime. Asad compromised by tacking on a provision that stated that the president of the Republic had to be a Muslim and by making a habit of regularly attending Friday prayers. He went so far as to generate a *fatwa* (a religious ruling) that 'Alawism represented the fifth school of Sunni Islam. The limited victories of the 1973 war and his close association with Egypt and Saudi Arabia counted in his favor, whereas his participation in Kissinger's peace diplomacy in the war's aftermath counted against him. Syria's involvement in the Lebanese War in 1976 on the side of the Maronite Christians against the preponderantly Sunni Palestinian forces and their Muslim allies was extremely unpopular. At the same time, dissatisfaction was mounting with regard to excessive 'Alawization of the Syrian government, rampant inflation, and widespread rumors of corruption centering around Asad's own brother, Rif'at. In 1976–77, the *Mujahidun* group began an energetic campaign of agitation and assassination directed against Alawi leaders, security agents, party professionals, and others associated with the Ba'th regime. In an attack on the Military Academy at Aleppo in June 1979, *Mujahidun* members gunned down eighty-three Alawi artillery cadets. This triggered a near civil war between the government and the Islamic groups that lasted until March 1982, ending with the three-week siege and bombardment of the northern city of Hama which left around twenty thousand dead.

By the late 1970s, the Islamic opposition had grown into an immense armed revolutionary movement of more than thirty thousand followers. The radical *Mujahidun* group under 'Adnan Sa'd al-Din had succeeded in unifying the Islamic movements of the north and reabsorbing the more moderate mother organization, the Syrian Muslim Brotherhood of Damascus. The new unified organization assumed the general title of the Syrian Muslim Brotherhood. Islamic ranks were further consolidated in October 1980 with the establishment of *al-Jubhah al-Islamiyyah fi Suriyyah* (The Syrian Islamic Front), which included the new Syrian Muslim Brotherhood, the old ʿAttar faction, some *ulama*, and other small Islamic groups. ʿAdnan Saʿd al-Din was the prime force behind it, whereas Saʿid Hawwa, a disciple of Qutb, was its primary ideologue (Sivan 1985, 43–45).

In a charter published in January 1981, the Front appealed to Alawis to abandon the "Asad brothers" and avoid civil war, called for a lifting of government repression and a return to rule of law based on *shura* (consultation), and demanded that the government stop its intervention in agriculture and cede its control of public industries to the workers. The charter also stressed the Front's commitment to "Islamic socialism," *jihad* to transform the secular state into an Islamic state, and unbending hostility toward Israel and Zionism (Dekmejian 1985, 116). Despite the radical ideology of the influential Saʿid Hawwa, in exile for some time, the Islamic movement in Syria combined the moderate ideological attitude of the Egyptian Muslim Brotherhood with the tactical militancy of the radical *Takfir* and ILO groups. Unlike in Egypt, Sunni violence against the regime did not require elaborate justification because the Alawi-led regime was clearly a non-Sunni—in other words, heretical—regime. Some Islamists also cited Ibn Taymiyya's "Fatwa on the Nusayris [Alawis]" which pronounced Alawis to be more alien to Islam than Christians or Jews (Sivan 1985, 106). The conflict was also fueled by the more thoroughgoing secularism of the Baʿth party.

The Islamic movement in Syria is different from that in Egypt because it more clearly represents a sectarian and class conflict. In essence, it is the opposition movement of the Sunni middle and upper classes of the northern towns against the Alawi regime in Damascus that relies on a large peasant and lower-class base. The different sociological makeup of the Syrian Islamic movements as compared to the Egyptian movements is expressed in the fact that the ideology of the Syrian Islamists is, although tactically militant, theologically quite moderate. Theirs is a simpler political struggle between confessional groups and has much less of the deep moral and religious messianism present in the more radical Egyptian groups.

Islamic Opposition in Iraq: The Voice of Shiʿi Opposition in a Baʿthist Sunni-Dominated State

Whereas the Islamic movement of Syria generally represents the opposition of the Sunni majority to the Baʿth regime dominated by the small ʿAlawite minority, the Islamic movement in Iraq represents the opposition of the Twelver Shiʿa community (roughly 55 percent of the population) to the Baʿth regime dominated by the Sunni Arab minority (roughly 22 percent). The Shiʿa ulama of Iraq were involved in the uprising against the British in 1920 and then again in disturbances in 1922 and 1924 but since then had grown cautious and avoided involvement in political affairs. The overthrow of the monarchy and the revolutionary atmosphere that accompanied it, however, posed new challenges to the Shiʿa clerics. Specifically, the Iraqi Communist party had risen to a dominating political position and Marxist ideology was seriously threatening the social and moral authority of the *ulama*. Religious *fatwas* were issued denouncing the Communists, but that was hardly effective in stemming the Marxist tide. Marxism spoke to a large set of social problems that directly affected the people, and it promised a way out of problems into a better future. To compete with Marxism, Islamists had to point to an Islamic alternative that could also boldly face these pressing issues and outline a road toward economic and political justice. The task of interpreting and elaborating this alternative Islamic ideology was taken up by Muhammad Baqir al-Sadr, a leading Iraqi Shiʿa cleric. Sadr played a leading role in the politicization of Shiʿism in the twentieth century, and his influence over Shiʿa movements in the Arab world as well as in Iran, through his personal relationship with Ayatollah Khomeini, was considerable (see below).

Several groups and parties emerged in Iraq to combat the spread of Marxism and secular Baʿthism. Hizb *al-Daʿwah al-Islamiyyah* (The Party of the Islamic Call), founded in 1968–69 by a number of Shiʿa clerics, was one of the earliest of these movements and was loosely identified with Sadr as well as with Sayyid Muhsin al-Hakim ap-Tabatabaʾi of Najaf (d.1970) (Batatu 1981a, 588). Another organization, *al-Mujahidun* (Holy Warriors), was established by religiously oriented graduates of modern schools and colleges after the Iranian revolution in 1979. The

Mujahidun also regarded Baqir al-Sadr as something of a mentor although they stood firmly against the intervention of the *ulama* in the political life of the country. Indeed, they were closer to former Iranian President Abulhasan Bani Sadr's outlook and blamed Iran's clerics for the confusion in which Iran's revolution wallowed. Both of these organizations drew their membership largely from the impoverished Shiᶜa slum town of al-Thawra, which constitutes about one-fourth of the population of greater Baghdad (Batatu 1981a, 578). But the most influential Islamic organization in the 1980s was the Supreme Assembly of the Islamic Revolution in Iraq (SAIRI). Established in 1982, it was a grouping of leading Iraqi clerics, many of whom fled or were exiled from Iraq after the Iranian revolution and the execution of Sadr by the Iraqi government in 1980. It received the full official backing of Khomeini, and, based in Tehran, it controlled areas of Iraqi territory occupied by Iran and considered itself poised to take over power in Iraq (Mallat 1988, 81). Its ideology was almost identical with that of the Tehran regime, and it was led by Muhammad Baqir al-Hakim and Mahmud al-Hashimi, both in exile in Tehran. The power of the movement, however, was limited for several reasons: (1) it could operate only indirectly within Iraq, (2) there were significant political splits within the leadership, and (3) no charismatic figure emerged to replace Sadr or to play the role of a Khomeini.

Nevertheless and not surprisingly, the Shiᶜa population within Iraq had become significantly radicalized by the Iranian revolution. Ayatollah Khomeini, a close associate of Sadr, had left Iraq only in 1978. After the Islamic revolution in Iran in 1979, riots broke out in Shiᶜa areas demanding the overthrow of the Baᶜth regime and the establishment of an Islamic state. In addition, several Baᶜthist officers were assassinated and an attempt was made on the life of Mikhail Yuhanna, alias Tariq Aziz, the foreign minister and number-three man in the regime. The Baᶜth responded with severe repression that split the RCC and prompted Saddam Husayn, who had just elevated himself to the presidency in July 1979, to conduct a thorough purge of the party, which led to the execution of twenty-two top leaders. Baqir al-Sadr, heralded by the new Islamic regime in Tehran as the "Khomeini of Iraq," was promptly arrested. He was executed, along with his sister Bint al-Huda, in April 1980. His death fixed his image in the firmament of Shiʿa martyrdom and gave added zeal to Shiʿa opposition to the Baʿth. Acts of subversion and sabotage continued with enthusiastic support from the Khomeini government in Tehran, most notably a suicide bomb attack on the secret police headquarters in Baghdad that destroyed the building and left more than eighty top agents and officers dead (Taheri 1987, 164). The Baʿth regime, however, was able to outmaneuver its Shiʿite opposition. Using tactics of repression and co-optation, it kept the Islamic opposition off balance, and through its war with Iran, it fanned old Arab-Persian hostility that helped shade over Sunni-Shiʿa differences.

Relations between the Baʿth regime and the Shiʿa opposition took a turn for the worse in the aftermath of the Iraqi invasion of Kuwait in August 1990 and the subsequent confrontation with the American-led, U.N.-sponsored coalition of Western and Arab states in 1991. Overtures from the American administration and the apparent weakening of the Iraqi regime encouraged segments of the Shiʿa leadership to attempt rebellion. Large segments of southern Iraq, including Basra and other important towns, slipped from Baghdad's control. As the 1991 Gulf War came to a close, however, the Baʿth regime redeployed forces previously engaged at the front to areas of domestic unrest, not only in the Shiʿite south but also in the Kurdish north. By 1992, the abortive rebellion had been crushed and repression had returned to levels higher than had prevailed previously.

Islamic Movements in Lebanon: Protagonists in Confessional Conflict

The collapse of the Lebanese Republic in 1975 was almost as serious an indictment of nationalism as the 1967 war although in this case it was primarily an indictment of regional, rather than pan-Arab, nationalism. The collapse in 1975 seemed to show that even in the most prosperous and modernized Arab country, the nationalist structure was only a rickety framework that could scarce contain the more potent religious and sectarian identities that it claimed to supersede. The outbreak of sectarian strife and the wave of kidnappings and massacres carried out on the basis of religious affiliation underscored the primacy of religious over secular and national identities. Meanwhile, the Lebanese-Palestinian inter-Arab dimension of the conflict, which had been played out previously in Jordan in 1970, seemed to reaffirm the bankruptcy of Arab nationalism. In the words of Saʿid Shaʿban, leader of the Islamic Unification movement, or *Tawhid*, in Tripoli, "Pan-Arabism has been tried but did not foster any coming together. Territorial nationalism has been experimented with in Lebanon and brought us nothing but destruction and devastation. Therefore, we call upon one and all: come back and worship Allah, your Lord" (Sivan 1985, 47).

Both the Sunni and Shiʿa communities in Lebanon have undergone a significant Islamic resurgence. One of the principal ideologues in the Sunni community, Fathi Yakan, was a student of the radical thought of Qutb and Maudoodi. He had started out as an Arab nationalist but realized the contradictions between Arab nationalism and Islam at an early date. In 1964, he founded *al-Jamaʿa al-Islamiyya* (The Muslim Association) to help propagate his views. The more militant expression of Sunni fundamentalism arose only in the late 1970s in the northern town of Tripoli far from the influence of Beirut and close to the centers of Sunni resistance to Alawi Baʿthist rule in northern Syria. This *Tawhid* movement of Saʿid Shaʿban took a fiercely uncompromising position vis-à-vis nationalism or secularism. He and his followers proved hostile to the governments both of Beirut and Damascus and enjoyed close links with Khomeini's Iran. They exhibited the outspoken anti-Westernism of the Shiʿa movements and called for the establishment of an Islamic Republic in Lebanon (Wright 1988, 59). In Beirut and Sidon, other Sunni-populated coastal towns, the Sunni community avoided an excessive drift into fundamentalism largely to distinguish itself from the newly arrived Shiʿa community that was challenging Sunni control over these cities and articulating its Shiʿism in stridently Islamic fundamentalist terms.

The mobilization of the Shiʿa community began mainly along sectarian lines in the 1960s under the leadership of the charismatic Persian-born cleric, Musa al-Sadr. Sadr combined the symbols of Shiʿism with a vigorous populist political campaign aimed at catapulting the large Shiʿa community of Lebanon to its rightful place in the Lebanese political and economic system. His movement, *Harakat al-Mahrumin* (Movement of the Dispossessed), was not a particularly revolutionary one. It was essentially reformist and sought to advance the cause of the Shiʿa community within the secular nationalist, but heavily sectarian, context of modern Lebanon. The collapse of the Lebanese state in 1975, the disappearance of Musa al-Sadr while on a trip to Libya in 1978, and the Islamic Revolution in Iran in 1979 all served to radicalize the Shiʿa community.

The mainstream Shiʿa political movement that Sadr had established, upon the outbreak of the 1975 war, formed its own militia called Amal, meaning hope; its Arabic letters represented the acronym for *Afwaj al-Muqawamah al-Lubnaniyyah* (Units of the Lebanese Resistance). After the Iranian Revolution, Amal's authority in the Shiʿa community was challenged by Hizballah (Party of God), which was established in 1982 under Iranian tutelage. Nominally under the spiritual leadership of Sheikh Muhammad Husayn Fadlallah and the operational control of Husayn Musawi, the movement was largely controlled from Iran through the several thousand Iranian Revolutionary Guards that were stationed in the Lebanese Biqaʿ valley. Unlike Amal, which was content to work within the traditional framework of secular politics as a representative of the Shiʿa community, Hizballah was committed to the complete overthrow of the Lebanese political system and the establishment of an Islamic state similar to that of Iran. With ample funding and support from Iran, Hizballah became a potent force among the Shiʿa community and played a leading role in combating Western and Israeli influence.

The Ideology of the Islamic Movements

Sunni Activist Thought

Hasan al-Banna: Setting the agenda. Almost without exception, the Sunni Islamic activists of the twentieth century recognize Hasan al-Banna as the founder and first martyr of modern organized political Islam. Unlike Afghani, whom many revere as the first herald of an Islamic response to the West, Banna went beyond exhortation and pamphleteering to develop an organization and a plan of action that found ready adherents among a population now keenly aware of the

Western challenge. He represented "the unique embodiment of Sufi spiritualist, Islamic scholar, and activist leader" who could provide charisma and leadership for a dynamic political Islamic movement (Dekmejian 1985, 70).

Much of Banna's thought was influenced, among other sources, by that of Ibn Hanbal (d. 855), Abu Hamid al-Ghazali (d. 1111), and Ibn Taymiyya (d. 1328), especially as interpreted by Rashid Rida. Ibn Hanbal opposed the open rationalism of the Greek-influenced Mu'tazalite school in the ninth century. He called for a return to orthodoxy and a more literal interpretation of Holy Law based more heavily on revelation than reason. Ibn Hazm, a theologian and vizier in Muslim Spain, had also championed a return to orthodoxy as did the eleventh century theologian al-Ghazali, who developed an elaborate analysis and refutation of Greek rationalism. Ibn Taymiyya, however, was the most direct inspiration because he combined the perspicacity of an able and orthodox theoretician with the courage and enthusiasm of a political activist and defender of the faith. He recognized no authority but that of the Qur'an, the Sunnah, and the practice of the early community. He bitterly opposed innovation and favored vigorous *jihad* and open *ijtihad*. Born in Syria, he fled the Mongol invasion as a child and continued to agitate against the Mongols from the Mameluke sultanate of Egypt throughout his life. The Mongols had adopted Sunni Islam, but Ibn Taymiyya refused to accept their Islamic credentials because he insisted that they had transgressed against the Shari'a. He participated in several wars against them and was jailed several times for his actions. This brilliant and vigorous defender of orthodox Islam, especially with his legitimation of revolution and rebellion, was an attractive model not only for Banna but for other Islamic thinkers of the time. In addition to his influence on Banna and Rida, he provided the theoretical foundation for the Wahhabi movement and influenced the thought of Maudoodi and Qutb. Most importantly, Ibn Taymiyya's credentials within the Sunni tradition were unimpeachable, and although he preached rebellion, conservative *ulama* would be hard put to condemn his message as outside of the faith. This was a strong weapon in the hands of Banna and his followers.

What is important to note about Banna and what sets him apart from his illustrious predecessors—Rida, Abduh, Afghani, or even Ibn Kathir and Ibn Hazm in earlier times—is that he chose to take his message not to the *ulama*, the intellectual elite, but directly to the masses. This probably reflects his Sufi background and proved to be the key to success in the era of mass politics. Indeed, Banna faulted the *ulama* for having let the Islamic community fall so deep into decline. Neither did they formulate new and reformed interpretations of the faith nor were they able to defend Islam against the religious, intellectual, moral, and cultural assaults of the West.

For Banna, the crux of the problem in the Islamic countries was that Islam no longer held the central position in ordering society and the lives of its members. It had become marginalized by the encroachments of the Christian West and the weakness and decadence of a corrupt Muslim elite. The seventh article of the credo of the Muslim Brotherhood explicitly declared, "I believe that the secret of the Muslims' backwardness is their estrangement from religion, and that the basis of reform should be a return to the precepts and judgments of Islam" (quoted in Abdel-Malek 1983, 46). Banna saw the crisis of Muslim countries manifested in many spheres. In the political sphere, Islamic countries, once proud, unified, and independent, had succumbed to Western colonialism and internal division and partisanship. In the economic sphere, usury had become widespread and foreign companies controlled the wealth and assets of Muslims. In the intellectual sphere was great disarray and widespread atheism. In the social sphere, virtue had given way to sensualism and pornography, legislation had descended into the hands of parliaments, and the organization of education and the upbringing of children had strayed from the authority of Islam. Finally, at the personal psychological level, the individual seemed to be suffering from what Banna himself diagnosed as "despair, apathy, cowardice, and selfishness" (Banna n.d., 117). He argued that contemporary Muslim society was in such disorder as to lead "either to revolution, or to extinction, and both are crimes that history will never forgive" (Banna n.d., 342).

Writing in the interwar period, Banna emphasized that although the West had made its contribution to civilizational progress in some spheres over the past centuries, it was now in decline. Its political principles were leading it into tyranny and dictatorship, its economic principles were leading it into depression and unemployment, and its social principles were leading it into moral decay and revolution (Banna n.d., 168). In the capitalist democratic West he found an excess of individualism, moral degeneracy, class warfare, social chaos, a weakening of the family, debasement of women, subservience to capital, and racism. In the communist world he saw atheism, tyranny, and international dictatorship. In both societies he saw rampant materialism and spiritual emptiness. As the East had led the world in the age of Moses, Jesus, and Muhammad, it was time again now for the East to serve as a guide and a beacon for the rest of the world.

For Banna, the main purpose of the *Ikhwan* organization was to call people to the message of Islam contained in the Qur'an, the *sunna* (the tradition of the Prophet), and the practice of the *salaf al-salih*. Banna was confident that the Islamic call was not far from the hearts of his compatriots, ingrained as it was in their culture and their daily lives. Given the familiarity of the population with Islam, the Islamic call had the power of simplicity and directness. The *Ikhwan* slogan proclaimed simply: "God is our purpose, the Qur'an is our constitution, the Prophet is our leader, *jihad* is our path, and martyrdom for the sake of God is our noblest wish" (Banna n.d., 11). As an indigenous creed, Islam had the advantage also over communism and nationalism of preserving the cultural, intellectual, and political independence of Muslim societies. As a widespread and familiar creed, it also had the advantage of being able to provide Muslim societies with an indigenous source of power and self-esteem.

What Banna called for first in his followers was a spiritual reawakening to Islam. He called for a life of faith and piety and urged his followers to familiarize themselves with the totality of the Islamic message from its personal to its political, social, and economic aspects. Reform had to begin with the individual and his return to the ways of Islam. These reformed Muslims would join together in the *usar* (families) of the *Ikhwan* organization. As these families multiplied, their influence over polity and society would bring about a general reform of the political and economic institutions of the society. Much of Banna's call was directed to the moral and spiritual reform of the individual. Individuals must understand and internalize the principles of Islam, they must reform their thoughts and behavior accordingly, and they must dedicate themselves to promoting the cause of Islam in their society (Banna n.d., 117). They must join with other like-minded individuals in love and trust. At the general societal level, they must labor with others to establish a *nizam Islami* (an Islamic order), in which Shariʿa would be the law of the land and Islam the ordering principle of cultural and social life.

Banna saw the mission of the *Ikhwan* in bringing about an Islamic order as divided into three stages. In the first stage, propaganda, or spreading the call of Islam among the people, organization could be rather loose, and there was no need for great hierarchy. In the second, preparation and mobilization, the promising elements within the *Ikhwan* would be selected, organized, and trained for the final stage. "It is a period of Sufism in the spiritual sphere, and militancy in the sphere of action" (Banna n.d., 15). In the final stage, execution, *jihad* would be declared from which there would be no turning back; "Either success or martyrdom." Banna himself never fully and unequivocally declared the inauguration of this last decisive phase. He was concerned about holding back some of the overhasty young activists among his followers and also worried about the ill-preparedness of the *Ikhwan* to face the organized repressive apparatus of the state. As Banna warned, "O Muslim Brothers, and especially the enthusiastic and hasty among you . . . he who wants to pick a fruit before it is ripe or pluck a flower before its time, I am not with him under any circumstances" (Banna n.d., 254). "At the time when you have mobilized 300 battalions . . . at that time ask me to lead you into the stormy sea" (Banna n.d., 258). Furthermore, as his remarks on revolution reveal, he was apprehensive about the uncontrollability of violent revolutionary action once it got under way. In any case, it was up to others in the 1960s and 1970s, especially Sayyid Qutb and his followers, to declare open *jihad* not only against the secularist government but in some cases against the society at large. The main objective of the *Ikhwan*, he insisted, was not to seize the reigns of government themselves but to ensure the implementation of Islamic laws and principles by the government. Whoever accomplishes this, he insisted, the Brothers would support (Banna n.d., 273).

Banna admitted that he had no detailed blueprint for an Islamic political system. Indeed, he considered such details to be only marginally important (Banna n.d., 359). He did, however, have a basic concept of what an "Islamic order" would involve. To begin with, an Islamic state was a central necessity in any Islamic order, for in Islam there was no separation between *din wa dawla* (religion and state). The pillars of such a state were roughly as follows: (1) the Qur'an was to be considered the fundamental constitution from which all authority and legislation would flow. The Qur'an would be seconded by the *sunna* and the practices of the early community under the first four caliphs. (2) The government was not to be autocratic but to operate on the principle of *shura,* or consultation, as mentioned in the Qur'an: "And their affairs are a matter of consultation among them" (Qur'an 42: 38). (3) The ruler was not free but bound by the Law of God and the will of the people as articulated by their leaders and learned men (*ahl al-hal wa al-ʿaqd*). He argued that such a system had been most perfectly realized during the reign of the first four caliphs (Banna n.d., 359). (4) Islam, however, was not rigid and could be adapted to different forms as long as the essence was preserved. An Islamic state could, for example, be constructed on the parliamentary model with elections serving to select *ahl al-hal wa al-ʿaqd* and the parliament serving as the locus of *shura* (Banna n.d., 366). He opposed the proliferation of political parties, however, because he regarded them only as sources of division and weakness. The goal was unity in the path of God. If there were two parties, then one of them, at least, must have strayed from God's path.

The *Ikhwan* also involved themselves in economic affairs. Unlike Christianity, Islam is unapologetically concerned with the material conditions of Muslims in this life, and, accordingly, Banna and the *Ikhwan* devoted much attention to matters of economic justice and the welfare of the poor. Indeed, the third article of the Muslim Brotherhood credo read: "I believe that a Muslim must work and earn money. . . . I promise to work and to earn my living, to save for the future, to pay the *zakat* [religious tithe], to set aside part of my income for charitable deeds, to encourage any useful economic project, to give preference to the products of my own country and those of other Muslim countries, not to practice usury in any respect, and not to lose myself in matters lying beyond my competence" (quoted in Abdel-Malek 1983, 46). As interpreted by Banna, Islam required the elimination of usury, the nationalization of natural resources, respect for private property, industrialization, the abolition of the stock market, the establishment of *zakat*, full employment, land reform, labor legislation, a social security system, and so forth. In short, the economic program was a mildly socialist one tailored to fit more traditional Islamic economic practices (Banna n.d., 391).

The Muslim Brotherhood illustrated their serious interest in economic matters by establishing a number of economic enterprises of their own. The purpose behind these ventures was to promote national economic independence, to prove the viability of Muslim economic practices, to provide employment and income for the poor, and to gain some earnings for the Muslim Brotherhood organization itself. Aside from a successful printing and publishing industry, the Muslim Brotherhood had significant ventures in commerce, engineering, and industry (Mitchell 1969, 275). These enterprises were hit hard in the crisis with the government in 1948 and never recovered their full size. Nevertheless, this activity provided the Muslim Brotherhood with inroads into the labor class and promoted their claims to represent the Egyptian worker.

The brotherhood also placed a strong emphasis on education, and from its early years in Ismaᶜiliyya was active in establishing and running schools. Banna opposed the influence of the Christian mission schools and criticized the government for promoting secular education. He favored an education grounded in religious moral teaching although complemented by a strong schooling in the modern technical sciences that Muslims had to borrow, at this juncture, from the West. Banna also took an active interest in matters of public health, social welfare, and social reform. The Muslim Brotherhood developed an extensive network of clinics, dispensaries, and hospitals, established development teams to help villages overcome problems of water and electricity shortages, poor roads, and unsatisfactory housing facilities, and actively campaigned to prohibit wine, gambling, and prostitution and to impose media censorship in the interests of morality and religious rectitude.

Banna insisted that the Islamic movement had no serious conflict with nationalist movements as long as those nationalist movements stayed within their proper limits. After all, the nation, whether it was the Egyptian or Arab nation, was the first community that the individual naturally turned to with thoughts of social reform and progress. It was natural and acceptable that people should organize to some degree within their natural geographic or cultural boundaries as each family was organized within itself. In other words, a true Muslim appreciated the love of the fatherland promoted by nationalists. He supported the nationalists in their call for national liberation and independence. He agreed with their attempts to organize and strengthen the national community. The true Muslim, however, could not accept the revival of pre-Islamic *jahili* customs, nor the glorification of race, nor the principle of competition and conflict between nations of the same faith (Banna n.d., 106–7). The Ikhwan's basic difference with the nationalists, said Banna, was that "we consider that the boundaries of a nation are ultimately determined by the dispersion of a common creed or faith, while they consider them to be defined by physical and geographical obstacles" (Banna n.d., 105). In other words, Banna's nationalism, like that of Afghani, was clearly Islamic nationalism.

His patriotism for Egypt, however, and his hostility for its enemies were both quite passionate. "There is no contradiction between the Islamic call and devotion to the defense of Egypt" he insisted (Banna n.d., 69). Defending Egypt, however, was simply part of every Muslim's duty to defend Islam and to defend Muslims against injustice and oppression anywhere. He rebuked the Egyptian secular nationalists of his time who held up the nation, a grouping of mere men, as the ultimate source of temporal authority. These he accused of *shirk,* assigning partners to God. "The ultimate and only real relationship possible to men," he said, "is with God, not with other men" (quoted in Mitchell 1969, 264). In fact, nationalism, according to Banna, was not possible without religion, for what manner of loyalty to family or nation could one have without religion, beyond that of selfish self-interests?

He opposed Pharaonism, Phoenicianism, and Syrianism as futile attempts to base identity on artificial and profane myths. He was more favorable toward Arabism, however, because the Arabs, he argued, were at the center of Islam, and the Arab identity was deeply intermixed with the Muslim identity. After all, the Prophet himself had said "the Arabs are the first Muslims," and "if the Arabs are humiliated, then so is Islam." Indeed, "Islam," Banna proclaimed, "will not be revived until the Arab peoples unify their word and liberate their lands" (Banna n.d., 70). The final and ultimate loyalty of every Muslim, however, must be to the Muslim nation, and not to any lesser nation. In the interest of this Islamic nationalism Banna actively favored a restitution of the caliphate and endeavored to spread his movement to other Muslim regions beyond the borders of Egypt.

It is apparent that Banna's thought was quite wide ranging. It defined the contemporary crisis as resulting from an estrangement from true Islam. It called for activism and provided an organizational framework within which to channel this activism. Its political program strongly agitated for gradual but meaningful reform. Its social program promoted Islamic virtues and practices and combated religiously proscribed evils. Its economic program was welfare oriented with an emphasis on autarky, state control of large enterprises, and social justice within a general system of private property. Banna was a man of great oratorical aptitude. He was a charismatic figure whose enthusiasm breathed life into the ideology he elaborated and the organization he founded. His death was the greatest blow to his movement. Since his death, the Muslim Brotherhood has been an organization of lesser dynamism and vitality.

Sayyid Qutb: The radical reformulation. The main ideological transformation of the Sunni Islamic movement in the Arab world after its founding by Hasan al-Banna was carried out by Sayyid Qutb. "As a militant ideologue, Qutb presided over the generational transition from the Brotherhood's atrophied fundamentalism to the youthful extremism of the 1970s" (Dekmejian 1985, 90). From a movement of social and political reform, Qutb sowed the seeds for the growth of a more radical branch of the Islamic movement that considered contemporary Muslim society to be in a state of abject *jahiliyya* (ignorance and religious unbelief) and advocated a vigorous program of moral, social, and political *jihad* against society and its leaders.

Qutb was born in 1906 in Asyut Province and received a rigorous religious education from an early age (Haddad 1983, 68). At the age of thirteen he was sent to an uncle in Cairo and pursued a more secular educational path, finally graduating from Cairo University with a degree in literature. He received a post in the Ministry of Education but eventually left it to devote himself to reading and writing, still mostly in the field of literature. A trip to the United States in 1948 to study educational administration stimulated an ideological transformation in him that had begun with disenchantment over Britain's war policies and general Western support for the establishment of Israel. Alienated and embittered, his experience in the United States, where he saw strong American support for Israel and hostility toward the Arabs and Muslims, confirmed his abandonment of Western secularism and his reorientation toward Islam as an identity and an all-embracing faith and ideology. His first book, *The Struggle Between Islam and Capitalism,* published in 1952, was an expression of this reorientation. His subsequent work, *In the Shadow of the Qur'an* (1953), was strongly influenced by Maudoodi and provided the theoretical outlines of his radical outlook that he would elaborate in later years. He joined the *Ikhwan* organization upon his return from the United States in 1950 and headed its propaganda section. He was a consultant to the Free Officers regime for a few months in 1952. In 1954, he was arrested with many others and served ten years of a fifteen-year sentence. Released in 1964, he published his most well-known work, *Milestones on the Road* (1964). He was jailed again in 1965 and finally executed in 1966.

To understand the roots of Qutb's thought, we should turn first to the thought of the Indian Muslim thinker Abu Aʿla al-Maudoodi who was the primary influence on Qutb. Maudoodi (d.1979), one of the foremost Muslim thinkers and writers of the twentieth century, was a leading activist in the Islamic movement in India and, after partition in 1947, in Pakistan. His thought became known in the Arab world through the efforts of his main Arabic translator, Ali Nedvi (Sivan 1985, 23). In his major works, *Jihad in Islam, Islam and Jahiliyya,* and *The Principles of Islamic Government,* Maudoodi developed the theory that the Muslim community had slipped back into unbelief comparable to the unbelief with which the Prophet found himself surrounded in Mecca. Maudoodi was the first Islamic writer to depict the crisis of Islam in such extreme terms and the first to advocate the type of activism that easily followed from such a radical diagnosis—an all-out *jihad* carried out by a small group of organized and committed true believers to reintroduce Islam into a society that had come to be Islamic in name only. Maudoodi articulated a conclusion that Rashid Rida and others had been stumbling toward for some time, namely, that a compromise between Western modernity and Islam was not possible but that a complete triumph of Islam was a necessary prerequisite for the revival and progress of the Muslim community. It was this radical attitude that began to find adherents in the Arab world in the late 1950s after the loss of Palestine and the disappointment with both liberal constitutional and military authoritarian regimes. Sayyid Qutb's thought had been growing increasingly radicalized during the 1940s. In an encounter with Ali Nedvi in 1951, Qutb found much that was attractive in the thought of Maudoodi and came to adopt the outlook of Maudoodi and Nedvi in his writing.

Qutb's central thesis was that contemporary Muslim society had abandoned Islam and that the Muslim community had, therefore, ceased to exist. True Muslims, then, were in the same position that the Prophet Muhammad and his followers had encountered in Mecca. As Muhammad and his followers withdrew from Mecca (*hijra*), regrouped in Yathrib, and declared *jihad* on the unbelievers of Mecca and the Quraysh tribe, so present-day true Muslims had to recognize the unbelief of their compatriots, withdraw from their society, and declare a *jihad* "of tongue and sword" upon it in order to bring it back under the mantle of Islam. In Qutb's words,

The Muslim community is a community of people whose life, thoughts, conditions, institutions, values, and standards all flow from Islam. . . . [T]his community—with these characteristics—has ceased to exist ever since governance according to God's law disappeared off the face of the earth. . . . This community must be brought back into existence. (Qutb 1964, 6)

We are today in a *jahiliyya* like the *jahiliyya* the Prophet faced or even darker. Everything around us is *jahiliyya*. . . . Even much of what we consider Islamic culture, Islamic sources, Islamic philosophy, or Islamic thought, is also a product of this *jahiliyya*. (Qutb 1964, 17–18)

Qutb traced the beginning of the eclipse of Islam all the way back to early centuries when the teachings of the Qur'an became overlayed with the philosophy and logic of the Greeks, the mythology and imagination of the Persians, the scripture of the Jews, and the theology of the Christians. For a rebirth of the Muslim community, Qutb advocated a purification from all these corrupting accretions and a return to the pure source, the Qur'an. Moreover, Muslims should turn to the Qur'an not in the spirit of contemplation or entertainment but in the spirit of action. "Our first aim is to know: what does the Qur'an want us to do?" (Qutb 1964, 18). The Qur'an, then, was not simply a book of God's teachings but of God's commands that must be obeyed here and now.

Qutb's exegesis of the Qur'an made clear what he believed God had revealed. First, contemporary society was not Islamic but comprised unbelievers: "Whoso judgeth not by that which God hath revealed: such are disbelievers" (Qur'an 5:44; Qutb 1965b, 110). Since the Egyptian state was a secular institution that applied human-made not divine law, then it was a government of unbelievers. The fact that the authorities included the Shariʿa as an occasional source of legislation did not bolster their legitimacy: "Believe ye in part of the Scripture and disbelieve ye in part thereof? And what is the reward of those who do so save ignominy in the life of this world, and on the day of Resurrection they will be consigned to the most grievous doom" (Qur'an 2:85).

Qutb's quarrel is not with the government alone, for he alleges that the entire society which calls itself Islamic is, in fact, not so. "An Islamic society is not simply one made up of individuals who call themselves Muslims, when the laws of Islam are not the laws of the society, even if these people prayed, fasted, and made the pilgrimage to Mecca. And the Islamic society is not that which invents for itself its own Islam—other than what God revealed and the Prophet explained—and calls it 'modern' or 'advanced' Islam" (Qutb 1964, 105). The societies that consider themselves Islamic are in fact *jahili* because "they grant to entities other than God the characteristics of divinity: they grant domination and sovereignty (*hakimiyyah*) to something other than God, and derive from it their institutions, laws, values, standards, customs, and traditions" (Qutb 1964, 92). To these societies as to their governments applies the verse, "Whoso judgeth not by that which God hath revealed: such are disbelievers" (Qur'an 5:44).

The Qur'an reveals, says Qutb, that the aim of every Muslim should be not to reconcile Islam with barbaric society but rather to purge society of any and all un-Islamic elements. What is needed is a revolutionary transformation not a political compromise. The first step along this difficult path is for the true Muslim "to raise himself above this barbaric society and its values and ideas. We must not compromise with it in any of our values or ideas even a little. Islam and this society are on a crossroads: if we go one step in the direction of the *jahili* society we will lose our way and our path" (Qutb 1964, 19). Despite the difficulties and the challenges, the true Muslims must follow the same tortuous path followed by Muhammad's early community of believers who encountered many difficulties but whom God rewarded with victory (ibid.).

In effect, Qutb was accusing of apostasy nearly all contemporary Muslims except the small band of Islamic activists who had withdrawn from society and rejected its norms. *Dar al-Islam* (the abode of Islam), therefore, had become a small and narrow place, whereas *dar al-harb* (the abode of war) was all around. "Every land that persecutes the Muslim in his beliefs, and pushes him from his faith and nullifies his Shariʿa, is properly *dar al-harb* even if in it are his family, his clan, his nation, his property, and his commerce" (Qutb 1964, 145). "O ye who believe! Choose not your fathers nor your brethren for friends if they take pleasure in disbelief rather than faith. Whoso of you taketh them for friends, such are wrong-doers" (Qur'an 9:23). As for how to behave toward the abode of war, the injunction of the Qur'an is clear and categorical: "And fight them until persecution is no more, and religion is all for God" (Qur'an 2:93).

In the context of the persecution of Islamic activists by the Nasir regime and the increasing secularization of Egyptian life through the socialist reforms of the government and the domination by the state of religious institutions, Qutb's message had a strong appeal. The defeat of 1967 helped confirm Qutb's charges that Egyptian government and society were of unbelievers and was a consolation to the Islamists who had already received many blows. "If ye have received a blow, the [disbelieving] people have received a blow the like thereof. These are [only] the vicissitudes which We cause to follow one another for mankind, to the end that Allah may know those who believe and may choose witnesses from among you" (Qur'an 3:40). "That which befell you, on the day when the two armies met, was by permission of God, that He might know the true believers" (Qur'an 3:166).

Except for the crucial transformation in outlook about the boundaries of *dar al-Islam* and *dar al-harb* and the uncompromising revolutionism of its adherents, this new ideology shared many of the same aims with the earlier, more moderate, and reform-oriented ideology developed by Banna. Indeed, Qutb's debt to Banna and thinkers such as Ibn Taymiyya and Ibn Hanbal is clear and openly acknowledged. The new radicals still aimed to bring into being the good and true Muslim, reform him and reform his society, establish an Islamic government, promote union among the Islamic countries, revive the caliphate, and work toward the spread of Islam to all humanity. Moreover, there was a general commonality of thought on matters of economics, public welfare, international relations, and so forth, except that the radical groups tended to take more extreme positions in these matters than the Muslim Brothers who evolved into a rather moderate political force.

By streamlining the principle of the Islamic imperative and by drawing an analogy to the early Muslim community, Qutb had hit upon a potent activist formula. The problem, the absence of Islam from society, was clear; the solution, a withdrawal from society followed by consolidation of power and *jihad*, was equally direct. Qutb's thought formed the ideological basis for the majority of the radical Islamic groups that emerged in the 1970s. Not only the *Takfir*, ILO, and *Jihad* groups in Egypt, but also others, such as *Kata'ib Muhammad* and *al-Tawhid* in Syria and Lebanon set their agenda according to Qutb's thought. Some differences, however, did emerge with respect to the exact interpretation of Qutb's ideas. Some, such as the ILO and most of the Syrian groups, restricted the open *jihad* declared by Qutb to the government and its supporters. Others like *Takfir* and *Jihad* took the more extreme interpretation of Qutb's thought and declared open *jihad* on society at large. Indeed, this ambiguity had not been firmly resolved in Qutb's writing because whereas in some places he seemed to excuse the people for their estrangement from Islam and to explain that once the government was reconstituted along Islamic lines the people would quickly revert to Islam (e.g., Qutb 1964, 63), in other places he stated simply that these people were not Muslims despite their protestations, hence, they were in *dar al-harb* and *jihad* against them to bring them around was legitimate. In other words, in contrast to the Qur'anic dictum "There is no coercion in religion" that Qutb occasionally cited (e.g., Qutb 1964, 63), he also cited verses advocating a more aggressive approach.

The ideology of an activist Islam as developed in modern Arab Sunni thought by Banna and Qutb, among others, had considerable coherence. Although the Muslim Brotherhood and, later, more radical groups differed on the delimitation of *dar al-harb* and on the approach to improving society, their basic convictions about the source of Islamic society's problems and the ultimate goal of the reinstitutionalization of Islam in those societies were quite similar.

Shi'ite Activist Thought: The Millennial Perspective

The several million Shi'a of the Arab world are concentrated in the northern Gulf territories of Iraq, Saudi Arabia, and some of the smaller Gulf sheikhdoms, as well as in Lebanon. They constitute a majority in Iraq and Bahrain and at least a plurality among the various religious groupings of Lebanon. The Shi'a of Islam, as opposed to the Sunnis, are those Muslims who took the side of Ali, the Prophet's son-in-law, in the dispute over the succession to Muhammad after the Prophet's death. Deviation from true Islam began, according to Shi'a tradition, when the companions of the Prophet unjustly overlooked Ali, a member of the Prophet's family and the first male convert to Islam, for the stewardship of the Islamic community. Three caliphs were chosen from outside the Prophet's household before Ali was invested as caliph. His tenure was shortlived, however, as he was poisoned in A.D. 661. The truly dark period of Islam for the Shi'a began with the claims of Mu'awiya, a member of the Umayyad tribe who had fought against Islam in its early years, to the caliphate. Hasan, Ali's oldest son and the Prophet's grandson, feebly contested Mu'awiya's claim but then conceded defeat to the established power of the Umayyads in Syria and withdrew to pursue a more contemplative life in Mecca. Upon Mu'awiya's death in A.D. 680, Ali's younger son, Husayn, challenged the legitimacy of Mu'awiya's designated successor, his son Yazid. Opposing Mu'awiya's plans to make the caliphate an inherited dynastic office akin to kingship, Husayn and a band of his followers upon the invitation of some elements in Iraq, rode from Mecca toward Baghdad. Intercepted by Yazid's army at Karbala on the tenth day of the month of Ashura, Husayn's forces were decimated, he was killed, and his head was sent back to Damascus. The events at Karbala, the martyrdom of Husayn, and the persecution of the believing Muslims at the hands of nominally Muslim political tyrants, form the central theme and reference point of Shi'a history. "Every day is Ashura, and every place is Karbala" (slogan quoted in Ajami 1986, 141). The defiance of Husayn and his companions was transformed into an internalized and bitter righteousness while the story of Karbala underlined the profound pathos of Shi'a history and the futility of open revolt. After the disappearance of the Twelfth Imam (the twelfth of the descendants of the Prophet, the first of whom was Ali and all of whom were considered legitimate and infallible leaders of the Shi'a community), the revolutionary zeal of the community waned. The revolution of true Islam and the restitution of justice and equality would be carried out at the end of time by the occulted Twelfth Imam who would return to put things aright. Many of these themes would be exploited by Shi'a activists and ideologues to lend depth and direction to their movements.

Muhammad Baqir al-Sadr of Iraq and Musa al-Sadr of Lebanon were the two most influential Arab-based Shi'a clerics of recent decades.

Ayatollah Muhammad Baqir al-Sadr: The power of theory. Muhammad Baqir al-Sadr was born in Najaf in 1930 to an Arab family renowned for its learning in the Shi'a world. He rose to the religious station of Ayatollah and became one of the leading theologians of the contemporary Shi'a world. He was regarded with special esteem by his followers in Iraq because he was one of the few Arabs to be considered a *marji'* (source of imitation) in a Shi'a religious establishment dominated by Persians. He wrote prolifically, decrying the secularism into which society had sunk and elaborating a comprehensive and systematic Islamic alternative to the Marxist and secular nationalist ideologies that had become dominant. Unlike his colleague, Ayatollah Ruhollah Khomeini, with whom he developed a close relationship during the latter's exile in Iraq, Sadr was a relatively quiet and serene man, not given to daring political action despite the provocative content of his writing.

The development of Sadr's thought can be divided into three periods. In the first, Sadr was primarily reacting to the fall of the Iraqi monarchy in 1958 and the spread of Marxist and nationalist ideologies. In his two most influential works of this period, *Falsafatuna* (Our Philosophy) published in 1959 and *Iqtisaduna* (Our Economy) published in 1960, Sadr addressed the issues of social and economic reform. He engaged in lengthy critiques of both Marxism and capitalism, faulting the former for its dehumanizing materialism and the latter for its exploitative nature and describing an "Islamic alternative" based on traditional Islamic law and philosophy (Mallat 1988, 75). Not hesitating to employ Marxist terminology, he provided Islamic definitions of landownership, labor, raw materials, production, distribution, and so forth.

His economic views also reinforced his theory of the Islamic state, which was based on the rule of the jurisprudent and was adopted in part by Khomeini. "God is the source of all power," he declared, "the only legislator, and the sole owner of all the earth's resources" (Batatu 1981a, 579). From this, he deduced that the political or economic domination of one human over another is a violation of God's prerogatives and that humans are to live in political and economic freedom under the rule of God. Along these lines he called for a "social revolution" against political injustice and economic exploitation with the aim of establishing an Islamic state. This state would be headed by the highest *marjiᶜ* or *mujtahid* (religious scholar) in the Shiᶜa clergy. He would govern with the consent of a Council of One Hundred representing the *ulama*, and the assistance of a popularly elected assembly of *ahl al-hal wa al-ᶜaqd*. This scholar-king would in effect be the deputy of the Absent Imam and the head of the executive, judiciary, and legislative branches of government. The Islamic state would implement the Shariᶜa and in the economic sphere would prohibit usury, regulate income according to effort and need, fight monopoly, promote a narrowing of class disparities, provide a measure of economic security, and provide free education and health services to all (Batatu 1981a, 580).

In the second period of his literary life, Sadr wrote *al-Bank al-La Rabawi fil-Islam* (The Non-Usurious Bank in Islam) and *al-Usus al-Mantiqiyyah lil-Istiqra*ʾ (The Logical Bases of Induction). Both were rather technical and apolitical works, and the first, at least, may reflect Sadr's attempt to influence the rapidly growing banking industry in the first years of the oil boom which brought great prosperity to Iraq. The last period of his life is marked by a narrowing and repoliticization of his concerns focusing on the increasing Sunnization of the Iraqi regime and Shiʿa attempts within Iraq to redress the sectarian imbalance. These tensions were only heightened by the Islamic Revolution in Iran. When Sadr announced his intention to lead a procession to Tehran to salute Khomeini, he was arrested by the Baʿth government and later executed with his sister, Bint al-Huda.

Although Sadr's ideas were not entirely original, his thinking was lucid and his writing style was simple and powerful. He was revered by a generation of Arab Shiʿa activists, and his writing represented a high point in recent Shiʿa thought. With his passing, Arab Shiʿa movements would lose much of their intellectual stature.

Musa al-Sadr: Mobilizing the Lebanese Shiʿa community. Musa al-Sadr (no relation to Muhammad Baqir) was born in Iran in 1928 to a family of Shiʿa learning. He came to Lebanon in 1959 and elbowed out traditional Shiʿa leaders to promote a populist political awakening of the Shiʿa community and to mobilize it in demands for economic and political justice. Sadr's main constituency was the Shiʿa community of the battered South. Trapped between the cycle of attack and retribution established by the Palestinians and Israelis and the closedness and intransigence of the urban political establishment in Beirut dominated by Maronites and Sunnis, the Shiʿa came increasingly to constitute an impoverished and rootless underclass. The traditional feudal leaders of the Shiʿa had capitalized on Shiʿa insecurities and feelings of inferiority and strived to maintain control of their constituencies. Moving away from their villages and flocking by the thousands to the cities, however, the Shi⟨a, especially the young among them, were ripe for a new style of leadership. Sadr, a tall, turbaned, and charismatic figure, held out new hopes to the Shi⟨a community. Forsaking the diffidence and defeatism of a persecuted minority, he recast Shi⟨a history to imbue his movement of progressive political activism with a sense of religious-inspired moral courage and righteousness that grew to messianic proportions after his disappearance while on a visit to Libya in 1978.

Musa al-Sadr was keenly aware of the evocative power of the story of Karbala and employed it to depict Shi⟨a Islam as a continuous revolution against injustice and tyranny. With Husayn, Sadr argued, "Islam was born again in its true form oriented toward the liberation of the oppressed" (Sadr 1982, 87). The revolution of Husayn was a revolution of a just and righteous cause against the forces of oppression and tyranny. As did all heavenly religions, God's final religion delivered through his Prophet, Muhammad, had "one purpose: to war against the self-proclaimed gods of this world and the tyrants, and to raise up the weak and persecuted . . . but when the weak had almost secured victory they found that the tyrants had changed their clothing and beaten them to the spoils; they started to rule in the name of religion and to wield the sword in its name" (Sadr 1979, 10). Although Sunni political thought historically developed in ways that accommodated and legitimated the rule of tyrants and that taught obedience to their rule among the believers, Shi⟨ite thinkers maintained a sustained opposition to what they regarded as injustice and usurpation and preached a mixed message of obedience in situations of physical necessity but an underlying attitude of nonallegiance to the established political system. Sadr was keenly aware of this distinction and emphasized its revolutionary potential. Shi⟨a history, declared Sadr, was "a history filled with persecution and oppression at the hands of powerful authorities" (Sadr 1982, 60), but the rebellion of Husayn was not a historical fact that was to be simply remembered and mourned but a timeless call for rebellion against injustice, tyranny, and impiety.

Sadr played masterfully on this theme of Shi⟨a history. His community was the dispossessed community portrayed in history. The blows delivered by Israelis, Palestinians, and a careless Lebanese government echoed the blows at Karbala. Although time had not come to an end, the Lebanese state itself was coming to an end and a new reckoning, a new beginning, was at hand. Indeed, Musa al-Sadr transformed the Shi°a tradition of weakness and defeat into a galvanizing source of revolutionary defiance and activism. This defiance began to turn militant in the mid-1970s upon the outbreak of the Lebanese war. In a famous speech in Ba°albak, he proclaimed, "We do not want sentiments, but action. We are tired of words, feelings, speeches. . . . We want our full rights completely. . . . What does the government expect? What does it expect except rage and revolution? Arms are the adornment of men!" (quoted in Wright 1988, 62)

Unlike in Sunni activist circles, the revolutionization of Shi°a tradition was a rather straightforward ideological affair. Where Sunni tradition interpreted legitimate Islamic rule very broadly and advocated loyalty to even only nominally Islamic rulers, Shi°a tradition "held to a comprehensive vision of the political order that usually did not congrue with the political systems that existed. . . . the teachings of the Imams and the *fatwas* of the learned men (*faqih*) [were] full of frank positions [in opposition] to deviant regimes and tyrants" (Sadr 1982, 52).

Although Shi°a leaders had perforce come to emphasize the need for pragmatism and accommodation in the face of overwhelming force over long periods of political persecution, the essential message of Shi°ism was still fairly revolutionary. Hence, unlike the transformation wrought by Qutb, Sadr's contribution was not so much a radical reinterpretation of Shi°a Islam as it was an evocation of strong revolutionary themes that were quite centrally present in Shi°a tradition.

Aside from his call to political activism and self-assertion vis-à-vis the state and the dominant groups, Musa al-Sadr's program focused on the needs of the poor. He charged the government with being corrupt and uncaring and endeavored to impel it into action through a program of organized mobilization and protest. His message was not without its contradictions. In a climate of increased sectarian polarization he reached out to other communities and emphasized the essential unity of all religions even as he organized the Shi°a into a politically self-conscious and combative political entity. Addressing an audience in a Christian Catholic church in Lebanon, he said, "Religions were all one when they served the one goal: a call to God and to the service of humankind" (Sadr 1979, 10). He invoked the compassion of all heavenly religions and spoke of the divine messages of Abraham, Ishmael, Moses, Jesus, and Muhammad all in one breath. In the atmosphere of competing claims of Lebanese, Palestinian, and Arab nationalism, Sadr paid homage to all of them. He spoke fondly of Lebanon as the "country of humanity, and the shelter of the persecuted and the afraid" (Sadr 1979, 11). Avowedly a man of peace and an apparent admirer of Mahatma Gandhi, Sadr graduated quickly from conducting peaceful hunger strikes to galvanizing armed rallies with the slogan: "Arms are the adornment of men."

To the average Shiʿi of Lebanon, Musa al-Sadr, a religious man of distant Lebanese roots who had returned from a faraway land to succor his community, a man who was said to be a descendant of the seventh Imam, fit nicely and evocatively into the framework of Shiʿa tradition. His disappearance in 1978 completed his harmony with the Shiʿa past as it both echoed the martyrdom of Husayn and intensified the tension implied in the occultation of the Twelfth Imam. The movement he had founded and the Amal militia he had established after the outbreak of the Lebanese war in 1975 continued under the leadership of Nabih Birri, a lawyer and close associate of Sadr. Hizballah, the more militant Iranian-inspired rival of Amal, also claimed Sadr's mantle although it was more closely linked with the person of Ayatollah Khomeini.

The Appeal of Islamic Fundamentalism

All religions strike deep within the psyche. They appeal to basic categories of fear, hope, love, hate, reason, faith, and so forth, to gain a profound grasp on their adherents. Islam is no exception. The appeal of fundamentalist Islam can be explained by way of the categories of psychological strain described in chapter 1. In the sphere of identity, the effectiveness of an impassioned Islam is quite obvious. As Hrair Dekmejian noted, "As an ideology, Islamic fundamentalism bestows a new identity upon a multitude of alienated individuals who have lost their socio-spiritual bearings" (Dekmejian 1985, 52). This is especially relevant for new arrivals to the city from the more traditional countryside. Brought up in an environment dominated by Islamic symbols and rituals, newly urbanized rural people are alienated by the secularism of the urban environment and find a sense of connectedness and self-esteem through identification with Islam. Even for individuals with less religious backgrounds, Islam became a particularly prominent source of identity and self-esteem after the collapse of secular Arab nationalism in the late 1960s.

In the sectarian societies of the Levant, the Islamic identity in addition served as a simple communal identity that would sustain the individual in a social environment in which national identities had proven illusory. Although the ideologies of the Baʿth in Syria and Iraq and Lebanese nationalism in Lebanon had promised a national identity as the basis for social life, political life was still largely carried out along sectarian or ethnic lines with Arab Sunnis dominating in Iraq, Alawis in Syria, and Maronites and other sectarian elites competing for power in Lebanon. In these countries, the Islamic movement provided some of the same identity support that tribal or ethnic chauvinism provides elsewhere.

As a source of moral guidance, Islam could also be quite effective as it provided direction on nearly every aspect of individuals' moral lives and interactions with other people. In this respect, Islamism was far more powerful than any of the other competing ideologies. It defined people's relationships with God, with community, with family, and with themselves. It provided a complete moral worldview rooted in the Qur'an, enriched by centuries of cultural recycling, and pertaining to all aspects of religious, social, and individual life. It was in this sphere that Islam's psychological appeal was strongest because only Islam could provide an adequate response to the apparent corruption and lassitude of modernizing Arab society and provide moral bearings to individuals lost in an increasingly secular and amoral modern environment.

In the category of intellectual guidance, the Islamic movement tried to intellectually reinterpret modernity in categories that harmonized with religious tradition. Social and political realities were analyzed with regard to the extent to which they were "Islamic" or "non-Islamic". The condition of the individual vis-à-vis society and of the society vis-à-vis other societies was also explained in terms of religious affiliation and conflict. Estrangement from Islam was explained to be the root cause of almost all of society's problems, and a return to Islam was presented as the ultimate remedy. To be sure, however, many of the arguments of the Islamists remained rather vague and unspecific. The definition of what was or was not Islamic was often too facile, and the explanation of the complex social environment simply in terms of proximity or distance from an undefined "Islamic" ideal was not always satisfactory in an intellectual environment already exposed to the sophisticated outlooks of Marxists and Western-trained social scientists. Consequently, in the domain of intellectual strain, the fundamentalist Islamic worldview was only effective for those who unquestioningly accepted its simplicity but was more problematic for more critical thinkers.

As a means of channeling and releasing aggression as discussed in chapter 1, the militant Islamic movements were especially effective. They sharply distinguished between good and evil in the world, drawing on the categories of *dar al-Islam* and *dar al-harb* that form part of the Islamic tradition. In the struggle for the future of society and the world, there were only two forces, good and evil, and only two parties, God and his opponents. Society was just a stage for this grandiose universal struggle between the forces of light and darkness. In this sense, the Islamic movements could provide deeply satisfying targets of hostility, and by granting that hostility divine sanction, they could render the process of aggression-release that much more satisfying and complete.

The Social Dynamics of the Islamic Movements

The examination of the sociological dynamics of the Islamic movements must be divided into several categories because the movement sprang from different sociological origins in different countries and at different times. The principal geographic categorization lies between the Islamic movements in Egypt as opposed to those in the Levant countries of Lebanon, Syria, and Iraq. In the latter countries, the movements often expressed confessional divisions within the political system, whereas in Egypt the movement was a purely internal Sunni affair drawing its energy more directly from class and generational differences. Within Egypt, however, the sociological analysis of the Islamic activism of the 1940s and 1950s under the *Ikhwan* differs considerably from the more radical Islamic movements that emerged in the late 1960s and early 1970s.

From the perspective of class, the Islamic activism of the *Ikhwan* that peaked in the 1950s, as attested by Mitchell, drew its following from more or less the same circles that the Arab nationalists and the Marxists did, namely, the new middle class, especially the newly urbanized members among them. That newly urbanized members of the middle class would be attracted to a fundamentalist Islam is not surprising. Most had received an elementary religious education and had absorbed the conservative religious and moral outlook of their rural families. In the city, they were confronted with widespread secularism and lax moral and social codes. They felt all of this as an affront to their sense of order and interpreted it as an offense against God. The activist Islamic movements capitalized on this discontent and provided a haven and a second family to these alienated individuals. Islam, for these people, represented a means of self-definition and self-assurance in an urban environment in which they were sandwiched between a secular urban upper class and a frighteningly poor urban subproletariat. They sought to distinguish themselves from those members of the upper class who had lost their living relationship with Islam while separating themselves from the urban subproletariat that they feared to slip down into. A fundamentalist literalist Islam set them apart both from the secular classes above them and from the illiterate subproletariat beneath them. Furthermore, by relating material well-being to piety, it invested the economic struggle of this rising middle class with moral and religious significance. As Weber pointed out one century earlier in *The Protestant Ethic and the Spirit of Capitalism,* a puritanical religion can be an important source of identity and purpose for a precarious rising middle class.

Indeed, Islam for these individuals was no longer simply a faith they adhered to but a program of political action against the status quo. As such, Islamic ideology, if one may call it such, was one of the vehicles through which this new middle class endeavored to assert itself in the urban centers of Egypt in between the traditional ruling upper class and the almost equally traditional urban poor. The petty bourgeoisie was a newly arrived stratum eager to carve out a place for itself in the social structure and to reform society according to its own prescriptions. As it happened, however, in the competition for the right to represent this important class, secular Arab nationalism managed to defeat both activist Islam and revolutionary Marxism as the principal ideology of the petty bourgeoisie. The eclipse of the Islamic movement in this period is largely the result of nationalism itself and the scientific and secular aspects that formed part of the general ideology of revolutionary Arab nationalism that were still regarded at that time as the ultimate sources of political and economic success in the modern world. In any case, the first wave of Islamic activism can be understood in class terms as coinciding with that period in the 1940s and 1950s when the new middle class was making its major breakthrough into the political arena.

In generational terms, the connection between this early Islamic wave and the frustrations of a rising generation is quite plain. As mentioned earlier, the following of the Muslim Brotherhood was a distinctly youthful one. In that sense, it represented a generational group articulating its frustrations with and hostility toward a previous generation. The previous generation had adopted secularism, Westernization, parliamentary liberalism, and regional nationalism as pillars of their sociopolitical worldview. In opposition to this, the Islamic movement could offer a rising generation several antitheses to these themes: religion versus secularism, Islamization versus Westernization, rule of the *shari^ca* versus parliamentary liberalism, and Islamic nationalism versus regional nationalism. Through these categories a rising generation could distinguish itself from its predecessor and articulate its struggle with it. As the Islamic activism of the *Ikhwan* was eclipsed and suppressed by Arab nationalism and Nasir, the next Islamic upsurge had to await the crystallization of a new generational group in the aftermath of the 1967 war.

This second wave of Islamic activism in Egypt was represented by more radical organizations such as *Jihad, Jama^cat al-Takfir wa al-Hijra*, and the ILO. As reported by Ibrahim (1980), Fischer (1982), and Davis (1984), the membership of the new radical Islamic movements in Egypt still came—as in the first wave—from the petty bourgeoisie, especially the newly urbanized members among them. One must notice, however, that although the class label is still the same, this is not the same group of people. For the newly urbanized petty bourgeoisie that provided the backbone of support for the Islamic activism of the *Ikhwan* underwent urbanization in the 1940s and 1950s and by the 1970s had become thoroughly part of the urban social structure. Furthermore, that class had been largely secularized under the influence of Arab nationalism and the Nasirist state. In addition, the conditions that the immigrants to the city faced in the 1940s and 1950s were radically different from those similar immigrants would face in the 1970s. Whereas in the 1940s and 1950s immigrants could easily join a rapidly growing middle class at a time of economic expansion, the immigrants of later decades found a middle class already ensconced in an overcrowded urban social structure suffering economic stagnation. Naturally, the frustrations of these latter-day immigrants would be more intense and their interpretation of political Islam far more extreme and revolutionary.

In any case, the immigrants of the 1970s could not be integrated as easily into the urban social structure and currently represent a lower middle class that forms a slum belt around most of Egypt's cities. It is from these areas that the militant Islamic movements of the 1970s and 1980s primarily drew their following. This lower middle class was replaying a conflict with the now dominant middle class which that same middle class at one time waged against the dominant upper class. As the middle class adopted revolutionary Arab nationalism, with its secularism, social liberalism, and potpourri of concepts from both the Communist East and democratic West, the lower middle class, clamoring for admittance to the urban political arena, had to express its identity and agenda in different ways. Islamic fundamentalism was conveniently tailored to the political needs of this lower middle class because it was the antithesis of the secular nationalist ideology of the middle class. It could serve, therefore, as the expression of the basic conflict between these two classes. Of course, Islam was, in the first place, acceptable as a political ideology to these newly urbanized individuals for precisely the same reason that it was acceptable to the newly urbanized individuals of the 1940s and 1950s: it was a familiar ideology resonating with the conservative religious culture of the villages from whence they had come. The difference was that although the immigrants of the 1940s and 1950s had the option of adopting the ideology of radical pan-Arab nationalism, as it was an ideology as yet not claimed by any class, the immigrants of the 1970s faced a tighter ideological field. They had to choose an ideology that would contrast sharply with the ideology of the dominant middle class that they were struggling against.

In generational terms, the dynamics of the new wave of Islamic activism in Egypt are also quite apparent. As most researchers have confirmed, the more recent radical Islamic groups drew on a consistently young following. Indeed, Saad Eddin Ibrahim fixed the average age of the members of these movements at between 22 and 24 (Ibrahim 1980, 438). It is not surprising that in a crowded social environment like that of Egypt, such acute generational tensions should exist. As revolutionary Arab nationalism ended up being the ideological means for the generation of the 1950s to express its hostility toward the preceding generation, so radical Islam became the means of ideological expression for the youth of the 1970s and 1980s in their conflict with an older generation. It was a means for venting frustrations, discrediting a ruling generation, and putting forward an independent social and political agenda.

In Syria, Iraq, and Lebanon the variable of sectarian competition must be added to the elements of class and generation to get a better picture of the sociological dynamics of the Islamic movements there. In Syria, the Islamic movement was largely the expression of Sunni hostility to an Alawi regime. In addition, it enjoyed the support of the urban middle and upper middle classes of the northern towns who were opposed to the socialist policies of the Baʿth that favored the lower rural and urban classes and were also opposed to those policies that favored the businessmen and merchants of Damascus over those of the north (see Batatu 1981b and 1982; Hinnebusch 1982).

In Iraq, meanwhile, the Islamic movement was a manifestation of Shiʿa resentment toward Sunni rule. Furthermore, as in Egypt, it voiced the frustrations of a newly urbanized group of rural immigrants, who populated the slum belts—such as that of al-Thawra—around Baghdad and other Iraqi cities and were anxious to find a place for themselves in the urban social structure dominated by the secular Arab nationalist middle class.

In Lebanon, the principal Islamic movements expressed the hostility of the Shiʿa to a political system dominated by Maronites and Sunnis. The small Sunni Islamic movement in the northern town of Tripoli represented Sunni hostility to both Alawi and Maronite domination. It is very interesting to note that Sunni-Alawi hostility in the north evoked a religious response from the Sunnis, whereas Sunni-Shiʿa hostility in Beirut and the South evoked no such religious response. This was probably because the Alawis expressed themselves in secular terms, hence, opposition to them could be expressed in religious terms, whereas the Shiʿa expressed themselves in religious terms and opposition to them would have to be expressed in secular terms, in this case an outdated and feeble Arab nationalism. From the perspective of class, the Shiʿa movements in Lebanon, as did the recent Islamic movements in Egypt and Iraq, represented the hostility of a class of newly urbanized rural immigrants toward the established urban middle—and in the case of Lebanon, upper-class. The situation of the Shiʿa slum dwellers of Lebanon was especially desperate because they had been, for the most part, driven out of their villages in the south by ongoing battles between Israel and the Palestinians. The Sunni Islamic movement of Tripoli more closely resembled the movements of northern Syria in that it represented the opposition of a more traditional urban middle class to the domination of rural lower class Alawis.

From the perspective of generations, it is the case that nearly all the Islamic movements of the Arab Middle East draw their membership from among the youth. As in most cases of ideological politics, the ideology of radical Islam appeals most to impressionable, passionate, and frustrated youth, especially when the preceding generation chose secular nationalism as their ideological calling card.

The Legacy of the Islamic Movements

An evaluation of the legacy of the Islamic movements is a difficult and delicate matter. To their followers, the Islamic movements are a necessary element in the struggle to roll back secularism and establish an Islamic state that will presumably bring with it ideal social, political, economic, moral, and religious conditions under the grace of God. And indeed, even to the neutral observer, these movements represent a positive attempt to preserve and promote an embattled religious and cultural heritage in the face of thoroughgoing Westernization and secularization. They also provide a haven for alienated individuals and a channel for their integration into the modern urban environment. In addition, they have kept a large number of important moral and cultural issues on the political agenda. But still, from the perspective of the political or social scientist attempting to gauge the region's political and social future, the legacy of the Islamic movements is a troubling one.

First, they have articulated opposition to the authoritarian secular Arab nationalist regimes in such a way as to perpetuate many of the authoritarian elements of these dominant regimes. They have unwittingly preserved the idea of authoritarian government by opposing the authoritarianism of the Arab nationalist regimes with a promise of Islamic authoritarianism; thus offering to supplant one authoritarianism with another and in the process legitimizing the idea of authoritarian politics as such and keeping at bay any notion of democratic or popular government. The ruling nationalist vanguard is to be replaced by a ruling Islamist vanguard. Moreover, by challenging the legitimacy of the nationalist regimes on the basis of some divine sanction, they have preserved the idea that political legitimacy does not flow from the people but rather from some remote being or abstract idea. Whereas the nationalist vanguard rules in the name of Progress, or the Nation, or even the People, but only with a capital 'P', the Islamist vanguard is to rule simply in the name of God. In both cases, the authority of the people, understood in any democratic sense, is from the outset discounted.

Moreover, the Islamic movements have preserved the notion in the Arab world that politics is primarily a stage for messianic and mythological struggles of grandiose proportions. While the Arab nationalists draped their ordinary politics in rousing speeches about the rebirth of the Arab nation, the emergence of the New Arab, and the process of civilization, the Islamists describe politics in terms of a universal struggle between good and evil, between God and the Devil, and between Islam and non-Islam. Both discuss politics at levels of abstraction and reflection high above the everyday issues of political life. Lost in the shuffle is any practical idea of politics as "Who gets what, when, and how?" or the state as the manager of human and material resources and the trustee of certain political rights. By driving political discourse into lofty ethereal realms, the Islamic movements have conveniently helped the dominant regimes distract attention from more mundane but politically very relevant issues of political and economic development. Prince Otto von Bismarck once remarked about German politics, "We in Germany hold our ideals very high so that we may walk comfortably beneath them." By setting the political agenda at such a high level, something similar has been taking place in the Arab world.

Furthermore, by articulating their opposition to existing political systems in uncompromising revolutionary terms, demanding an overthrow *of* the system not a change *within* the system, they have kept Arab politics in a mode of existential crisis in which all methods are allowed and no holds are barred. They have allowed contemporary authoritarian regimes to claim that every form of opposition to their rule and their policies is a threat to the very existence of the state and, hence, is deserving of immediate repression rather than gradual accommodation. By discrediting the entire basis of legitimacy of the nationalist regimes, the Islamic movements helped preserve and promote the politics of naked coercion. Whereas political opposition may lead, over time, to the evolution of some system of give and take between political in-groups and out-groups—a set of approximate political "rules of the game"—the revolutionary opposition of the Islamic groups enables ruling elites to continue to postpone the emergence of any process of give and take and to govern in a fashion wherein the only rules are those of direct coercion.

As the Marxists and radical Arab nationalists did before them, the Islamists participate enthusiastically in the popular chorus of vilifying the West as a political, moral, and economic entity. The effect of this in everyday political terms is that it increases the comfortable isolation and insulation of existing governments from Western standards of political legitimacy. Through blanket condemnation of the West, myriad principles of human, civil, and political rights can be discredited. What threatens the authoritarian control of the state can be conveniently denounced as inauthentic, alien, un-Arab. Under an Islamic regime, ruling elites could similarly reject objectionable political demands by categorizing them as "un-Islamic." Communist states long justified the repression of various movements and demands by labeling them under the catch-all categories of "bourgeois" or "reactionary" or "antirevolutionary," and so forth. Although it worked for many decades, the Soviet and Chinese regimes found it increasingly difficult to isolate their societies from "Western" demands regarding human and political rights. By reinforcing the Arab nationalists' condemnation of the West, the Islamists have further postponed the opening of Arab society to certain notions of political life currently embodied in the working democracies of the West.

Finally, the Islamic movements have contributed to a dangerous increase in religious and sectarian tensions throughout the Arab world. A rise in religious and sectarian tensions is normal in the turbulent process of modernization the world over, but while nationalism consciously endeavored to avoid social disintegration in the religiously heterogeneous Arab world by promoting common themes of culture and history and focusing loyalties on the all-inclusive secular state, the Islamists have served to exacerbate problems of religious and sectarian identity. This has contributed to serious tensions between Muslims and Christians in Egypt, Muslims and non-Muslims in Sudan, Sunnis and Alawis in Syria, Sunnis and Shiʿis in Iraq, and among the various religious and sectarian communities of Lebanon.

CHAPTER FOUR

Marxism

The Communist Parties and the New Left

The Communist Parties

Although their influence receded in the 1970s and 1980s, Communist parties and groups played a central role in the genesis and development of ideological political life in the modern Arab world. Many of the Communist parties were founded in the early 1920s and, thus, represent the oldest organized political parties in the Arab world. In that respect, they served as a model to other activists especially in the nationalist camp. By example, they showed how a modern political party should be organized, how it mobilizes popular support and participation, how it develops and propagates an ideology, how it operates underground if repressed by the government, and how to prepare for an overthrow of the political system and the ultimate seizure of power.

In addition to the influence of their example of party organization, the ideology of the Communists itself had a profound influence on Arab political life. They were the first to introduce elaborate theories of class conflict, Western imperialism, socioeconomic revolution, and economic justice. At a time of rising class tensions, these themes would prove crucial in galvanizing political participation and challenging political systems that preferred to ignore such issues. The theme of imperialism was especially effective after the loss of Palestine in 1948, giving profound social, economic, and political meaning to the defeat.

While the Communists introduced progressive issues of social and economic justice into the political debate, they also introduced a set of more dangerous themes under the cloak of an impressive pseudo-scientific social philosophy. They justified the use of force in politics, discredited liberalism and democracy, encouraged violent revolution, justified state repression, legitimated social strife under the guise of class conflict, demonstrated the power of party regimentation and party propaganda, and justified state ownership and regulation of the economy. Many of these themes were incorporated into revolutionary Arab nationalism and influenced the orientation of military and one-party regimes in Egypt, Syria, Iraq, Sudan, Algeria, Yemen, and elsewhere.

The History of Arab Communism

Early socialist and Communist beginnings. In the intellectual sphere, non-Marxist socialist thought of late-nineteenth century Europe had found its way into the Arab world through a number of writers in Egypt, most notably, Shibli Shumayyil, Farah Antun, Niqula Haddad (Syrian Christians), and Salamah Musa (an Egyptian Copt), all of whom decried the backward socioeconomic conditions of contemporary Egypt and proposed radical progressive reforms (especially Musa's *al-Ishtirakiyyah* (Socialism) (Cairo 1913) (see Reid 1974, 177; Rodinson, 1981, 192, and Batatu 1978, 373). Significant from the Islamic point of view was al-Kawakibi's strong attack on tyranny and the wealth of the upper classes and his exploration of the communistic aspects of what he considered authentic Islam in *Taba'i‘ al-Istibdad* (The Characteristics of Despotism). Notable in the political arena were two events, both relatively confined to Christian Mount Lebanon: a peasant rebellion in 1858 against some of the large landholding families of the mountain, the only rebellion of its kind in the region (Issawi 1982, 148) and a literary rebellion around 1908 that had an intense egalitarian streak accompanied by a sharp opposition to the priesthood as upholders of the inequalities and oppression of the traditional world (Batatu 1978, 371–72). Intellectuals who had participated or lived through this latter rebellion would later participate in the founding of Communist parties in Lebanon, Syria, and elsewhere.

Important to the story of the arrival of Marxism to the Arab world also, however, is the role of the Armenian *Hentchak* (Bell) organization established in 1887. This party played a central role in spreading socialist and Communist ideas in the Ottoman empire before the war (Batatu 1978, 371–72). Among its members were founders later of the first Communist cells in Lebanon. In 1924–25, they also helped found the Communist party of Syria and Lebanon. But it is through the Jewish community, especially through Jews newly arrived from Europe, that modern Communist formations took recognizable shape.

The Bolshevik Revolution had a significant impact in the Arab world. It illustrated that revolution against the forces of the status quo was possible and gave credibility to a utopian philosophy that had now triumphed in Europe's largest nation and had become a vibrant world force to be reckoned with. In the struggle against the dominance of Britain and France in the aftermath of World War I, the Bolshevik Revolution was generally welcomed by nationalists as a force that would help weaken the Western powers and assist the Arab countries in achieving their independence despite the fact that the ideology of the revolution itself remained alien to most Arabs. Rashid Rida, an orthodox Muslim scholar and a conservative nationalist, welcomed Bolshevism as a counterweight to the Western capitalist powers in an article written just after the war. "'Bolshevism,'"he declared, "is only another name for socialism, and socialism means the liberation of the workers from capitalists and oppressive governments. Muslims must hope for its success, since they too are workers and suffer from the same oppression, and if socialism succeeds, the subjugation of peoples will end. True, Communism is not in conformity with Islamic law, but neither are the activities of the European governments" (in Hourani 1970, 304). Despite this generally friendly Arab attitude toward the revolution in Russia, when the Executive Committee of the Third International organized a conference for the Oppressed People of the East at Baku in September 1920, among the 1,891 delegates, only 3 were from Arab countries (Samarbakhsh 1978, 106).

The story of the evolution of Communist parties in the Arab world begins in earnest in the 1920s and is a complex and multifarious one. Because a country-by-country approach might capture many of the regional specificities of Communist development in the Arab world but fail to highlight the important cross-country changes that the Communist parties went through, often reflecting changes in the foreign policy of the Soviet Union itself, I rely on an approach that emphasizes the broad historical phases of the evolution of Communist parties in the Arab world. In doing so, I follow the periodization outlined by Agwani (1969).

The evolution of the Communist parties. Phase 1 (1920–35) was a period of doctrinaire purity in which most of the Arab Communist parties of the Middle East got their start. In the early 1920s, flushed with their own triumph, the Bolsheviks were hopeful that revolution would soon sweep the colonized world; in the Arab world, their hopes were shared by "a handful of middle-class intellectuals who were mesmerized by the Bolshevik Revolution and its slogan of proletarian revolution" (Agwani 1969, 177). Together, these two groups set out to establish Communist parties and preach Marxism and socialism throughout the Arab world. Their efforts met with very limited success. The movement was still very small and heavily reliant on minority religious and ethnic groups; its propaganda was very abstract and had not yet found its proper voice in the Arab social and cultural milieu; and finally, these nascent groups had to contend with Western-governed or dominated political regimes that kept close track of their activities. Nevertheless, the Communist parties of Egypt, Palestine, Lebanon, Syria, and Iraq all got their start in these years, and their future development and identity would be deeply influenced by these beginnings.

In Egypt, the Communist party of Egypt (CPE) was founded in 1922 under the leadership of Joseph Rosenthal, a Jewish jeweler of Alexandria. The members were predominantly Greek, Jewish, and Armenian, and they organized unions and a few early strikes among predominantly foreign or minority laborers (Laqueur 1961, 31–37). Although party leadership eventually moved into Arab hands, the movement membership remained predominantly from minorities, reflecting the makeup of the urban proletariat of the time (Batatu 1978, 379–82). After a series of strikes, the CPE came into conflict with the new Wafd government of Saʿd Zaghlul and was outlawed in

1925. Driven underground, the CPE quickly collapsed. Attempts by the Comintern to resuscitate it during this period were fruitless (see Laqueur 1961, 31–36; Batatu 1978, 379–82).

In Palestine, Marxism had its beginnings among the small minority of Jewish Communist immigrants from Europe as well as some far left members of the Jewish labor movement. The Communist party of Palestine (CPP), an almost completely Jewish organization, was formed in 1922 and admitted to the Comintern in 1924. The party declared itself bitterly opposed to what it considered the reactionary, nationalistic, religious, utopian movement of Zionism. "It is the main task of the party," the CPP declared, "to fight against Zionism in all its forms, to expose the bankrupt Zionist bluff" (Laqueur 1961, 77). In addition, it vowed to fight against imperialist and Arab landlords. A splinter faction of the CPP, meanwhile, raised as its slogan: "Leave the Zionistic Hell!" (ibid.). Needless to say, this position isolated the CPP in the Jewish community. By 1925, the party began to broaden its base to attract more Arabs, and, in 1933, a Palestinian Arab, known as "Musa," rose to the leadership of the party (Agwani 1969, 12). The Revolt of 1936–39, however, nearly destroyed the party, as the CPP threw its support to the Arab Higher Committee and many of the Jewish members either left the party or left the country altogether. Many of the Arabs joined several of the more mainstream Arab parties. As in Egypt, Communism would not resurface as a potent force in Palestine until several years later in the early 1940s.

The founding of the Communist party of Syria and Lebanon represented the coming together of several groups. Around 1922, two Lebanese Christians, Iskandar Riyashi and Yusuf Ibrahim Yazbeck, founded a moderately socialist journal, *al-Sahafi al-Taʾih* (The Wandering Journalist), advocating a classless society, communal landownership, and internationalism (Odeh 1985, 91). Not really Marxists, these intellectuals reflected the socialistic thinking of the Lebanese literary rebellion of 1908. They were contacted by members of the CPP and asked if they would establish a branch of the CPP in Lebanon. Instead, Yazbeck and Riyashi, with a few others, formed their own *Hizb al-Shaʿb al-Lubnani* (Lebanese People's party) in 1924. In 1925, they were joined by an Armenian Communist organization led by Artin Madoyan, and together they founded the Communist party of Syria and Lebanon (CPSL) (Agwani 1969, 14). Armenian dominance in the party was replaced by Arab in the early 1930s with the entrance into the Central Committee of Khalid Bakdash, Farjallah Helou, Nikola Shawi and Rafiq Rida, all of whom would play prominent roles in the party's leadership over the following decades. A Lebanese, Fuad al-Shamali, led the party between 1928 and 1936 until Khalid Bakdash returned from a two-year course of study at the Communist University of the Toilers of the East (KUTV) in the Soviet Union. With Moscow's help, Bakdash secured the leadership of the CPSL and led it (or, after 1944, its Syrian branch) for decades afterward.

In time, the CPSL emerged as the foremost Communist party in the Arab world partly because the CPSL managed to maintain its core leadership when other Communist parties were constantly losing leaders to the jails or the gallows; many of the leaders of the 1930s were still prominent in the 1980s. In addition, however, one must not discount the cultural centrality of Syria and Lebanon, especially Beirut, for the Arab Middle East nor the influence of Bakdash himself who rose to considerable prominence in international Communist circles.

The growth of the Communist movement in Iraq took place in relative isolation from its development in Egypt, Palestine, Lebanon, and Syria. Laboring under a much more oppressive British-supported monarchy and suffering from the most acute class disparity in the Arab world, the conditions for the emergence of Iraqi Communism were quite distinct. Batatu traces the beginning of Iraqi Communism to Pyotr Vasili, an Assyrian Iraqi educated in Soviet Georgia and a professional Bolshevik revolutionary (Batatu 1978, 404). Vasili returned to Iraq in 1922 and was central in gaining adherents to Marxism and establishing a number of Communist organizations. In that same year, for example, *Jam'iyyat al-Ahrar* (The Society of Liberals) was established, which espoused a radical liberal, feminist, pan-Arabist, anti-religious line. It came to be known as the Anti-Religious party and attracted much hostility. Hounded by the authorities, lacking a sizable middle-class audience, and riddled with divisions and splinter movements, organized Communist political activity in Iraq did not amount to much until Yusuf Salman Yusuf (alias "Fahd" [Leopard]), a Christian Baghdad-born Chaldean, brought together various Communist and pseudo-Communist groupings to establish the Communist party of Iraq (CPI) in 1934. The party, under intense harassment from the government, remained small and weak until the early 1940s.

This first phase of Communist development between 1920 and 1935 was characterized by an obsession with "ideological purity and organizational viability" (Agwani, 1969, 178–79). In this period, the movement was very intellectualized and groups disputed with the zeal of latter-day medieval scholasticists over the finer points of Marxist doctrine. At the same time, a number of the Arab Communist movements had their organizational beginnings and made their first inroads into labor unions, the political arena, and public consciousness.

In this period, the Arab Communist parties were still highly dependent on the Comintern and followed its policy recommendations rather closely. This was detrimental to the nascent parties' interests after the sixth Comintern Congress in 1928, for example, when Stalin turned away from a conciliatory policy vis-à-vis the national bourgeoisie of Asia and Africa toward a more radical revolutionary policy. The extant Communist parties in the Middle East had to abandon burgeoning contacts with more mainstream nationalist groups and isolate themselves in the political arena. Nevertheless, Arab Communist parties made use of this time to tighten their organization and test the mettle of their leadership and membership. The professional revolutionaries that would carry Arab Communism to prominence in the 1940s and 1950s almost all had their formative party years in this difficult period.

The first breakthrough occurred during phase 2 (1936–46). The seventh Comintern Congress, held in 1936, reflected Stalin's apprehension about the rise of fascism in Europe and abandoned the sixth Congress's emphasis on ideological purity and revolutionary militancy. Instead, Communist parties around the world were directed to participate in National Fronts with almost any and all parties willing to take a stand against fascism. In the Arab world, this meant that Communist parties were directed to drop their reservations about cooperation with parties of the bourgeoisie and even seek conciliation with the mandate powers. The proletarian revolution, it was posited, must await the defeat of fascism. Despite the embarrassing ideological reversal that this entailed, the new policy left the Arab Communist parties a freer hand to make their way in their local political arenas. Thus, for the first time, for example, the CPSL joined with several other parties in an Anti-Fascist League established in 1938.

The Soviet-Nazi pact of 1939 shook the credibility of Arab Communist parties because they had, after only three years, declared another *volte face* in their positions. Now, suddenly, the war against fascism was to be suspended and a position of neutrality was to be assumed toward what was announced to be simply a war among capitalist countries. It is a measure of the indigenous strength and emerging independence of the CPSL that it, alone among Arab Communist parties, did not go along with the new Soviet policy. In any case, the Comintern returned to recommending a policy of anti-fascist national fronts after the German attack on Russia in 1941. With the Soviet Union now in the war, the mandate powers took a more favorable view of local Arab Communist parties because they could now be used as part of the anti-Axis war effort. They could be especially effective in combatting fascist propaganda, which had been gaining favor among Syrian and Arab nationalists ever since the mid-1930s.

Nineteen forty-three was an important year for Arab Communism not only because it saw the dissolution of the Comintern but also because it witnessed the victories of the Red Army in Stalingrad and elsewhere that would carry the Soviet Union to superpower status. As Bakdash himself argued in his address to the second Congress of the CPSL held between December 29 and January 3, 1943–44, the dissolution of the Comintern was a great boon to Arab Communist parties. First, it left them freer to adopt programs and policies more in tune with the conditions of their national surroundings. Second, and more importantly, "it eliminated the reason that many hesitated to join the party—the reason that the party belongs to an international movement of foreign origin" (Bakdash 1944, 32). The events of the war itself, however, besides the policies of the Comintern, the Soviet Union, or the Arab Communist parties, had a profound effect on the fortunes of Arab communism.

1. The victories of the Red Army over the formidable German army, as well as the occupation of Eastern Europe, rendered the Soviet

Union an awesome world power and seemed to prove the vitality of Marxist ideology. As Bakdash himself noted, in a society that admires strength and "glorifies . . . patriotism, courage, manliness, defiance, and dignity," the victories of the Soviet Union had an especially favorable impact (Bakdash 1944, 7). Whereas the strength of Britain and France in the 1920s had convinced the nationalist mainstream that liberal parliamentarianism was the path to national revival and power, and the rising strength of Nazi Germany in the 1930s had attracted patriots to fascism, the great victories of the Soviet Union now attracted many Arabs to the formulas of Stalinist Marxism.

2. In the struggle for national independence from Britain and France, the Soviet Union by the mid-1940s had replaced the Axis powers, as the main challenger of Anglo-French power. Because many Arab nationalists had lined up with the Axis powers, expecting their eventual victory, the defeat of the Axis powers embarrassed some among the nationalists and allowed the Communists to pick up some of the following lost by the pan-Arabists. Furthermore, the Arabs had never experienced Russian imperialism and, thus, could welcome its appearance on the world stage without the negative associations of Western imperialism. As the Beirut-based Communist journal *al-Tariq* declared, "Russia never subjugated our country and does not snatch our bread or deprive us of our freedom and independence" (*al-Tariq*, Beirut, 8 [Oct.–Nov. 1949], 28).

3. As Britain and France were weakened by the exertions and expenditures of the war, the movement for national independence in the Middle East gained momentum. The Allies had precipitated this trend by using the promise of independence as a propaganda weapon against the Vichy French and as a palliative to offset the hardships and discontent generated by the war. The hardships and dislocations generated by the war, as well as the presence of large Western armies in Egypt and the Levant, had a strong disruptive effect on economic and political life. All these factors brought forth a new political climate in which the Communists, like the nationalists, could find new and eager recruits. The Communists were especially successful in channeling labor unrest linked to the economic fluctuations of the war. Moreover, unlike in the early 1920s, there was now a larger working class and intelligentsia from which to recruit members and leaders.

In Egypt, the Communist movement that had died out in the 1920s began to show new signs of life in the early 1940s as the Soviet Union joined the Allied war effort. In 1941–42, a number of Marxist groups emerged in Cairo and Alexandria still, as before, dominated by Jews and other minority members. Two of the most significant groups, the Mouvement Egyptien de Liberation Nationale (MELN), founded in 1942 by Henri Curiel, a bookseller and scion of a millionaire Jewish family, and *Iskra*, established in 1942 by another Jew, Hillel Shwartz. The MELN supported the British-sponsored Wafdist rise to power in 1942 under Nahas Pasha and consequently enjoyed good relations with the government and gained some influence in the bureaucracy, the press, trade unions and even the Wafd party (ibid.).

As in other Arab countries, the Communists in Egypt could take advantage of the disruptive effects of the World War. During the war, Anglo-Egyptian forces alone in Egypt employed more than three hundred thousand people, and as the war ebbed, rising unemployment and inflation generated political unrest. Both the MELN and *Iskra* gained much influence in labor unions and played a central role in the strikes of February 1946 that led to serious clashes with the government and triggered a government crackdown later that summer. In May 1947, the MELN and *Iskra* merged to constitute the Mouvement Democratique de Liberation Nationale (MDLN) with a membership of around fifteen hundred (Agwani 1969, 45). This organization comprised the nucleus of the broader Communist movement in Egypt that would emerge in the 1950s.

Between 1936 and 1946, the CPSL in Syria and Lebanon fared quite well. Its anti-fascist position allowed it to reach out for alliances with other political parties and eased tensions with the French mandate power although relations with the openly fascist Syrian Social Nationalist party deteriorated. Conditions under the French improved after the coming to power of Leon Blum's Communist-backed Popular Front cabinet in Paris in 1936. The party line during these times emphasized "maximum cooperation with France, mobilizing public opinion against the fascist menace, and a broad national front resting on a moderate political and economic program" (Agwani 1969, 18). The party intensified its recruitment efforts and set up its first front organization, *Muʾtamar Mukafahat al-Fashiyyah* (The Anti-

Fascist League) whose inaugural Congress in May 1939 attracted many prominent non-Communists. Even though the CPSL stuck to its anti-fascist position, the party suffered setbacks after the Nazi-Soviet Non-Aggression Pact of 1939 as the French authorities clamped down on the party, banned its publications, and jailed Bakdash, Farjallah Helou, and other party leaders. The CPSL returned to favor, however, as soon as the Soviets joined the war in 1941.

The CPSL adapted to the independence of Lebanon and Syria in 1943 and 1944 by splitting in two, with Bakdash heading the Syrian branch and Farjallah Helou heading the Lebanese branch (Odeh 1985, 92). The new National Charter adopted during the second CPSL Congress held in December–January 1943–44 called for complete national independence and sovereignty and recommended a host of progressive social and economic reforms in both Lebanon and Syria. Indeed, this decade around World War II was an auspicious one for the CPSL; it gained acceptance within the nationalist mainstream and expanded its membership from an estimated three hundred in 1936 to around twenty-five thousand ten years later (Samarbakhsh 1978, 112). The two party branches contested parliamentary elections in 1946 with four Lebanese and two Syrian candidates making impressive showings although not victorious.

In Iraq, the late 1930s continued to be years of strong repression. In 1938, the Iraqi parliament passed into law decrees prohibiting Communism and stipulating strong punishment for its sympathizers. Unlike the CPSL, the CPI went along with the Soviet Union's *volte face* between 1939 and 1941, making its position even more precarious vis-à-vis the authorities. It also supported Rashid Ali Gaylani's abortive pro-Axis coup of April 1941. But 1941 was also the year when the energetic Moscow-trained Fahd took final control of the CPI. Aided, crucially, by a tolerant British attitude toward the Communist movement after the Soviet Union joined the Allied war effort, Fahd forged the small and beleaguered CPI into a formidable political force. Like his counterparts in Syria and Lebanon, he could take advantage of rising Soviet prestige, declining British power and credibility, a revived national independence movement, and widespread public and labor unrest linked to the deprivations and dislocations of the war. The close association of the pan-Arabists in Iraq with the Axis powers eventually rebounded to the favor of the Communists when the Axis powers lost ground. As the monarchy grew more repressive throughout the 1940s, the Iraqi Communists gained increasing legitimacy as leaders of the opposition, partially because they were most proficient at withstanding government repression and operating underground and partially because the government tended to label any and all opposition to its policies as "Communist" (Laqueur 1959, 339). By the mid-1940s, the CPI had grown to include more than ten thousand secret members and many more sympathizers, thus surpassing in size the National Democratic party, the largest legal party in the country (Batatu 1978, 404). Strong among urban and oil workers, it also swept the schools and universities and dominated the prisons.

The CPI held its first party congress in secrecy in 1945 and set out a National Charter that differed from its Syrian counterpart mainly in its more pronounced revolutionary militancy. The party was declared to be, unequivocally, the "party of the working class," and the struggle with the monarchy and bourgeoisie was expressed with undisguised hostility (Laqueur 1961, 187). The charter also expressed far more caution about cooperating with other parties than did the CPSL charter, reflecting the strong class tensions and conflicts that prevailed in Iraq, and wariness toward the machinations of the formidable Iraqi secret police.

In Palestine, as mentioned earlier, the revolt and riots of 1936–39 almost destroyed the party. The CPP support for the Soviet-Nazi entente of 1939–41 also did little to improve its position either with the British authorities or within the Jewish community. In 1943–44, with Soviet power in the ascendant, a number of young Arab intellectuals, including Emil Tuma and Emil Habib (later joined by Fuad Nassar), left the CPP and founded their own Communist organization ʿUsbat al-Tahrir al-Watani (League for National Liberation) [LNL]) (Laqueur 1961, 110). The CPP, weakened and still predominantly Jewish, joined the Jewish Histadrut labor federation in 1945. The LNL supported the Arab Higher Committee's general stand vis-à-vis the Zionists and, with a card-carrying membership of around one thousand, it gained very strong influence among the Palestinian Arab labor force that had swelled to more than forty thousand owing to war-related government projects and expenditures (Agwani 1969, 31, 182).

The period between 1936 and 1946 was one in which Arab Communist parties made their first significant inroads into Arab political life. A positive Soviet attitude toward cooperation with other parties and the mandate regimes as well as a leftist government in Paris opened the way for the Communists to make progress through political coalition making and compromise. After the Soviets joined the Allied war effort, the Communists enjoyed tolerant government attitudes and growing prestige as the Soviets turned their initial defeats into impressive victories. Pervading all was growing labor unrest and an accelerating national independence movement that generated political ferment in which the Communists could find new and eager recruits.

Phase 3 (1947–54) consisted of a tug of war in the international arena which coincided with the dissolution of the Soviet-Western wartime alliance and the dawn of the Cold War. Concentrating now on evicting the Western powers from the Middle East, the Soviet Union urged Arab Communist parties to reverse their cooperation with local regimes and revert to a position of intense antagonism toward the pro-Western national bourgeoisie. This drove Arab Communist parties into alliances with such opposition groups as the Muslim Brotherhood, the Ba'th, and others. In the domestic arena, the economic hardship caused by postwar retrenchment and the devastating shock of the loss of Palestine intensified the political ferment of the war years to revolutionary levels. The period began very badly for Arab Communist parties with a Soviet decision to support the United Nations' partition plan of 1947 and the subsequent establishment of Israel in 1948. Still heavily dependent on the Soviet Union, Arab Communist parties went along with the Soviet decision, which itself was a reversal of three decades of Soviet policy. Needless to say, this alienated the Communists from the political mainstream, caused a crisis of conscience within most Arab Communist parties, and precipitated a wave of government repression.

In Egypt, Syria, and Lebanon, the Soviet decision of 1947 prompted the outlawing of Communist parties. In Iraq, the reaction was rather more severe; the government came down with full weight on the Communist movement, jailing many of its leadership and executing Fahd and other top leaders. Although the repression and loss of public support suffered by Arab Communist parties as a result of their position on Palestine was severe, this period of harassment and persecution was not without its benefits. The escalation of government repression led to a streamlining and tightening of party organization that had become rather loose in the expansive years of the mid-1940s and to the purification of the Communist movement from those elements who were really more nationalist than Communist. Furthermore, underground and in the prisons, the Communists developed strong contacts with other radical opposition groups from which cooperation and alliances would flourish in the early 1950s.

In general, the early 1950s were far more propitious years for Arab Communist parties than were the late 1940s as the memory of early Soviet support for Israel began to recede and the relationship between Israel and the West, especially the United States, became increasingly apparent. Opposition to Israel, Western imperialism, and the local governments that had been powerless to oppose Israel's creation, coalesced into national fronts of wide ideological diversity. In Egypt, the MDLN, now headed by Saʿd Sulayman, after Henri Curiel's deportation in 1950, made much headway in the severe unrest of the period although it did not have much of a hand in the riots of January 1952. By 1952, its membership had grown to more than five thousand. It welcomed the military coup of 1952 because a number of Marxists were among the Free Officers group, but the regime and the Communists soon parted ways as the regime reached a new accord with Britain, signed an unpopular agreement over the Sudan, and jailed a number of nationalist and Communist leaders (Botman 1986, 351). Driven underground, the MDLN struck up alliances with the Wafd and the Muslim Brotherhood although its own influence was unsurpassed in the universities and trade unions.

In Syria, the Communists, banned by the repressive Shishakli regime (1949–54), joined the Muslim Brotherhood, the Baʿth party, and Hurani's Arab Socialist party in an opposition National Front alliance. In 1954, Bakdash ran and was elected to the Syrian parliament, becoming the first avowed Communist to become a member of an Arab parliament. In Iraq, the party managed to get back on its feet in 1951 under the leadership of a young Kurd, Bahaʾ al-Din Nuri (Batatu 1978, 662). Despite Nuri's capture in 1953, the party rapidly gained strength and joined a National Front alliance in 1954 with the National Democratic party, the Istiqlal party, and the Ba'th (Samarbakhsh 1978, 118). The Communist movement in Palestine was disrupted by the war of 1948–49 and the tumultuous events surrounding the establishment of the state of Israel. While the Jewish-dominated CPP had joined the Histadrut in 1945, a number of Arab Communists returned to Palestine—now Israel—in 1949 and founded the Arab Communist party of Israel. As the only political party allowed to the Arabs, this party soon attracted the sup- port and vote of the Arab population living within the borders of the new Jewish state. On the West Bank, now occupied by Jordan, the LNL led by Fuad Nassar was renamed the Communist party of Jordan (CPJ) and joined the Ba'th and the newly formed National Socialist party in opposition to the Hashemite regime and its pro-British policies (Agwani 1969, 73). A number of Communist candidates running, unlike Bakdash, as independents, entered the October 1954 election campaign. Two, from Nablus and Hebron, were successful.

The second breakthrough occurred during phase 4 (1955–58). Three events outlined the political landscape of this period: the conclusion of the Baghdad pact, the Czech arms deal, and the nationalization of the Suez Canal. The first forced the Soviet Union into a more favorable stance toward Arab nationalism; the second opened the door for Soviet alliance with Arab nationalist regimes; and the third compelled Soviet and Arab Communists to revise their negative ideological view of the "Arab national bourgeoisie."

The new receptivity of the Soviet Union to the nationalist movements of the developing world had been prepared by Stalin's death in 1953 and the accession of the more open-minded Khrushchev to power in 1954. The changes in the Soviet attitude were articulated and confirmed in the Twentieth Party Congress of the CPSU. A distinction was made between "national liberation" and "social liberation" with the postulate that full national sovereignty had to be attained before the ground for social revolution could be prepared. It was argued that national bourgeoisies, such as those in Egypt and Syria, once they moved out of the imperialist orbit, were capable of leading progressive national liberation movements. It was the duty of the Communist parties and the proletariat they supposedly represented to co-operate with the national bourgeoisie and support its efforts. As for the transition from capitalism to socialism, it was now resolved that this transition could be effected through gradual and peaceful means and did not require a radical proletarian revolution.

In this phase between 1955 and 1958, the position of the Egyptian Communists improved appreciably. Having come to oppose the Free Officers regime as reactionary and repressive, the MDLN decided to reorient its policy after the Czech arms deal to one of all-out support for Nasir. Nasir responded by freeing Communist prisoners. The Suez War of October 1956 greatly improved their image as Soviet prestige soared through Soviet threats against the West and offers to send volunteers. Indeed, the MDLN did send volunteers to fight on the battlefront. As Nasir's turn to the East was confirmed, Marxists of various stripes streamed into the press and educational and cultural institutions. Enjoying respectability and freedom, Egyptian Marxists maintained an influential position in Egypt until their clash with Nasir over the UAR and the Iraqi revolution in 1958.

In Syria, the Czech arms deal and the reassessment of Soviet attitudes helped Bakdash negotiate an alliance with the Bacth Socialist party. Through this combined front the Communist Party of Syria (CPS) gained prominence and several cabinet seats. Uncomfortable with the alliance, however, the Bacth were able to capitalize on apprehensions about the growth of Arab communism and Soviet influence to break the alliance and rally a number of prominent Syrian politicians and army officers to help them weaken the Communists and to further Arab unity by urging Nasir to accept a hastily drawn Egyptian-Syrian unity plan.

In Iraq the CPI paralleled the National Front tactics of the CPS with the establishment of the National Unity Front in 1957 incorporating the Bacth, the National Democratic party, the Istiqlal party, and the Democratic party of Kurdistan (DPK). Aside from the addition of the DPK, the alliance was similar to that of 1954. The front called for Iraq's withdrawal from the Baghdad pact, an opening toward the socialist bloc countries, and a series of political and economic reforms. Although the CPI had no direct hand in the July 14, 1958, coup that unseated the monarchy and brought Abd al-Karim al-Qasim to power, the front helped bring about the political conditions necessary for the coup and welcomed it warmly.

On the West Bank and in Jordan, the CPJ continued its alliance with the Baʿth and other opposition groups and played a significant role in the unrest leading to the dismissal of Glubb Pasha. In October 1956, three Communists running on the National Front ticket gained seats in parliament. The front's leader, Abd al-Qadir Salih, was granted the agriculture portfolio, thus becoming the first Communist government minister in the Arab East. Reaching its peak strength in this period, the CPJ could count around one thousand card-carrying members (Agwani 1969, 155).

Phase 5 (1958–63) was an extremist interlude. The merger of Egypt and Syria in 1958 with the consequent banning of the Communist parties and the Iraqi revolution of the same year in which the Communists and anti-Nasirists gained the upper hand precipitated a showdown between Nasir and the Communists. Emboldened by their rapid advances in the previous period and the dominance of Iraq's Communists in the Iraqi Revolution, Communists in Egypt, Syria, and Iraq demanded a larger share of political power. Although Qasim, the new Iraqi leader, was relatively responsive to Iraqi Communist demands, Nasir came down hard on Syrian and Egyptian Communists. Even in Iraq, the Communists soon outlived their usefulness for Qasim and gradually lost their influence which had grown to impressive proportions. The extremism of this period was motivated by a disillusionment with the authoritarianism of Nasir and the Baʿth and a newfound confidence regarding the political power of the Communists generated by the successes of the Communists in Iraq. In ideological terms, Arab Communist parties now revived their opposition to the "bourgeois nationalism" of Nasir and the Baʿth and insisted that the Communist party itself would take the lead in the struggle for national liberation.

In Iraq, the CPI had not been directly involved in Qasim's coup but had participated actively in the unrest that preceded it. With the overthrow of the monarchy, thousands of political prisoners of all persuasions were released. The Communist party machine emerged intact from underground after twenty-four years of repression and set about freely mobilizing support. The Baʿthists and Istiqlalists also benefited from this brief period of liberalization and clamored loudly for unity with Nasir's UAR. Qasim grew fearful of the pan-Arabists. He suspected that Nasir and the Ba'th, with the support of Abd al-Salam al-Arif, his second-in-command, planned to unseat him and subjugate Iraq to Egyptian rule. This led to a clash with the pan-Arabists in which Qasim adopted the Communists as a convenient ally. Through their overwhelming domination of the Supreme Military Courts (the revolutionary people's courts established in the early weeks of the revolution) and the People's Resistance Force (PRF, a revolutionary militia force established in August 1958) the Iraqi Communists led a fierce campaign to root out Ba'thist, Istiqlalist, and any other Nasirist elements from all sectors of Iraqi society. Their power was crucial in quelling a Ba'thist-Nasirist military revolt in the town of Mosul in March 1959. In their opposition to the pan-Arabists, the CPI also enjoyed an alliance with the DPK, whose leader, Mullah Mustafa Barazani, just returned from thirteen years of exile, feared the Arabism of the Ba'th and the Nasirists.

With the Ba'thists and other Nasirist parties out of favor, the popular euphoria that attended the overthrow of the monarchy was translated into vast numbers of recruits for the Communist party, which declared itself in full support of Qasim. The Soviet Union also favored a weakening of the pan-Arabists to chasten Nasir, who had proven quite uncontrollable. A procession of more than one million people at the close of a Communist-organized Partisans of Peace conference in Baghdad in April 1959 illustrated the strength of the CPI. With their growing influence, the Communists began to demand a greater share of power from the Qasim government in which they still had no formal position. Although he grudgingly admitted two Communist sympathizers to his cabinet on July 13, 1959, he also began to take measures to curb their influence. In June, he released a number of detainees, many of whom were of the Communists' right-wing opponents; at the same time he began to reduce their influence in the people's courts and the PRF. After a bloody clash between Arab Communist activists and native Turkomen in Kirkuk on the anniversary of the revolution, July 14, 1959, in which more than one hundred Turkomen, including women and children, were killed, Qasim moved vigorously against the Communists. He neutralized the PRF and dismantled numerous other Communist front organizations. In public, the Communists were decried as anarchists and terrorists. To further undermine their influence, Qasim established a rival Communist party, under Dawud al-Sayigh, that was pliant to his wishes. The CPI, weakened and embattled, was forced back underground. To make things worse, on February 8, 1963, Arif led a Ba'thist coup against Qasim that ushered in a period of vicious retribution in which the Ba'thists killed or jailed thousands of Iraqi Communists. The CPI was decimated by this campaign, which abated only after Arif's own countercoup against the Ba'th on November 18.

In Syria, upon the formation of the UAR, Bakdash refused to disband the Communist party, a condition that Nasir had insisted on before accepting unity. "We declared," Bakdash said, "that we were for Arab unity but that we would never vote for anti-democratic principles and would never agree to disband our party." "In any case," he continued, "the Communist party has no authority which could disband it" (*World Marxist Review* 1, no.1 [September 1958], 62–64). In taking this position, he had the support of the Soviet Union and Iraqi and other Arab Communist parties. Moreover, after the 1958 Iraqi Revolution, feeling that the balance of forces was tipping in favor of the Communists, Bakdash issued a list of thirteen demands as conditions for lending his party's support to Egyptian-Syrian unity. Nasir reacted forcefully to this challenge, calling the Communists "stooges of imperialism and Zionism" and rounding up hundreds of them in Syria and Egypt as well. Bakdash was out of Syria in self-imposed exile but Farjallah Helou, head of the Lebanese Communist party, was captured in Damascus and later died in UAR prisons. Bakdash welcomed the secession of Syria from the UAR in 1961 although the conservative regime that carried out the secession continued a policy of repression against the Communists. Nor did the situation improve with the March 1963 coup of the Syrian Ba'th who, like their counterparts in Iraq, carried out an effective, if less ferocious, campaign against the Communists.

During this period, the Communist clash with Nasir precipitated serious crises in the CPS and other Arab Communist parties because the Communist party had come out not only against Nasir, whose successes at Suez and elsewhere had made him an Arab national hero but also against the first successful experiment in Arab unity. In Syria, a number of prominent party members led by Rafiq Rida defected from the party, criticizing Bakdash's supposedly anti-Arab position and his authoritarian control of the party.

In addition to the divisive tensions within the Arab Communist movement generated by the clash with Nasir, another source of division that arose in this period was the Sino-Soviet rift. This polarization of the international Communist movement had its effects in the Arab world by providing an alternative rallying point for disgruntled Communists. The Sino-Soviet rift emerged in the late 1950s as China, eager to move out from under Soviet tutelage and exercise its own international influence, faulted the Soviet Union on a number of counts. It opposed the Soviet Union's new attitude of "peaceful coexistence" with the capitalist world and ridiculed the Soviet claim that capitalism would somehow "crumble of itself." In the third world, it criticized Soviet support for national bourgeoisies and rejected the proposition that a nonrevolutionary path to socialism existed through so-called "non-capitalist" development. This, Peking claimed, was nothing but state capitalism. In brief, the Chinese staked out a militant position for themselves to the left of the Soviet Union.

Chinese influence in the Arab Middle East, however, was circumscribed. Although the Chinese government had established diplomatic relations with Egypt, Syria, and Iraq in the 1950s, its preoccupation with its internal problems and the predominance of Soviet influence precluded any widespread Chinese influence. A number of factors in the Arab world, however, favored the modest flowering of Chinese influence during this period. Among Arab Communists, on the one hand, those dissatisfied with the Soviet-inspired policies of the Arab Communist parties' central leadership needed an alternative international Communist rallying point; opponents of the Communists, on the other hand, especially the Baʿth, for example, saw in the promotion of pro-Peking Arab Communist splinter groups an opportunity to fragment and weaken the Arab Communist movement. Other Communists simply felt more at home with the militant revolutionary stands of the Chinese than with the neo-conservatism of the Soviet Union. In any case, a number of small pro-Peking Communist groups emerged in Iraq, Syria, and Lebanon despite their denunciation by the older Communist parties.

Phase 6 (1964–1989) saw the charting of a "new road" to socialism.

Evolution in both Soviet and Egyptian policy in the early 1960s combined to undermine the extremist position of the Arab Communist parties in 1958–63. After the Cuban missile crisis in 1962, Soviet policy toward the third world turned markedly more cautious. The struggle with the capitalist West was now to be conducted through "peaceful competition" in the expectation that the internal contradictions of capitalism would be enough to undermine Western power. In third world countries themselves, the militant revolutionary attitude of earlier Communist movements was no longer deemed necessary because the international environment was said to have been transformed by the rise of a powerful bloc of socialist states. Under the tutelage of these socialist states, developing countries could traverse the road to socialism without passing through capitalism and the violence of the class revolution. In such a scenario the role of the indigenous Communist party was downgraded in favor of cooperation with a "progressive national bourgeoisie" which had supposedly led the struggle for national liberation and now held power in many developing countries. This position, of course, was reminiscent of the position in the early Khrushchev years between 1954 and 1958.

In Egypt, the positions of the Arab Communist parties were overtaken by Nasir's socialist decrees of July 1961 and the National Charter of 1962. In a few deft moves, Nasir had established state ownership of most of the economy, put a 100-feddan ceiling on land ownership, secured a 42-hour work week, and instituted a number of other leftist reforms. Whereas in 1959, Bakdash was accusing Nasir's regime of being a reactionary, right-wing regime interested only in the imperialistic expansion of markets for the "Misr Bank group" and the Egyptian bourgeoisie, in 1964 he observed that "[t]oday, the conditions are ripe for Egypt to take the non-capitalist path" to socialism (*World Marxist Review* 2, no. 11 [November 1959], 29; 7, no. 8 [August 1964], 53). After Nasir had released a great number of Egyptian Communists partly as a goodwill gesture to the Soviets and partly as a way to rally support for his socialist decrees, the Egyptian Communist party made the rare decision to disband itself and urged its members to join Nasir's Arab Socialist Union (ASU).

In Syria, the CPS remained in opposition to the Baʿth until the left wing of the Baʿth came to power in a coup led by Salah al-Jadid in

February 1966. Subsequently, the CPS returned to favor, Soviet-Syrian relations were strengthened, Bakdash ended eight years of exile in the Soviet Union and the socialist countries, and a token Communist was admitted to the new cabinet. The position of Syrian Communists was further legitimized in 1972 when the CPS joined the Baʿth in an officially sponsored progressive National Front.

In Iraq, the CPI remained in opposition through the late 1960s and early 1970s until 1972–73 when two of its members were admitted to the cabinet and the CPI joined the Baʿth in a nationally sponsored National Front. Whereas in Egypt the Communist party had simply dissolved itself, in Syria and Iraq, the power of the Communist party was soon outstripped in size and organization by the state-supported ruling Baʿth parties.

In Lebanon, the Communist movement gained some momentum in the radicalized atmosphere of Beirut in the early 1970s and secured a place for itself in the alliance of Palestinian, Druze, Muslim, and leftist forces that took on the Maronite militias in the fighting that overwhelmed the country in 1975. In Jordan, a small Communist opposition movement maintained itself despite continual setbacks at the hands of King Husayn's vigilant internal security forces.

As did the establishment of the UAR, the Arab defeat of 1967 caused a crisis in many Arab Communist parties and led to a number of splits and desertions. The most serious crisis was within the CPS, which around the time of its Third Congress in June 1969 almost split into two parties over differing positions on Israel, Arab unity, and Bakdash's leadership. The rising generation of leaders raised in the heyday of Nasirist nationalism and severely stung by the 1967 defeat put Arab unity and the destruction of Israel high on their list of priorities. The old guard, however, led by Bakdash and supported by the Soviet Union, insisted that the slogan of Arab unity was best left to the nationalists and that Israel was an established social and political fact that the Arabs had to come to terms with. Struggle against the reactionary classes of Israel was legitimate but a war against the Jewish nation in its entirety was mere nationalistic chauvinism (Syrian Communist Party 1972, passim). In Iraq, the party did split into two in the aftermath of the 1967 defeat. Tensions had been brewing within the party over the leadership's docile opposition to the Arif regime and its equivocal position on Kurdish rights. The new party, calling itself the CPI-Central Command (CPI-CC) supported Kurdish rights to secession, advocated a militant revolutionary attitude toward the government and the bourgeois ruling class, and strongly condemned as treasonous the participation of two CPI members in the 1972 Ba'th cabinet and the joining of the CPI with the Ba'th in the National Front of July 1973. The CPI-CC represented one of the handful of Maoist-leaning Communist groupings that emerged in the 1960s. Its unrelenting opposition to the Iraqi Ba'th was vindicated after the collapse of the Communist-Ba'th alliance in 1979 and the return of the CPI to underground opposition.

As is apparent, the history of the Communist movement in the modern Arab Middle East is a complicated one. Influenced by the vicissitudes of international events and the repressive measures of hostile governments, its presence varied greatly in size and stability. Nevertheless, it had a great influence on the political evolution of the Arab Middle East both in party activity and ideological sophistication and remains to this day one of the distinctive strains of Arab ideological thought.

The Ideology of the Communist Parties:
Marxism Tailored to the Arab World

The thought of the Arab Communist parties was scarcely original. It drew, often imperfectly, from the thought of Marx, Lenin, and Stalin as articulated and elaborated by the Comintern and other Soviet institutions. Over time, however, especially after the dissolution of the Comintern, Arab Communist leaders worked their own views and insights into a Marxist analysis of the conditions of their respective countries and the Arab world generally. Different parties offered slightly different analyses, but they all shared a basic emphasis on class awareness, the dynamics of imperialism, and the imperative of economic justice and progress. It is beyond the bounds of this book to review Marxist-Leninist thought, but it is appropriate to present the attitudes of the Arab Communists on some of the principal issues facing Arab society in their time.

The fundamental ideological contribution of Marxism in the Arab world is that it replaced the complacency toward poverty with a modern explanation of its causes and a fiery commitment to its alleviation through political agitation and economic progress. Thus, it raised important issues in one of the most highly charged areas of politics, an area that had been left unexploited by pre-Baʿthist Arab nationalists and the earlier Islamic movements. The reforms that the Communists called for were of critical significance. Uppermost was the demand for the intensification of the struggle against imperialism and its local feudal and reactionary allies in the interest of true political and economic national independence. This demand was accompanied by a call to strengthen ties with the socialist bloc countries and to seek their alliance. In the domestic political arena, the party consistently called and agitated for political liberalization and respect for democratic constitutional procedures. This position was important to help ward off government restrictions and persecution. But most importantly, the Communists emphasized the need to carry out a long list of socioeconomic reforms. Bakdash described them as follows in the 1943–44 CPSL Congress:

Attention to agriculture, the encouragement of commerce and national industry, the protection of small producers, the emancipation of the peasant from ignorance, backwardness and disease, the equitable distribution of the tax burden, the insurance of affordable living expenses for the masses, attention to thinkers and artists, the enactment of just labor laws, attention to youth, the national education of children, protection of the family from misery and ignorance, raising the status of women, attention to the health of mother and child, and the spread of education in city and village. (Bakdash 1944, 86)

Under the slogan of A Free Nation and a Happy People, Fahd's CPI listed its demands in its 1945 National Charter as follows:

We struggle for the true independence of our country . . . for a democratic constitutional government system . . . for the provision of necessary foodstuffs to the masses . . . for the industrial development of our country's economy and the exploitation of its natural resources in the popular interest . . . for the promotion and modernization of agriculture . . . for the dissolution of foreign and local monopolies . . . for the protection of the peasant from the feudalist and the equitable redistribution of land . . . for the unionization of labor, the protection of the political, economic, social, and health interests of the worker, and the enforcement of just labor laws . . . for a tax system that eases the burden of the small producer . . . for the expansion of education fully and equally for both sexes and the promotion of social and athletic life through clubs . . . for the equality of women in all political, social, and economic affairs . . . for equal status for minority groups such as the Kurds, Turkomen, Armenians, and Yazidis . . . for the better care of the soldier and the reform of the army to render it more democratic and progressive . . . for closer relations with the Soviet Union and the other democratic countries . . . for cooperation with the Arab countries in political, social, cultural, and economic matters. (Yusuf 1976, 133–37)

It was the Communists more than any other group that paid close and detailed attention to such matters of practical concern as economic progress and socioeconomic welfare. Moreover, they translated these concerns into a list of detailed demands for which they lobbied as a party. This part of their message was no doubt attractive to the lower and lower-middle classes; consequently, the Baʿth and Nasir had to adopt most of these demands in their efforts to win over the lower classes. Stripped of their Marxist philosophic baggage and rechristened under the symbols of nationalism, these demands found a permanent place among the progressive nationalists.

Notable in its absence from the Communist reform program was the call for the establishment of socialism. Unlike the revolutionary Arab nationalists, the Communists avoided the use of the term *socialism* to describe their social and economic agenda. This is partially because, in strict Marxist terms, the Arab world was in no way socially or economically prepared for true socialism and partly because, before Nasir, the term had an odious negative connotation popularized by ruling civilian and religious classes hostile to Marxism. Bakdash explained the absence of a call for socialism as follows:

He who reads our National Charter will find it empty of any reference to socialism. . . . But this is in no way an ideological retreat. . . . A country that suffers from colonialism and agricultural and industrial backwardness cannot attempt right away to establish a socialist system, it can only struggle to achieve national liberation and to rid itself of the trappings of the middle ages in its economic and intellectual life. . . . Yes, we are a revolutionary party . . . but the revolution we seek today is not a socialist revolution but a democratic national revolution. (Bakdash 1944, 88–90)

The CPS, of course, spread the ideas of Marxism throughout the political intelligentsia and popularized theories of internal class struggle and international imperialist domination. These concepts would be adopted by the Baʿth and the Nasirists and form a large part of the socioeconomic content of Arab nationalist ideology. The particular attitude of Communist parties toward the national ruling class, whether it was the large landed and comprador bourgeoisies of, say, Egypt, Syria and Iraq of the 1930s and 1940s, or the petty bourgeoisies of later years, took various forms. In part, this reflected the changing directives emanating from Moscow about the desirability of alliance with or opposition to the national bourgeoisie.

The rationale for alliance with the petty or national bourgeoisie was first provided by Lenin, who insisted that this class was leading opposition to Western imperialism in Asia and Africa and was, therefore, a progressive force that would destroy the twin shackles of foreign imperialism and domestic feudalism to set the less-developed countries on a rapid course of economic progress, the culmination of which would be the proletarian revolution and the establishment of socialism. Furthermore, he believed that these nationalist bourgeoisies in turning against imperialism would also unleash forces that would suppress the harsher face of capitalism and guide the country along a noncapitalist course of economic progress. Within this outlook, alliance with the national bourgeoisie was recommended although not without simultaneous commitment to struggling against this bourgeoisie for more concessions to the lower classes. This was the dogma from Moscow in the years roughly between 1921 and 1927 (when Moscow was preoccupied with its massive internal challenges and was optimistic about such nationalist movements as those of Zaghlul in Egypt, Mustafa Kamal in Turkey, Reza Khan in Iran, and Chiang Kai Chek in China), 1935 to 1947 (when Moscow urged cooperation with the ruling class and even the imperialist powers to help defend the "democratic" world against the fascism of Germany and Italy), and again after 1954 (when Khrushchev rededicated the Soviet Union to cooperation with the nationalist movements that had seized, or were in the process of seizing, power in the postcolonial world). Soviet directives were especially influential before the dissolution of the Comintern in 1943.

A hostile position toward the national bourgeoisie was recommended by the Soviet Union between 1927 and 1935 (when Stalin grew disillusioned with the rightist and pro-Western turn of the nationalist movements in Turkey, Iran, and China) and again between 1947 and 1953 (in the early Cold War years in which an aging Stalin still clung to his bitter conviction of the late 1920s that the nationalist forces of the third world were inherently pro-Western). The "class versus class" position recommended by the Soviets to Arab Communist parties in these periods did considerable damage to these movements in the public eye because they were accused of being subservient to a foreign power in opposition to the popular national cause. These difficult periods, however, did generate more powerful party organization and helped filter out many elements who were, in truth, more dedicated to the nationalist than the Communist cause. Communist party attitudes toward the ruling class, however, were also conditioned by political circumstances in the different Arab countries. Temporary political alliances with the political mainstream, as in Syria with the Ba'th in the mid-1950s, for example, would generate positions and arguments advocating such alliances and justifying them in reinterpretations of scientific socialist philosophy, whereas political conflicts, such as those of the Iraqi Communists with Arif and the Ba'th in 1963, would generate the opposite position with the requisite arguments to refuse any such alliance.

Marxism, of course, is an internationalist philosophy officially hostile to the categories of European nationalism. In Marxist theory, the modern nation-state has its origins in the growth of capitalism and bourgeois relations of production and the triumph over feudalism. In this early phase of socioeconomic development, nationalist ideology plays a progressive historical role. Beyond that point, however, nationalist ideology can play a dangerous reactionary role by obscuring class differences and promoting chauvinism and imperialism. In the end, nationalism is to be superseded by internationalism, a higher and more final universal identification of the proletarian with all members of the class worldwide.

Because the Arab world was still in the early stages of socioeconomic development, most Arab Communists could justify support for nationalist movements, as was made abundantly clear time and time again by Bakdash. Indeed, the Communist parties claimed to be at the heart of the national liberation movement. This is not to say, however, that they did not often differ on the nature or identity of the relevant national unit. The main controversy in this sphere was with the Arab nationalists with whom the Communists most frequently took exception. From the materialistic Marxist perspective and given the emphasis of Communist thought on social and economic realities, the Arab nationalist case, based heavily as it was on commonalities of language, culture, and sentiment, came in for frequent criticism. The objection, basically, was that there were too many serious economic and social differences among the Arab countries to say that a unified Arab nation existed. As Stalin had insisted, to exist in actuality, a nation must have a common economic life. They were ready to accept that relative linguistic and cultural homogeneity indicated the potential for an Arab nation, but they balked at the Arab nationalist assertion that such a nation was already a reality. Bakdash, for example, accepted the proposition that Arab unity had a real basis. "The Arabs," he admitted, "belong to a common race speaking a common language and with a common culture"; "however," he warned, "ever since the downfall of the great Arab state that had its capital first in Damascus and later in Baghdad, the Arabs have lived for centuries in different countries and under different conditions" (*World Marxist Review*, 2, no.11 [November 1959], 31). Nevertheless, the Communists did occasionally accommodate themselves to the Arab nationalist position especially in the period of close cooperation with Nasir and the Baʿth between 1955 and 1958.

Arab Communists had additional reservations about Arab nationalism. In its early manifestation in the Arab Revolt of 1916, Arab nationalism was heavily suffused with religious overtones and was led by no less a religious figure than the Sherif of Mecca. In the interwar period, it was the favorite slogan of the upper bourgeoisie. In the late-1930s, it began emulating the authoritarianism and chauvinism of the European fascist powers. Aside from the encouragement lent Arab nationalism by Axis propagandists, the movement also enjoyed British imperial encouragement. It was only until the rise of the Baʿth and Nasir in the 1950s and the break with the capitalist West later in the decade that Arab nationalism could finally lay some claim, according to Marxists, to being a socially progressive movement.

Arab Communists, however, never took an unequivocal position on Arab unity. In general, they acknowledged that working toward closer ties and cooperation between Arab countries was a good thing, and they rarely wrote off the possibility of some eventual unification of Arab lands. But for the immediate future, they cautioned against thoroughgoing unity and advocated instead a looser form of federation that each Arab country could join voluntarily when it had reached an appropriate stage of national liberation and socio-economic development.

The issue of Arab unity was first seriously addressed at a conference of Arab Communist party delegates held for this purpose in the fall of 1935 (Yusuf 1976, 337). They decided that the slogan of unity was impractical because of the differences between Arab countries in "level of development, types of political systems, and internal conditions" (ibid.). The delegates agreed instead on the goal of an "Arab Union," a federation to which Arab countries would join and in which they would maintain a high level of autonomy. The Communist position veered much closer to the Arab nationalist position between 1955 and 1958, adopting the progressive nationalist argument that Arab unity and social revolution were interdependent because the ruling classes that kept the Arab world divided were also the classes that upheld social oppression, and the working classes, presumably, wanted Arab unity not only for sentimental reasons but for practical reasons, wanting to be part of a viable, strong, and independent national economy. The political clash with Nasir and the Ba'th, however, confirmed the Communists in their skepticism about Arab unity. Their final position, articulated in the early 1960s, was that any move toward unity between two Arab countries must be preceded by serious "democratic reforms," and "complete liberation from colonialism" and that unity must be established on a federal basis with "due regard for the specific conditions of each country" (*World Marxist Review* 5, no. 5 [May 1962], 42).

The Communist position on Arab unity was probably their most politically controversial position. It caused serious splits in the Communist movement both in the aftermath of Communist opposition to the establishment of the UAR and in the aftermath of the 1967 defeat when many Communists called for Arab unity as a means to stand up to Israeli power. Its internationalism was also a source of constant embarrassment, because it was frequently accused of being an alien movement controlled by a foreign government. The Communists responded by arguing that alliance with the Soviet bloc was necessary to face the international challenge and might of imperialism and insisted that despite their links with Moscow, they were an autonomous and indigenous political force. As Bakdash insisted, "The Communist party is a pillar of the national movement: the movement's aims are the party's aims, its program is the party's program, and its dreams are the party's dreams" (Bakdash 1944, 78).

With regard to the Communist position on religion, Batatu quotes a chant that was heard briefly in Basra in 1929 at a demonstration organized by a proto-Communist group called the Association of Liberals:

> And the people came in droves
> and asked—not knowing
> who had fallen:
> "Who is this? Tell us, we implore."
> "It is God," we said, "that tyrannized
> and whom land and sea have banished"   (Batatu 1978, 408)

This rather brazen antireligious attitude was paralleled in speeches and pamphlets in which Communists "linked religion to misery, showed the prophets to have been nothing but selfish in their own time, and declared themselves sickened to see how priests and *ulama* continued to fool the people" (ibid.). The association came to be known as the Anti-Religious party, and, needless to say, gained itself a multitude of enemies.

In light of this brief experiment, and as any sensitive activist in the Arab world would have surmised, it was decided that the issue of religion should be avoided altogether. The association between Communism and atheism had been made all too openly by the *ulama* and the pro-Western ruling class. To minimize the burden that such a reputation placed on Communist parties in a religious culture like that of the Arab world, avoidance was considered the best policy. Henceforth, Communist appeals referred only to class and to nation and avoided any mention of religion. Bakdash, it is true, being a Sunni and sensitive to popular sentiments, would occasionally venture into an enumeration of some of the communistic aspects of Islam, and on occasion would invoke one or another verse of the Qur'an or *hadith* to lend credence to a point he was putting across. "We invoked Arab tradition and incorporated the best of the wisdom of our forefathers and their customs into the heart of the national liberation movement. We adopted in our political struggle the holy Qur'anic verse: "Their affairs were a matter of consultation among them," and the sacred *hadith*: "He who aids a tyrant, God puts that tyrant in power over him" (Bakdash 1944, 76). In practical political terms, however, the Communists were undoubtedly out to destroy the political, economic, and cultural influence of the *ulama* whom they considered pillars of the backward, exploitative, traditional status quo.

In sum, the ideology of the Communist parties focused mainly on socioeconomic issues and opposition to imperialism. It drew eclectically from the traditional Marxist literature and played an important role in pushing socioeconomic issues to the forefront of Arab political consciousness.

The Appeal of Communism

To understand the appeal of Communism to large sections of the urban population of the 1950s and 1960s, one begins by looking at what the Communist movements had to offer in the four categories of psychological strain outlined in chapter 1: a need for a sense of identity, a need for moral guidance, a need for intellectual guidance, and a need for the venting of pent-up frustration through the release of aggression. These categories of psychological strain and how the Communist ideology interacted with them are quite relevant given that the middle and lower classes that provided the following for the Communist parties suffered quite acutely from them.

In response to the crisis of identity, Marxist ideology could speak to three important segments of society. First, to the politically conscious members of any of the lower classes, it offered a class identity that helped them define themselves in contradistinction to the members of the upper class with whom they might share a national and religious identity but against whom they felt a certain economic and political opposition. Second, to members of ethnic and religious minority groups, it offered a definition of social solidarity that bridged the gap between them and the Arab Sunni majority. Third, to members of the alienated intelligentsia, it offered an identity and a role as the necessary vanguard of class revolution. Having said this, however, it should be noted that class identities have traditionally been weak in the Arab world and that the atheism and internationalism of Marxist ideology continually militated against the spread of strictly Marxist class-based identity patterns; in terms of identity, pure Marxism would always take a back seat to Arab nationalism. In the end, revolutionary Arab nationalism was able to strike a more marketable balance between the class identities of Marxism and the more accessible identities of nationalism.

Meanwhile, in response to the crisis of moral confusion, the Marxist movements, like the Arab nationalist movements, also did not have much to offer. To be sure, much in the writings of Lenin and Marx addressed itself to the prescribed values and behavior of Marxist activists. Most importantly, they were to conquer their selfishness, purge their characters of "bourgeois" values, and dedicate themselves wholly to class struggle. But, after all, Marxist philosophy is based on a historical materialist perspective and has no room for strict moral imperatives. Whatever ethical prescriptions existed were based on utilitarian considerations to promote the socialist revolution rather than on any absolute moral standard. In this sphere, Marxist ideologues had nothing to match the moral agenda of the Islamic fundamentalists who had a long list of divine moral commands backed by centuries of tradition.

It was in response to the crisis of intellectual confusion, however, that Marxist ideology was most effective. As Maxime Rodinson noted, Marxism provided an "attractive ideological synthesis: an up-to-date conception of the world, a universal explanation of the imperialist phenomenon, which was the fundamental problem for these regions, a practical method of modernization and development, prescriptions for organization, strategy, and tactics, a theory of ethics giving moral force to urgent secular aims, and even an aesthetic theory in which the artist too had a place in the active ranks" (Rodinson 1981, 198). This was especially attractive to members of the Western-educated intelligentsia who had been introduced to the categories of modern European thought but were still thoroughly confused about their contemporary condition. Although Marxist philosophy helped explain reality for the intelligentsia, the wider, less-educated public, for whom Marxist philosophy was too complex, had to make do with simpler slogans of class oppression, Western imperialism, and revolution. The

Communist movements were most effective in this sphere because the entire orientation of Marxist philosophy was toward gaining an *understanding* of society through which one could more effectively promote progressive change. This passion for understanding was not matched by the nationalists or the Islamists. Again, though, the valuable explanation of reality provided by the Marxists was borrowed by the revolutionary Arab nationalists and became part of their package of ideas.

In the category of aggression release, one of the key psychologi- cal crises in strained societies, the Marxists were also quite effective. They divided the world into distinct categories of good and evil: capitalists and workers; oppressors and oppressed; imperialists and Communists. Thus, they could provide clear targets of aggression both within one's own society and in the international arena. Furthermore, within the logic of historical materialism, absolute and unrestrained hostility toward these targets was perfectly acceptable and did not need to be reined in by any moral or even political considerations. Conflict between classes was historically necessary, and, moreover, the ends justified the means. Lenin well understood the importance of aggression in the success of Communist movements. The Arab nationalists, who started only with national chauvinism as a source of aggression-release, soon adopted Marxist theories to lend more weight and intellectual credibility to their hostility. Even some among the Islamic activists could not ignore the aggressive potential stored in Marxist theories of class oppression, revolution, and Western imperialism. Indeed, such thinking eventually gave rise to a distinct left wing within the Islamic fundamentalist movements of the 1970s and 1980s.

Marxist ideology had a fair amount to offer in the psychological crisis areas of identity and moral confusion, intellectual disorientation, and aggression-release. In that sense, we can see how Marxism could be a part of an age of ideology in the Middle East in which individuals of various classes, groups, and backgrounds were looking for new ways to understand themselves and the world around them. It could compete with the nationalist and Islamic ideologies because whereas they offered accessible slogans of national and religious solidarity, the Marxists were the first to offer a modern rational worldview and to promote effectively the politically explosive slogans of class oppression and Western imperialism.

The Social Dynamics of the Communist Movement

From the perspective of class, the Communist parties, of the Arab Middle East shared largely the same base as the revolutionary Arab nationalist parties: namely, the petty bourgeoisie, or, more informally, the new middle class. The urban poor and the rural peasantry were notably underrepresented (Batatu 1978, 644). To the new middle class, qua class, Marxism provided a sense of identity and purpose. It explained that this class had an important and progressive role to play in the unfolding of political and economic history and provided an identity in contrast to the identity of the ruling upper class. Furthermore, Marxism provided a sense of legitimacy and inevitability to the overthrow of the ruling upper class by this rising middle class. It gave expression and meaning to the central class shift in the Arab Middle East of the twentieth century. Finally, it expressed the struggle of this new class against Western influence that continued even after it attained political power.

Ideological effervescence is always very high during times of class movement, and the Arab world is no exception. Although it began in the early 1920s, Marxist ideology only found a wide audience in the 1940s and 1950s when the new middle class was seizing and consolidating its power in Egypt, Syria, Iraq, and other corners of the Arab world. Marxist ideology legitimized revolution, showed the path to a successful seizure of power, and helped explain what to do once in power. In this sense, it had a lot to offer to a rising class. Indeed, Marxism was, along with revolutionary Arab nationalism, one of the two ideological battering rams used to destroy the legitimacy and credibility of the conservative postwar regimes and bring about their overthrow. Although Marxists and revolutionary Arab nationalists were generally allies during the rebellion against the old order, once the old order was destroyed, the Arab nationalists proved more successful in spreading their ideology and eclipsing Marxism as the principal ideology of the newly empowered middle class.

In the forties and fifties members of previously excluded minority groups and new economic classes entered political power. For the first time, Alawis, Druzes, Christians, Kurds, Chaldeans, and members of other minorities found themselves at the head of mass political movements with vast Sunni Arab followings, and soon after that, in the highest offices of state. This invasion by minorities of the political arena required a legitimating ideology as did the assault of the new middle class on the bastions of the ruling upper class. Marxism was very effective in providing such legitimacy and encouragement for members of minorities because it based its appeal on principles of economic status to which members of all communities could relate. Marxism was more inclusive than Arab nationalism not only because it incorporated non-Arabs where Arab nationalism could not but also because it placed no emphasis on cultural history as the Arab nationalists did. Inevitably, this emphasis led the nationalists to acknowledge a central role for Sunni Islam in Arab history. Indeed, the Communist movement was heavily favored by the minorities. In the 1920s, the movement was led by Jews, Greeks, Armenians, Kurds, and Arab Christians; and although in the 1940s and 1950s, Sunni Arabs came to play a more central role, Kurds, Christians, Armenians, Shiʿa and other non-Sunni or non-Arab minorities continued to be dramatically overrepresented. It is not surprising, then, from this perspective, that the heyday of Communism coincided not only with the entrance of a new middle class to political power but also the entrance of members of previously excluded minority groups.

The rise of the Communist movement can also be analyzed from the perspective of generational opposition. In other words, as discussed in chapter 1, ideological waves can be examined not only from the perspective of class struggle, or interethnic or interconfessional competition but also from the perspective of intergenerational opposition. This is especially relevant in societies that are experiencing rapid population growth without sufficient economic and political development to accommodate the rising generation. In such societies, discontent will gather in the rising generation as its efforts to find a place for itself in the political and economic order are frustrated by overcrowding. Such a generational group, like the economic and ethnic group, needs an ideological cover, or battering ram, to fight its way into the political arena. Whereas economic and ethnic groups are constrained to adopt ideologies which favor their interests and reject others that do not, generational groups, having no particular political interests except empowerment itself, can embrace nearly any ideology as long as that ideology is antithetical to the ideology of their elders. Thus, the frustrated youth of the forties and fifties, flocked to the Communist movement as they flocked to the revolutionary Arab nationalist movement, and in many cases, the fundamentalist Islamic movements—anything but the discredited liberal conservative pro-Western nationalism of their elders.

The sociological dynamics of the spread of Communist ideology in the Arab Middle East of the forties and fifties from the perspectives of class, ethnic or confessional groups, and generational opposition elucidate the decline in the following of Communist movements after the fifties. Of course, the central reason for the decline of the Communist parties comes from their political defeat at the hands of the Arab nationalists led by Nasir in Egypt and the Bacth in Syria and Iraq at a time when the Soviet Union began to value its regional political allies more highly than its ideological sister parties. Other sociological factors, however, figure highly in understanding the ebb of Arab Communism.

From the perspective of class, the new urban middle class that had used communism as well as revolutionary Arab nationalism to break into power in the 1950s had been successful. The old ruling class had been unseated and new political regimes had been established to confirm this class's hold on political, economic, and cultural power. A revolutionary ideology was no longer crucially needed. The so-called revolution had already taken place, and the new urban middle class now had vested interests in the polity and economy.

From the perspective of minority groups, similar arguments apply. Once in power, minority groups could ease their reliance on revolutionary ideologies and rely instead on the normal levers of power provided by political and economic institutions to maintain and enhance their positions. Unlike identities of economic class, however, ethnic or confessional identities could not be easily transformed or forgotten. Christians would remain Christians and Alawis would remain Alawis regardless of their success in changing their economic status or breaking through to positions of power. In an area where a Sunni Arab majority still predominated, these labels would continue to be a problem. Consequently, minority attachment to Marxism continued even after its general decline in the 1960s. The new Marxist movements that emerged in the late 1960s and early 1970s reverted to a heavy representation of minority groups reminiscent, to some extent, of the levels of minority representation in the very early days of the Communist movement in the Middle East.

The generational swing away from Marxism (as well as revolutionary Arab nationalism) is quite clear and is delineated by the rapid growth of fundamentalist Islamic movements among the youth of the early 1970s. Whereas secular communism or nationalism were the modes of protest for the frustrated youth of the fifties and sixties, a new generational group sought to express its frustrations in an ideology radically antithetical to the ideology of the preceding generation, which had now acceded to positions of established power. In a crowded and frustrated social environment, the ideology of one generation promotes the growth of an opposing ideology in the succeeding generation. Such was the case with communism and revolutionary Arab nationalism, whose influence ebbed as a rising generation searched for distinctly different ways to express their frustration and hostility toward the previous generation.

The Legacy of the Communist Movements

The most lasting contribution of the Communist movements in the sphere of ideology and political culture is their critique of laissez-faire capitalism and their emphasis on social and economic justice. They provided much of the ideological cover for the disenfranchisement of the landed and big business class, the takeover by the state of the majority of economic resources, and the redistribution of land and wealth to the middle and lower classes. Indeed, it was in large part the ideology of the Communists that was behind the Arab socialism of Nasir and the Baʿth. The Communists made poverty a potent political issue and focused political attention on issues of wealth distribution and economic development. They introduced a host of progressive social and economic themes that were previously absent from the agenda of Arab politics.

They also introduced the ideas of class interest and class conflict that were almost absent from Arab political consciousness and that later became common currency. While this helped clarify some real economic and political issues, it also provided a facile excuse under which new regimes could lash out at their opponents and challengers, confiscate their property, and restrict their freedom under the rubric of legitimate class struggle. Indeed, the idea of legitimate class struggle had a dangerous effect on the heterogeneous societies of the Fertile Crescent as it legitimized a form of internal warfare in societies deeply riven by ethnic and religious divisions in addition to economic class divisions. This was a far cry from the themes of political stability and communal and class coexistence that were, in effect, part and parcel of the Ottoman style of government. The legitimization of violence and the legitimate use of force in domestic politics contributed to the instability of many Arab regimes and provided a cover for those regimes that finally could harness enough force to subdue their enemies and impose a form of political stability based far more on terror than on consent or consensus.

Of course, the idea of the vanguard party, which they also introduced, was quite effective in sweeping away any notions of liberal democracy that had feebly taken root in the interwar period. The concept of a vanguard party of the Leninist type appealed to political and military activists. It gave their ambitions a grandiose importance and a profound legitimacy. It legitimized a violent takeover of power and the preservation of the political power thus acquired through a combination of coercion and propaganda, what Machiavelli called force and fraud. The idea of a vanguard party bypassed the need to pay formal attention to the views and wishes of the populace. Even the oppressed classes were not presumed to know what their proper interests were; the vanguard party acted on their behalf and without their consultation. On such an ideological basis, any notions of the legitimacy of public opinion and the importance of elections in representing the interests of the people disintegrate into nonsense.

The influence of the Communists was also seminal in introducing notions of imperialism into Arab political culture. Whereas the ideas of class conflict and the vanguard party helped define the domestic political arena, the theory of imperialism helped define the perception of the Arab world's relationship with the West. In essence, Communists provided the ideological tools for a dramatic vilification of Western politics, economics, and culture. A similar vilification was carried out on the radical right by the Islamic fundamentalists; the Communists provided the rationale for a vilification from the radical

Left. Of course, such vilification is normal and typical of developing countries struggling against colonial powers. In the hands of the new revolutionary Arab regimes, however, this encouraged a severe isolation of Arab societies from outside, or Western, influences. Although this was convenient for nascent regimes concerned with their internal security and stability, it boded ill for domestic political life because it swept a whole set of issues off the political agenda; issues such as political and human rights, liberalism, and democratic process could be conveniently suppressed as Western bourgeois notions.

Important, as well, was the Communist legitimation of rebellion and revolution against established governments. In its traditional form, Arab Sunni political culture was essentially conservative and frowned on revolt or revolution. Political stability and social solidarity were generally esteemed even in cases of unjust government. The Communists, however, introduced an interpretation of politics in which revolution was necessary, inevitable, and part of the progressive evolution of history. They helped provide the ideological framework within which the overthrow of governments in the majority of countries of the Middle East took place. This legitimization of revolution not only contributed to the overthrow of existing regimes but also meant that the new regimes would have to guard against overthrow as well, for the principle of revolution, once promulgated, could not easily be repealed. The new regimes, therefore, had to contend with the political instability that they had introduced with a growing emphasis on surveillance, coercion, and terror to protect against the constant threat of rebellion or revolution.

Finally, their attitude toward ideology itself is worth noting. As Elias Murqus, a former member of the Syrian Communist party, noted, "In general, Arab Communism is characterized by the absolute separation of theory and praxis and by a large gulf between general dogma and any specific practical activity. Loyalty to principles turns into rigid, meaningless dogmatism and political elasticity ends up as unlimited opportunism" (quoted in Tibi 1986b, 22). This is especially obvious in the career of the Syrian Communist party itself, which reversed ideological positions several times on cues from Moscow and pursued contradictory political lines according to the changing political climate of the times. This cynical attitude toward ideology divorced from actual political practice became a central facet of Arab ideological party life and was especially destructive within the Baʿth party whose Syrian and Iraqi branches pursued mutually hostile regional ambitions while spouting identical Arab nationalist slogans.

Moreover, Communists were keenly aware of the power of ideology and were well versed in the practice of propaganda. Although they believed that they had a precise and profound understanding of social and economic realities, they were aware that the ideology they promoted in their pamphlets and party speeches was a carefully engineered set of attitudes and ideas designed to appeal to key sectors of the population that would be in a position to support the vanguard elite who, alone, supposedly knew what was going on. They understood the power of propaganda and consciously used ideology to galvanize and manipulate public opinion. They were not averse to reversing their stated positions overnight if it suited their political purposes and were prepared to back it with freshly contrived pseudo-scientific arguments. In a word, the Communists illustrated to other Arab elites how opinions, attitudes, and ideologies could be manipulated to serve the interests of an elite. This reduced the level of political debate in the Arab world from the fairly civilized pamphleteering at the turn of the twentieth century to the crude mass propagandizing of the post–World War II regimes. The Communists showed how politics and politicians could dominate culture and the mind. In the process, they paved the way for the new regimes of the region to seize control of all organs of opinion and debate and impose a stifling monopoly on thought.

The New Left

The decade of the 1960s was characterized by a drift to the left within the Arab nationalist movement. The roots of this leftward drift lay in the principles of Marxist socialism grafted onto Arab nationalism by the Baʿth and Nasir. Nasir turned to his version of socialism earnestly in 1961–62 with the announcement of the Socialist Decrees and the National Charter. Within the Baʿth party, serious left-center differences became apparent in the October 1963 Sixth National Congress held in Damascus (Ismael 1976, 28). Criticism was leveled at Aflaq and the old guard for presenting only the symbols of socialism without any rigorous socioeconomic analysis. In 1965, the left wing of the Syrian Baʿth party seized power in Syria and dismissed both Aflaq and Bitar. In 1966, members of the Syrian Baʿth left wing also founded their own organization under Yasin al-Hafiz, *al-Hizb al-ʿUmmali al-ʿArabi al-Thawri* (Arab Revolutionary Workers' party)(Tibi 1981, 178). Within the ANM, Nayef Hawatmeh, Muhsin Ibrahim, and other younger party leaders were confronting the conservative nationalism of Habash and others. This leftward drift was strengthened and radicalized by the Arab defeat in the 1967 war.

The causes for the pre-1967 leftward drift include the following: (1) a leadership that had come to maturity in the 1930s and 1940s when the simple struggle against mandate domination was the dominant ideological theme was being challenged by a generation of the 1950s in which revolution, socialism, opening to the Soviet Union, and struggle against Western capitalist imperialism were the dominant themes. The 1950s were also a decade in which Arab Communists in Syria, Iraq, and elsewhere enjoyed unprecedented predominance; thus, Arab nationalists throughout the Arab world were exposed to their ideas. (2) The rudimentary socialism of the Baʿth and Nasir had raised more socioeconomic demands than their regimes could satisfy; a renewed concern with the principles of socialism reflected the concern among many party activists to bridge the broadening chasm between what the state promised to deliver and what socioeconomic good it could actually provide. (3) Awareness was growing among Arab nationalists that a new ideological effort was needed to add onto the simple romantic nationalism of Aflaq and the old guard an effective set of social and economic directives capable of guiding reform within the complex arena in which the Arab nationalist regimes found themselves. The poetic prose of Aflaq was inspiring, but it had nothing to say about housing, economic development, agricultural productivity, land reform, and so forth.

Furthermore, the defeat of 1967 laid bare the pretensions of Arab nationalism. In a matter of days, Israel had completely devastated the forces of two of the Arab world's most progressive and most powerful states and had occupied large territories on the Egyptian, Jordanian, and Syrian fronts. A mood of bitter disillusionment settled over the Arab world. Much has been written about the disappointment and disillusionment generated by the defeat of 1967. Suffice to say, it forced a split in the Arab nationalist movement between those who wished to cling to the Nasirist model and advocated only reform and those who decided that the whole ideology and political structure erected by nationalism was hopeless; the latter group turned to radical Marxist revolutionary activism as the path to redemption. The pre-1967 leftism of the Ba‘th and the Nasirists was superseded by this new leftism in which Arab socialism was now considered an insincere and inherently flawed program.

From the ANM emerged a number of Marxist parties, such as the Popular Front for the Liberation of Palestine (PFLP), the Popular Democratic Front for the Liberation of Palestine (PDFLP), the PFLP-General Command (PFLP-GC), and others that staked out the far left of both the Arab and Palestinian nationalist movements. In the intellectual arena, a number of thinkers emerged, such as Sadiq al-Azm and Elias Murqus, who led their colleagues in a reassessment of the Arab nationalist legacy and suggested a course of revolutionary upheaval.

The Splintering of the ANM and the Emergence of the Marxist Popular Front Organizations

The leftward drift of the ANM had paralleled that of the Ba‘thist and Nasirist movements in the 1960s. At the same time, however, it was losing its organizational coherence as the central leadership of Habash gave way to a decentralization of party policies and programs in different regions of the Arab world. The ANM branches of Kuwait, Yemen, Dhofar, and Palestine preserved their institutional independence, whereas the branches of Iraq, Syria, Egypt, and Lebanon merged with or dissolved into larger Ba‘thist or Nasirist groups. While the Kuwaiti, Yemeni, and Dhofari branches carried on in their local concerns, the Palestine branch attracted Habash and many of the central leadership of the ANM. After all, the ANM had been established as a reaction to the loss of Palestine in 1948; its concern for Palestine had always distinguished it from the less Palestine-centered worldviews of Nasirism and the Ba‘th.

In the mid-1960s, the influence of the Palestine branch of the ANM was being challenged in Palestinian refugee camps by a new Palestinian nationalism promoted, most notably, by Arafat's Fateh organization. This new Palestinian nationalism spoke directly to Palestinian concerns and disseminated a popular message of empowerment and guerilla warfare. The ANM's position toward Palestinian liberation had advocated a pan-Arab approach in which the conventional armies of the Arab regimes would engage and defeat the Israelis. Responding to the new militant Palestinian nationalism whipped up by Fateh, Habash renamed the Palestinian branch of the ANM, the National Front for the Liberation of Palestine (NFLP) and delved into guerilla activity as early as 1964 through the NFLP's newly established military arm, the Youth of Vengeance (Kazziha 1975, 84).

Fateh's call for popular armed struggle was simple and straightforward; it claimed little ideological complexity. For the more intellectual leadership of the ANM, however, this simple populist appeal to armed struggle seemed naïve, ill thought-out, and smacked of the discredited populism of Arab nationalism. For Hawatmeh, Habash, and others, a dedication to armed struggle necessitated a more "objective" analysis of the successful wars of liberation carried out in the century. This need inevitably led to the popular literature of Che Guevera, General Giap, and Mao Tse Tung, and the revolutionary writings of Lenin, Engels, and Marx. Thus, unlike the Communists or the leftists of the Ba'th or Nasirism, the ANM arrived at Marxism not primarily out of concern for class disparities and economic progress so much as out of a commitment to a war of liberation and, thus, to an ideology that would tend to strengthen such a war. Further distinguishing themselves from the approach of Fateh, Habash and the new ANM groups advocated a war of liberation not limited to Palestine alone but involving the entire Arab nation.

In December of 1967, Habash and several of his colleagues renounced their previous commitment to liberation through a conventional war waged by the standing armies of the Arab regimes and formed the Popular Front for the Liberation of Palestine (PFLP; a merger of the NFLP with a group called the Heroes of the Return and the Palestinian Liberation Front of Ahmad Jibril). The Jibril group soon left to form the PFLP-General Command. Nayef Hawatmah, who had joined the PFLP in early 1968 also left Habash to form his own, ostensibly more Marxist, Popular Democratic Front for the Liberation of Palestine (PDFLP). In 1970, a group of former ANM members formed *Munadhdhamat al-Ishtirakiyyin al-Lubnaniyyin* (the Organization of Lebanese Socialists). After the 1967 war the old ANM had effectively ceased to exist. Its branches around the Arab world had gone their separate ways. The core of Palestinian activists had abandoned the Nasirist ideology of the ANM and split into several revolutionary Marxist guerilla factions.

The Ideology of the New Left: Social Revolution and the Virtues of a People's War

The platform of the PFLP. According to these neo-Marxists, the modern history of the Arab world was characterized by the successive struggle of three distinct classes: the upper bourgeoisie, the petty bourgeoisie, and the proletariat. The upper bourgeoisie, consisting of large landowners and capitalists, led the fight for national liberation in the interwar period against the British and the French. Despite its successes in some countries, this class did not carry national liberation through to its stated goals. Instead of resolutely throwing out the imperialists, it soon became clear that this bourgeoisie sought only to share in the spoils derived from exploitation. They wanted not to overthrow the imperialist-organized system but only to be part of it. They ignored the objectives of Arab unity, and sought only to consolidate their privileges in the fragmented state system devised by the West.

Thus, the leadership of the bourgeoisie soon came into conflict with the "naturally progressive aspirations of the masses." In opposition to the bourgeoisie rose the middle class of intellectuals, professionals, enlightened officers, students, shopkeepers, and so forth—the petty bourgeoisie—which as a rising class at the time could lead the mass struggle against the upper bourgeoisie. In the late 1930s and 1940s this rising class articulated itself in various civilian and military parties and groups. The defeat of 1948 dealt a staggering blow to the upper bourgeois regimes. The petty bourgeoisie, with the support of the lower class of workers and peasants, broke into power and inaugurated a new political era in the Arab world. According to the PFLP, these petty-bourgeois Arab nationalist regimes, exemplified best by Nasir's regime in Egypt, played a progressive historical role and their accomplishments had to be recognized: they firmly evicted the British and French; they destroyed the power of the Arab bourgeoisie; they developed strong relations with the progressive socialist countries; and they introduced programs of social reform into the ideology of political liberation, such as land reform, nationalization of large industry and trade, public sector development projects, and so on (PFLP 1970, 62). Finally, Nasir brought Egypt into the mainstream of Arab nationalism and carried out the first Arab unionist project. Again according to the PFLP, however, the progressive policies of these regimes prompted the "imperialist" camp, led by the United States, to make a concerted effort to oppose them. The imperialists strengthened their support for Israel and for reactionary Arab regimes. To withstand this new imperialist assault, the progressive Arab regimes needed to mobilize the resources of their countries in the ideological, political, military, and economic spheres to their fullest extent. But here a contradiction arose between the class interests of the ruling petty bourgeoisie and the interests of the masses. Having become a ruling class, the petty bourgeoisie had also developed deep vested interests in the status quo. Its interests in industry, agriculture, and trade, unlike those of the bourgeoisie, had never been disturbed; its interests in the state, especially in the military and the bureaucracy, had also grown quite strong. Although it still opposed imperialism, its revolutionary momentum had been dissipated. It sought a continuation of the status quo, and it regarded the involvement and empowerment of the lower classes of workers and peasants as a threat to its position and privilege in society. It opposed a strategy of a popular war of liberation in the struggle with Israel because that would mean mobilizing and arming the lower classes. The war against Israel was only allowed to be waged by the conventional standing armies safely under the supervision of the petty bourgeois regimes.

But as the defeat of 1948 dealt a blow to the bourgeoisie, so did the defeat of 1967 deal a blow to the petty bourgeoisie (PFLP 1970, 65). It made clear that the petty bourgeoisie had outlived its usefulness in the development of the Arab world, and as it clung to its old formulas of Arab nationalism and struggle by conventional military means, a new struggle announced itself—the struggle between the petty bourgeoisie and the larger and lower class of workers and peasants.

These neo-Marxist groups, composed overwhelmingly of Palestinians, had a special understanding of the role of the Palestinian petty bourgeoisie. Because it was bereft of any state, the Palestinian petty bourgeoisie, represented in such organizations as Fateh, had been able to maintain a more progressive attitude than other Arab petty bourgeoisie (PFLP 1970, 40). For Palestinians, the struggle for the defeat of Israel and the liberation of Palestine was a direct and urgent concern for members of all classes. Nevertheless, the conflict between the petty bourgeoisie and the worker and peasant classes that was manifesting itself all across the Arab world, did emerge, although in a somewhat milder form, in Palestinian society. Since the disinheritance of the upper bourgeoisie, the Palestinian petty bourgeoisie had been leading the Palestinian revolution, but this class, like all petty bourgeoisies, could not be the central pillar in any thoroughgoing revolution because its leadership was by nature hesitant, confused, ambivalent, and cowardly, given the significant interests that it sought to preserve in any potential revolution (PFLP 1970, 36). As proven by revolutions from China to Cuba, it was only from the lower class of workers and peasants that able leadership could emerge.

The struggle between the petty bourgeoisie and the worker and peasant classes comprised politically the struggle for leadership in a revolution that concerned them both. The petty bourgeoisie, however, was still very strong; therefore, the parties of the worker and peasant classes, the PDFLP, PFLP, and so on, could not afford to challenge its leadership directly yet. An alliance should be sought in which the petty bourgeoisie and worker and peasant classes shared leadership while the latter developed its power and improved its organization. The two types of parties (e.g., Fateh representing the petty bourgeoisie and the PFLP representing the worker and peasant classes) each had a role to play. The program of this alliance between the Palestinian petty bourgeoisie and the worker and peasant classes, the National Front, would be quite direct—the inauguration of a commando war that would grow into a popular war of liberation (PFLP 1970, 27).

In the Arab world, the policies of the Palestinian petty bourgeoisie and the worker and peasant parties were quite dissimilar. Whereas Fateh and the PLO accepted as legitimate the Arab status quo and pledged not to interfere in the domestic affairs of other countries, the PDFLP and its sort, descendant as they were from a strong pan-Arabist background, recognized no such boundaries and considered the Palestinian revolution part and parcel of a wider Arab revolution. According to them, the alliance of imperialists, Zionists, and Arab reactionaries ranged against the progress and liberation of the Arab world was a formidable one (PFLP 1970, 53); only by banding together could the progressive forces of the Arab world, Palestinian or otherwise, gain the strength sufficient to mount a credible challenge (PFLP 1970, 76, 56).

For the time being, however, the example of progressive alliance established within the Palestinian movement between the petty bourgeoisie and the truly revolutionary parties should be followed in all other Arab countries. The parties of the worker and peasant classes should strike alliances with the currently powerful and marginally progressive petty bourgeoisie until such time as their own power and organization was sufficient for them to act on their own. The worker and peasant classes should use their growing influence to promote a policy vis à vis Israel of commando warfare and, eventually, popular guerilla war instead of the dead-end strategies of using weak Arab conventional armies against technologically far superior Israeli and American conventional power. The Arabs could overcome the enemy's technological advantage only by turning the war into a prolonged war of liberation in which determination and organization would carry the day, not technology and firepower. The final objective of such a war would not be to destroy the Jewish people or to subjugate them but only to destroy the "reactionary and racist" institutions of Zionism and to install in their place a "democratic state in Palestine in which Arabs and Jews live together on equal footing" (PFLP 1970, 88–90).

Beyond the Arab world, the Arab revolutionary forces sought the alliance of the socialist countries whose global influence could help challenge the global influence of the United States and its allies, who stood behind Israel and all reactionary Arab elements.

About the social and economic aspects of modernization that Zurayq, the early mentor of the ANM, had so emphasized, the attitude of the Popular Front organizations was quite direct. "The battle for Palestine will be with regard to the Palestinian and Arab masses an entry way to the civilization of the modern age and a conduit from the state of backwardness to the ways of the modern era. Through this struggle we will gain appreciation for the political realities of the day. We will do away with illusions and learn the value of facts" (PFLP 1970, 90).

As did the Communists before them, the Popular Front organizations avoided a direct confrontation with the symbols and ideology of Islam. For the most part, they sidestepped the issue of religion. It was quite obvious, however, that their program was one of thoroughgoing secularism deeply antithetical to any interests of the religious class or even the categories of the religious mind. Toward Communists, the Popular Front organizations had a more ambivalent position (Ismael 1976, 114, 117). The ideology of the Communists they largely accepted, but they faulted them for their attitudes and policies toward Arab unity and Arab interests in general. They criticized the Communists' highly equivocal attitude toward Arab unity and suspected their true motives in their support for the expropriation of Alexandretta Province from Syria in 1939, support for the partition of Palestine in 1947, support for the state of Israel in 1948, support for Qasim against the Arab nationalists in 1958, opposition to the UAR, and support for the secession of Syria from the UAR in 1961. They also criticized the Communists' blind support for the Soviets and hostility to the Chinese. In short, the Popular Front organizations accused the Communists of not being indigenous class organizations and, therefore, of being out of touch with the interests and sentiments of the masses. In this, the new Marxist groups contended, the Communists did a great disservice to Marxism-Leninism and to the Arab masses, for the latter came to confuse Marxism with the faulty and often anti-Arab positions of the Communist parties. The Popular Front organizations had to dispel that illusion and set Marxism-Leninism on the right course.

The loose organization of the petty bourgeois political parties had to be replaced by strong tightly knit structures that could be effective and enduring both in waging guerilla warfare against Israel and in inducting new members into the revolutionary war. Membership in the party, which was still predominantly of the petty bourgeoisie, had to be gradually but quickly replaced by a majority of members from the worker and peasant class, for it was from that class that clear-thinking and courageous revolutionary leadership would emerge (PFLP 1970, 106). Unlike other parties, the Popular Front organizations were to be fighting parties. Every member was to be directly or indirectly involved in the war for liberation. Either he was a fighter, or then an organizer, teacher, or propagandist supporting the fighters or bolstering their number (PFLP 1970, 121).

The Popular Front parties that emerged within the Arab and Palestinian nationalist movements after 1967 discredited the post-1948 regimes of the Baʿth and Nasir, criticized the mainstream Palestinian nationalist movement, blamed the weakness of the Palestinians and Arabs on social and class causes, and advocated a revolutionary People's War on the Chinese, Vietnamese, Cuban, and Algerian models that would at the same time do away with the Zionist state and the reactionary Arab classes and regimes that kept the Arab nation from developing the strength and vitality necessary to confront Israel and Western imperialism. An awareness of class differences, dissatisfaction with the Arab nationalist regimes, and a radical program of revolution and reform, however, was not confined to the Popular Front parties. It was also advocated by a number of formerly Arab nationalist non-party intellectuals who were driven by their shock at the Arab defeat of 1967 to reevaluate the content of their Arab nationalism.

Sadiq al-Azm: Intellectual as radical. Born to an aristocratic family of Syria, Azm was educated in philosophy at Yale and returned to teach at the American University of Beirut. Like many of his intellectual contemporaries, he was radicalized by the defeat of 1967. His writings in the aftermath of 1967 constituted, according to Malcolm Kerr, "the most scathing of all indictments of Arab society and culture" of recent times (Kerr 1971, 135). His outspokenness cost him his job at the American University of Beirut and the enmity of the religious establishment of Lebanon. Many of his positions were not original to him but had been espoused by Arab Communists and leftist members of the Baʿth or the Palestinian Resistance before him, but the Marxism that had penetrated other segments of society had not yet penetrated the Western-oriented intellectual community of Beirut for whom nationalism and liberalism had been the guiding principles since the time of Zurayq in the 1940s.

Azm's main critique, entitled *al-Naqd al-Dhati Ba'd al-Hazima* (Self-criticism After the Defeat), was published in 1968. He compares the Arab defeat of 1967 to the Russian defeat at the hands of the Japanese in 1904. Whereas the Russians took stock of their situation after their defeat and launched a massive revolution to transform radically the very foundations of their society, the Arabs, says Azm, concentrated on hiding from responsibility and putting the blame on others or on unseen forces, such as God.

Azm states the problem of Arab society in terms similar to those used by Zurayq before him. Attached first and foremost to narrow associations such as family, clan, or sect, Arabs are incapable of effective national organization and action. Furthermore, although they pose as members of the modern world, Arabs are deeply traditional in nearly every category of their lives. "The revolutionary Arab youth today is revolutionary politically, but in his heart, he is a trenchant conservative in social, religious, cultural, moral, and economic matters" (Azm 1968, 78). The change that has overcome the Arab mind and Arab culture has been alarmingly superficial. "We made room in our lives for the refrigerator, the television, oil wells, the MiG, radar, etc., but the mindset that uses these imported products has remained traditional—a mindset that belongs to the eras of tribalism, agricultural economies, and attachment to otherworldly things, eras prior to the industrial revolution and the scientific revolution. . . . Also our understanding of time, place, and professionalism did not change" (Azm 1968, 112–13). Borrowing from the Marxist vocabulary, he explains that the significant political and economic changes wrought by the Arab socialist regimes in, for example, Egypt, Syria, and Iraq, have not yet affected the ideological superstructures of Arab society. Although the material conditions of life have changed, the cultural and psychological attitudes have remained the same because the ideology of Arab socialism was vague and indistinct. It tried to make itself more acceptable by associating itself with Islam and other unscientific categories; in the process it lost its intellectual force and was unable to unseat the traditional belief-system (Azm 1968, 135–38).

For intellectuals, the task of cultural and ideological transformation was clear—to dismantle and discredit the traditional cultural system and to build in its place a rational scientific one in tune with the demands of the modern age. The task, then, was a revolutionary not a reformist one in which cultural progress could only be achieved by the defeat of the old cultural system and its dialectical supersession by a new modern one. Azm took the first step in this intellectual battle with his *Naqd al-Fikr al-Dini* (Critique of Religious Thought) published in 1969.

Returning to the defeat of 1967, Azm insisted that the only strategy that could secure victory for the Arabs was a popular war of national liberation on the model of Vietnam. The Arabs could not defeat Israel in conventional warfare because the Unites States had pledged that the Israeli army would not be defeated on the battlefield. But a war of national liberation on the Vietnamese model even the Americans could not thwart. For this purpose it was essential that "we transform the Arab countries surrounding Palestine to a North Vietnam: countries that participate in fighting, struggling, organizing, supporting, sacrificing, supplying, etc." (Azm 1969, 96). What was needed was an Arab Hanoi. Such a war would not only address the Arab need to regain the military initiative and liberate Palestine but would also provide the revolutionary intensity and focus for the cultural and ideological transformation of the Arab mind.

A people's war (as the 20th century history of such wars has shown us) helps weaken the traditional institutions and beliefs and participates in recreating the society along modern lines. . . . The direct and indirect participation of the individual in the resistance and in the popular war effort leads necessarily to a broadening of his horizons to absorb the existence of his fatherland and his nation and not just the existence of his clan and family. It also evokes in him a sense of his integral role in the national effort and national structures, and it inculcates in him the values of discipline, order, and appreciation of work and time and other such general considerations that are necessary in the establishment of a modern socialist state. (Azm 1969, 103–4)

Modern and traditional society and culture were irreconcilably opposed; the means for doing away with one and getting to work on erecting the other for the Arab world was through a popular war of national liberation.

In general, as can be readily surmised, Azm's position did not differ much from that of the Popular Front organizations. He shared their attitudes toward the Arab nationalist regimes: that they played a significant progressive role but that their petty bourgeois status prevented them from going further. He shared the Marxist-Leninist analysis of Arab society and politics, and he shared the commitment to a popular war of national liberation that would not only gain victory over Israel but also educate and discipline the nation. Indeed, Azm wrote on the new Marxist trends within the Palestinian resistance movement and welcomed their emergence (*Dirasat Yasariyya Hawl al-Qadiyya al-Filistiniyya* [Leftist Studies on the Palestinian Issue], Beirut, 1970). He argued that they arose in contradiction to the petty bourgeois regimes of the so-called progressive Arab countries; he warned that if these regimes were able to contain these revolutionary elements in the Palestinian resistance, then the Arab revolution would be defeated, for it was only through the vehicle of an ongoing popular war that the national revolution could take place (Azm 1970, 214).

The Social Dynamics and Appeal of the New Left

The New Left was a relatively small political movement confined to a number of tightly knit organizations; the intellectual trends that it represented, however, were more widely spread. In class terms, it appealed most directly to intellectuals and students of the middle class. What it offered was a reinterpretation of Arab nationalism (the central ideology of this middle class since the 1950s) based on radical Marxist categories. It appealed to intellectuals and students because it provided a highly intellectualized explanation of the defeat and showed what needed to be done to redress it. All in all, it promised to salvage Arab nationalism from the disappointments of the 1960s and give it renewed vigor and direction. The ideology of the New Left was also attractive to lower-class members of the Palestinian refugee population because it emphasized a commitment to a people's war of liberation against Israel. Thus, it gave members of the refugee population a central and dignified role in the nationalist program and a means of escape from the miserable conditions in which they lived. From the perspective of minority groups, it is noticeable that members of the Christian minorities were overrepresented in the movement. In many ways, it provided the only viable alternative for non-Muslims to the Islamic movement, which began to gain ground after 1967 as one of the principal responses to the bankruptcy of Arab nationalism. From the perspective of intergenerational opposition, the movement, like most ideological movements, was an overwhelmingly youth movement reflecting a hostility to the objectives and methods of the older Arab nationalist generation of the 1950s and 1960s. Finally, from the perspective of crises, the movement was clearly set in motion by the multiple crises of the collapse of the UAR, the splintering of the Ba'th, the near collapse of the Egyptian economy, the inconclusive Yemen War, and the abject defeat of 1967.

In the appeal of the New Left's ideology within the psychological categories discussed in chapter 1, several elements can be noticed. It offered class as a renewed source of positive identity within Arab nationalism after the Arab nationalist formulations that had emphasized social solidarity were discredited. This gave Arab nationalism new impetus, much as the formulations of the Ba'th had given Arab nationalism a new impetus after the defeat of 1948. It offered highly intellectualized theories of class struggle, revolution, and total war to treat the intellectual confusion that had set in after the defeat. Moreover, it put forward revolution and a people's war as moral imperatives to be engaged in totally. Finally, it provided ready and recognizable targets for the displacement of aggression in the petty bourgeois regimes that were stifling the development of the Arab nation and in the capitalist and imperialist powers that supposedly supported them. More importantly, perhaps, inspired by the Vietnamese and other models, it legitimized a new level in the use of violence for political ends both within Arab society and internationally. The New Left proclaimed the equivalent of total revolution and total war, and in such conflicts there were no rules or limits on the use of force. This, of course, provided some of the ideological foundations for the use of terrorism, which, in itself, is one of the most bitterly eloquent expressions of aggression.

The Legacy of the New Left

The legacy of the New Left is rather limited because the movement itself was of limited duration and scope. Although triggered by the

Arab defeat of 1967, it was also overtaken by the 1973 war in which the relatively conservative regimes of Sadat and Asad scored significant, if limited, victories. The victory of 1973 undermined the assumptions of the New Left about the hopeless weakness of traditional Arab nationalist regimes and even legitimized the authority of the "reactionary" Saudi regime that played a central role in the conflict through its oil embargo. The orientation of the New Left was also undermined by the accommodationist turn of regional politics after the war as both Syria and Egypt signed firm disengagement agreements and the latter pursued full peace with Israel. Within the Palestinian nationalist movement itself, the 1973 war marked the start of the PLO's long journey toward accepting and negotiating with Israel. The New Left lingered on in the Palestinian Popular Front organizations, which now abandoned most of their Arab orientation and concentrated on holding the militant leftist line within the increasingly moderate Palestinian nationalist movement.

Nevertheless, a distinct legacy of the movement can be discerned in the trends and characteristics of Arab political life in subsequent years. First, the ideological animation that they exhibited represented the final stage of the middle class's dependent association with ideology. In a sense, it signaled the end of the age of ideology for the middle class. With the decline of the New Left after 1973, no ideological movement arose to replace it within the dominant middle-class. The Islamic fundamentalist movements that grew throughout the 1970s and 1980s remained (except in Syria where there is a complicating sectarian variable) non-middle-class movements that sought to challenge that dominant middle class and its political and cultural power but, so far, with little success. The middle class itself remained true to its secular Arab nationalist origins, but its politics turned from the ideological to the pragmatic. This is not surprising; ideologies and ideological movements arise to provide guidance and psychological refuge in times of rapid and profound social change (see chap. 1). The middle class that rose turbulently to political center stage in the 1950s, however, has been more or less stably ensconced in that position since that time. No class since then has had the size and power to threaten its central position in society. Such stability and security gradually reduced its need for ideology whether as a political tool to fight for its dominant position or as a psychological crutch to escape from painful and confusing flux.

The New Left hastened the demise of ideological politics within the middle class, however, because it reinterpreted Arab nationalist ideology—the ideology of that middle class—in radical revolutionary ways that ran directly against that class's material and political interests. It reinterpreted Arab nationalism to mean a revolution against the middle class and a destruction of the political and economic institutions on which it thrived. In a sense, by hijacking Arab nationalist ideology and threatening the middle class with it, the New Left sealed that class's growing disillusionment and mistrust of ideological politics.

Within the Palestinian nationalist movement, its influence was slightly more long lived. Most importantly, it played a significant role within the PLO, which, after all, endeavored to be an umbrella organization for all Palestinian organizations and tendencies. Specifically, it was largely responsible for impeding the PLO's gradual drift toward accommodation. Providing the main opposition to the leadership of Yasir Arafat and Fateh, it preserved the PLO's commitment to confrontation with Israel well into the 1980s. Of course, the PLO finally broke away from the influence of the Popular Fronts in the late 1980s after its eviction from Lebanon in 1982–83 and the eruption of the *intifada* in the West Bank and Gaza in December of 1987. Several of the Popular Front organizations endure today under Syrian sponsorship in Lebanon and Syria although after Syria's confrontations with the PLO in Lebanon, first in 1976, then again in 1983 and, finally, in the bloody battles between PLO fighters and Syrian-backed Amal militiamen in 1986–87, association with the Syrian regime has greatly weakened these organizations' appeal among Palestinian audiences.

CHAPTER FIVE

Regional Nationalism

The Egyptian, Lebanese, and Syrian Cases

Egyptian Nationalism

The Formative Decades: ᶜUrabi, Kamil, and Zaghlul

The idea of Egyptian nationalism took root in Egypt in the late-nineteenth century. Aided by factors of geography and history and championed by able advocates, the idea was elaborated in the twentieth century to a rather sophisticated concept of the Egyptian nation: its history, its relations with the Arab and Islamic worlds, and its internal organization. Its foremost theorist was Ahmad Lutfi al-Sayyid (1872–1960). His fusion of Islamic modernism with Egyptian nationalism in favor of a liberal constitutional nationalist ideology dominated the thinking of the Egyptian ruling class in the interwar period. The tribulations of World War II, the shock of the loss of Palestine, and a perception of ruling class corruption discredited both this Egyptian ruling class and its regional nationalist ideology. Egyptian nationalism gave way to revolutionary Arab nationalism in the 1950s and 1960s and then to radical Islam in the 1970s and 1980s.

The first stirrings of modern Egyptian nationalism can be traced back to the shock of the Napoleonic invasion of 1798 and the encounter with European culture and power. The brief French invasion led to the collapse of the Mameluke state and the reestablishment of political authority under the rule of Muhammad Ali, an Ottoman officer of Albanian origin. He was impressed by the learning and technology of the French and set Egypt on a course of economic and political development. Despite the highly autocratic nature of his rule and his foreign roots, the economic and political institutions that he developed, such as banks, factories, a state army, and a government bureaucracy, provided an institutional focus for nascent sentiments of patriotism and national loyalty (Vatikiotis 1985, 49–52). Furthermore, he excited nationalist sentiment by asserting Egypt's power vis à vis Istanbul and cutting an imposing figure in regional and international politics. Despite the ultimate failure of his economic and military programs, his efforts provided an example and promise for future generations of Egyptians.

More importantly, however, the students he sent to Europe on educational missions to absorb the technical and scientific learning of Europe, such as Tahtawi and others, returned to Egypt with a host of ideas pertaining to nationalism and the philosophy of politics (Hourani 1970, 69). These returnees founded schools, which, in turn, produced a class of bureaucrats, officers, and civil servants independent of the traditional *ulama*-dominated Islamic educational system and immersed in the ideas of European nationalism and constitutional liberalism. This new intelligentsia rose to positions of responsibility in the Egyptian state and served as the key audience for the ideology of Egyptian nationalism that began to take shape in the late decades of the nineteenth century.

A nascent free press played the central role in articulating and disseminating the first formulations of Egyptian nationalism. The earliest newspapers in Egypt were founded primarily by Christian Lebanese immigrants fleeing the turmoil of the Lebanese emirate in the middle of the century. Unattached to the Ottoman or Islamic vision of political community and enjoying older relations with European culture, these Christians were easily attracted to secular nationalist principles. Because they were not native Egyptians, however, their patriotism for Egypt was not especially ardent.

In the 1870s, however, an indigenous nationalist movement emerged among the intelligentsia of Egypt to articulate dissatisfaction with the autocracy of the Khedive, the conservatism of the *ulama*, European domination, and the generally backward conditions of the populace. In 1877, an Egyptian newspaper called *al-Watan* (The

Fatherland) was established; in 1879, the *al-Hizb al-Watani* (the National Party), composed mainly of Egyptian military officers, was formed. In 1882, one of these officers, Ahmad ʿUrabi Pasha, led a revolt against the Khedive and the increasing British influence under the slogan "Egypt for the Egyptians." Abdallah al-Nadim, a gifted orator and the main spokesman for the ʿUrabi group, emphasized the need for national unity over and above Muslim-Coptic differences and decried foreign influence of all kinds whether it was European, Turkish, or Syrian-Lebanese. The ʿUrabi revolt was the first historical expression of modern Egyptian nationalism, and it left an indelible mark on the generation that witnessed it (see Safran 1961, 48–52). Nevertheless, the theory of Egyptian nationalism was still rather crude and undeveloped. Lacking serious theoretical foundations and unable to galvanize the support of a still largely apolitical population, the nationalist movement was easily contained by British forces that put an end to the revolt and moved in as the new de facto governors of Egypt.

The British occupation, however, also provided the conditions under which Egyptian nationalism could strike new roots and reach wider audiences. The British colonial occupation subjected Muslim and Christian Egyptians alike to roughly identical political conditions. This created a common pool of Egyptian grievances and aspirations, regardless of religious affiliation, that was unique in recent Egyptian history. Whereas under Islamic rule of successive regimes, political experience was largely determined by religious affiliation, with the Copts invariably at a disadvantage, British rule treated the native Egyptians first and foremost as Egyptians and imposed disadvantages on them primarily on that basis. This provided Muslims and Copts with common ground for the formation of a shared national identity and a common program of struggle and opposition. This experience, of course, was not unique to Egypt but also characterized the rapprochement of Christians and Muslims in the Arab East under various nationalist banners in opposition to European rule. Beyond providing Egyptians of both religious communities with a brief shared history, the relatively liberal policies of the British consul-general allowed and occasionally encouraged the development of an active press. The flourishing of journalism, especially as it moved from Lebanese into

Egyptian hands, played a central role in stimulating and shaping nationalist sentiment (Vatikiotis 1985, 179).

The man most responsible for fanning nationalist passions around the turn of the twentieth century, after the humiliation and disappointment of the British occupation, was Mustapha Kamil (see, e.g., Safran 1961, 89–90.). Born in 1874, Kamil received a modern education and graduated from a French law school in 1894. He had a charismatic personality and great oratorical talents. His activism and speeches gave momentum to a new nationalist movement that was the heartbeat of Egyptian politics for decades to come. Kamil demanded an end to British rule, a termination of the foreign capitulations system, and the institution of constitutional rule (al-Sayyid-Marsot 1977, 44).He founded *al-Liwa'* newspaper in 1900, which became the most prominent of its time and was the first entirely Egyptian-edited newspaper in Egypt (Vatikiotis 1985, 203–4). In 1907, he also cofounded the influential National Party, which would play a leading role in the struggle against the British. He died unexpectedly the following year.

In his brief decade of political activism, Kamil became a symbol of Egyptian defiance and a much adulated public leader. The populist style that he developed would become an attribute of Egyptian politics and would be reemployed in succeeding generations by Saᶜd Zaghlul and Gamal Abd al-Nasir. Kamil popularized a rudimentary concept of Egyptian nationalism that had become increasingly widespread among the European-influenced intelligentsia. He proclaimed that Egypt was a coherent and unified nation with roots in the ancient Pharaonic past, that it had a distinct history shaped by its particular geographic and climatic conditions and the specific history and genius of its people. Moreover, as it had proven from the very dawn of history, Egypt was capable of self-government. In his concern to rid Egypt of the British, Kamil sought French and Ottoman help and also the help of the Khedive himself. After his disappointment with France in the Fashoda incident of 1898 and the Anglo-French Agreement of 1904, he turned more earnestly toward Istanbul and often sang the praises of pan-Islamism and loyalty to the caliph. His political strategy and ambitions often introduced confusion and contradiction into his public positions. His attitude toward the distinction between secular and religious nationalism remained ambivalent and his program for the internal reform of Egyptian state and society remained unclear. Kamil was not primarily a thinker but a leader, an orator, and a politician. Kamil's role, however, in arousing national sentiment and establishing some fundamental pillars of its popular appeal was seminal for the success of Egyptian nationalism later.

The influx of great numbers of British troops into Egypt in World War I had a profound effect on the Egyptian population. Whereas before the war, British presence had been confined to a few regiments in a handful of key locations, the war turned Egypt into a British garrison and, thus, increased opportunities for friction between the British and the native population. The war also brought with it British promises of independence and Wilson's Fourteen Points that emphasized the right of self-determination of all peoples. At war's end, a number of leading Egyptians, including Ahmad Lutfi al-Sayyid, Saʿd Zaghlul, Abd al-ʿAziz Fahmi, Muhammad Mahmud, and Ali Shaʿrawi, all from prominent and wealthy families, formed a delegation (eventually known officially as al-Wafd [The Delegation]) to represent Egyptian national aspirations to the British at the European Peace Conference, but the Wafd found little responsiveness to its pleas among the Europeans. Opposition to British rule would still have to rely on domestic Egyptian support. When the British sent Zaghlul and several other of the Wafd leaders into exile in 1919, thinking to nip nationalist unrest in the bud, a wave of massive demonstrations broke out demanding a return of the Wafd and the end of British rule. The 1919 riots, or "revolution," as this period of unrest came to be known, engaged the population, both Muslim and Christian, to an extent well beyond that of the 1882 ʿUrabi revolt. It was a massive display of popular political participation that involved unprecedented numbers of Egyptians and that provided a popular base for the continuing struggle against the British (Safran 1961, 101). The British were forced to bring the Wafd leaders back and Zaghlul was quickly acclaimed as the hero of the revolution and the undisputed leader of the Egyptian nation. Under the leadership of Zaghlul, a one-time judge with religious training, the Wafd succeeded in negotiating with the British for independence (albeit with serious restrictions) in 1922 and for the establishment of a constitutional democratic govern-mental system in 1923. In these years, Zaghlul's predominance was unchallenged, and his name became almost synonymous with that of Egypt as captured in the popular rallying cry *kulluna Sa'd* (we are all Sa'd). The Wafd remained in or close to power throughout the inter-war period until the Free Officers coup of 1952. Under Nasir, Egyp-tian nationalism was soon replaced by Arab nationalism as the main ideology of the state. Revived somewhat by Sadat, especially as he began to move Egypt away from the Arab world and closer to the West, Egyptian nationalism today constitutes one of the main ele-ments of Egyptian political culture, sharing that arena with Arab nationalism and Islamic fundamentalism.

Although basically a movement led by the upper classes, the Egyp-tian nationalist movement, as embodied by the Wafd in the interwar period, enjoyed the support of large sections of the middle and lower classes. It mixed a romantic Pharaonic Egyptian nationalism with democratic political principles, and a laissez faire economic outlook with a relatively pro-Western foreign policy. But to understand the ideology of Egyptian nationalism one should turn to the thought of Ahmad Lutfi al-Sayyid, its main articulator.

The Ideology of Egyptian Nationalism:
The Contribution of Ahmad Lutfi al-Sayyid

Lutfi al-Sayyid was born in 1872 in lower Egypt to a wealthy land-owning family. He received religious elementary schooling but at thir-teen attended a modern private school in Cairo and then joined the School of Law (see Safran 1961, 90–93). He met the Islamic reformer and activist Jamal al-Din al-Afghani on a trip to Istanbul in 1893 and became a close friend of Muhammad Abduh in Switzerland during an extended stay there. In Geneva, also, he firmed up relationships with Mustapha Kamil and Sa'd Zaghlul, all members of Abduh's circle. Kamil's pro-Ottoman anti-British views strayed from those of his col-leagues, and in 1907, when he founded the National Party, Lutfi al-Sayyid declined to join and participated instead in founding the rival *Hizb al-Umma* (People's party), which took a more moderate and con-ciliatory stand toward the British. Lutfi became the secretary of the party and the editor of its newspaper, *al-Jarida,* for the seven years before the outbreak of the war. It was in the pages of this newspaper that Lutfi elaborated his views about Egyptian nationalism and Egyptian society and culture. In 1908, he helped found the Egyptian University and served as its director between 1924 and 1941 before joining the Egyptian Senate where he served until his retirement in 1952. He died in 1960. Through his copious written work, both in the form of journalistic essays and Arabic translations of Greek philosophic works, and through his influence in Egyptian higher education, Lutfi acquired the grateful title of *ustadh al-jil* (teacher of the generation).

The evolution of Lutfi's thought was strongly influenced by that of Muhammad Abduh. But as Lutfi's thought developed, what Lutfi borrowed most from Abduh was the latter's belief in the compatibility of Islam and reason and his commitment to gradualism in education and reform. He derived consolation from Abduh's views and took them to mean that Islam could be reinterpreted and marginalized. Indeed, Lutfi regarded Islam as constituting only one of several fundamental pillars of Egyptian society. Unlike for Abduh and Rashid Rida, Islam for Lutfi was not at the center of things but was just part of the social and cultural environment in which the individual developed. Despite an elementary religious education, Lutfi's exposure to Western education brought him under the influence of Plato, Aristotle, Locke, Rousseau, J. S. Mill, Darwin, Tolstoy, and others. He intended no refutation of Islam but relegated it to the realm of private worship and moral training similar to the place Christianity held in the West.

Most centrally, Lutfi's thought was shaped by the liberalism of John Locke, J. S. Mill, and the like. With Locke, he held that the individual's right to freedom of thought and speech, his right to equality before the law, and his right to private property were natural rights (*huquq tabi'iyyah*) (al-Sayyid 1937, 71). With Mill, however, he also believed that such individual liberties contributed to the greatest good of all. His adoption of both natural right and utilitarian theory betrays some intellectual eclecticism on his part but does not detract from his strong liberal commitment. In the political sphere, his philosophical liberalism dictated the limitation of government only to those spheres where its meddling was necessary and unavoidable, namely in the areas of defense, internal police, and the administration of justice (al-Sayyid 1937, 65). Government, to his mind, was an entity by nature hostile to the individual; any growth in its power was a direct loss of freedom for the individual (ibid.). The individual and the community—the latter represented in government through the majority—had naturally opposed interests (al-Sayyid 1965, 91). For individuals to develop in society, a compromise had to be struck between the interests of the individual and those of the community. That compromise was a limited government.

The creed of liberalism, or the creed of the liberals, demands that the community (in free countries) or the government (in Egypt) not be allowed to sacrifice the freedom of individuals and their interests for the freedom of the community or the government to act in public matters. This creed demands in essence that the government not have authority except in areas where necessity dictates its presence, as in the areas of police, justice, and national defense. In all other matters, authority should be left to private individuals and free associations. (al-Sayyid 1937, 65)

By limited government, Lutfi meant a constitutional government based on the legitimate rule of law and instituted as a parliamentary democracy with a largely titular monarch, somewhat on the contemporary British model. He campaigned loudly for the adoption of a modern liberal constitution for Egypt—something that was achieved, more or less, by the Wafd in 1923. "Our call for a constitution is not derived from a desire simply to imitate the civilized nations—it is not a luxury that we seek so we can boast and be proud, rather it is a necessity for progress and for security from tyranny" (al-Sayyid 1965, 99).

His concept of political community centered around the idea of the nation and, for his purposes, the Egyptian nation. Borrowing now from Aristotle rather than from the social contract theorists (Rousseau, Locke), Lutfi believed that the nation was a "natural entity" governed by "natural laws" (al-Sayyid 1946, 43–44). It was created by the same forces of geography and nature that created humans and because it was not created by humans, it, too, was born with a natural right to govern itself as it saw fit, and to be free from the enslavement of any other nation (al-Sayyid 1937, 74). The nation, he insisted, is distinct from the government, which is created by members of a nation for the purpose of government.

For Lutfi, the Egyptian nation is not a modern entity but a nation that was born in the distant Pharaonic past and has persisted, despite the vicissitudes of history, to the present day. "Our present nation is not distinct from our old nation for a nation is a unitary whole that does not admit of division or fragmentation. It is a nation whose social corpus was born on the day it established itself on this fatherland with its particular social order; it proceeded in its life from health to sickness, from sickness to health, till it developed to what it is today" (al-Sayyid 1965, 21). He acknowledges the many immigrations and emigrations in Egyptian history and the diversity of present-day Egyptians. But "none of us has doubts about our being a distinct nation. . . . We have a particular color, particular tendencies, and one common language. We have one religion for the majority and certain patterns in doing our work and virtually the same blood running through our veins. Our fatherland has natural boundaries that separate us from others. . . . We have an ancient history. . . . We are the Pharaohs of Egypt, the Arabs of Egypt, the Mamelukes and Turks of Egypt. We are the Egyptians!" (al-Sayyid 1965, 65)

Although he argues that nations are shaped by natural forces, he also holds that political communities are held together by common interests. "Both history and human nature teach us that nothing unites people but [common] interests, and if the interests of two people are at variance with one another, it is impossible for them to unite simply because of racial relationship or common religious belief" (al-Sayyid 1946, 99). According to Lutfi, a history of cohabitation in a common fatherland has produced in the Egyptians a set of common interests that constitutes the basis for their political community.

He rejected both pan-Arabism and pan-Islam as alternative formulations of political community. He denied that the various Arab or Islamic countries had significant shared interests and argued instead that they were in natural and necessary competition. With no common interests to bind them, Lutfi thought it foolish to assume that such various societies could be fused together on the flimsy basis of racial or cultural affinity. Furthermore, he considered Arabism to be a form of self-denial and self-loathing. "The Egyptian who claims to be above all an Arab or a Turk disdains his fatherland and his people, and he who disdains his own people disdains himself" (al-Sayyid 1965, 70).

In his critique of pan-Islam, he maintained that the political fragmentation of the Islamic world and the political unity between Muslim and Christian Egyptians proved that religion was no basis for political community. Lutfi did not address the issue of Islam being, unlike Christianity, explicitly concerned with organizing and regulating political life. He skirted this sensitive topic and made only occasional vague references to some of the liberal, just, and democratic aspects of the early Islamic period when the Community of the Faithful lived under the guidance of the Prophet and the Rightly Guided Caliphs. Lutfi went so far as to deny that a serious pan-Islamic movement existed. He claimed it was exaggerated by the British to weaken Egyptian nationalism and to scare the European powers into supporting British dominance in Egypt (al-Sayyid 1946, 101). He sought to defuse Islamic fanaticism in Egypt not only because he believed instead in the powers of reason and liberal government but also because he knew that the British used Islamic fanaticism as a pretext for prolonging their occupation and postponing independence.

All in all, his attitude toward Islam was far more radical than anything intended by Abduh. He agreed with Abduh that Islamic theology needed considerable reform to render it more compatible with the scientific and philosophic advances of the modern age. But unlike Abduh, he sought to divorce religion from government, withdraw it from the political sphere, and relegate it to the private realm. While Abduh saw a reformed Islam at the center of a vibrant and modern Islamic society, Lutfi saw Islam as only a marginal force in a generally secular society. Lutfi saw the attachment to a rigid and distorted understanding of religion as the cause of Egypt's backwardness and degradation. Hinting at Darwinism, Lutfi insisted that "there is nothing left for us, then, but to surrender the ideas and qualities which have caused our backwardness and to adopt change and evolution so that we may compete in the struggle of this civilized life" (al-Sayyid 1965, 75). He ridiculed the *ulama* class and blamed them for the stultification and decline of Islamic political life. He promoted the romantic image outlined by Afghani of an original Islamic community basking in the glory of equality, justice, democracy, and so on, but denied that Egypt or any other Islamic country could attempt to recreate that condition. The world was in constant flux. Those nations that did not successfully evolve would either be enslaved or simply disappear.

Like Abduh, he placed much faith in the power of education to create new generations and new social conditions. He devoted the largest part of his career to the reform and expansion of higher and lower education in Egypt, both as rector of the Egyptian University and as a man of letters. As a matter both of principle and utility, he insisted that educational institutions should be free from the control of the state and widely varied in their approaches. Freedom of inquiry and education was essential to the healthy evolution of society, and variety would allow citizens of different talents and abilities to realize their individual potential (al-Sayyid 1937, 76). Arabic was to be the language of education, with a strong effort to reconcile spoken and formal Arabic (al-Sayyid 1937, 123; Wendell 1972, 229). Religion—Islam for Muslims, and Christianity for Copts—was to provide the foundation for moral education in the first years of a child's schooling, giving way later to an education in the ethical philosophy of ancient Greece and modern Europe (Wendell 1972, 272–74). In all other matters, Egypt should import the learning and discoveries of Europe. Lutfi reassured his readers that such wholesale importation would not obliterate Egypt's character and identity because once imported into Egypt, all these innovations would "acquire our color,and adapt to our linguistic, religious and moral customs" (al-Sayyid 1965, 83).

Lutfi insisted that "progress is not achieved *except* through teaching and education" (al-Sayyid 1965, 56). By this, he partially meant the obvious—that general education would raise the standards of political, moral, and economic life. He also saw, however, an open and dynamic educational system as encouraging the emergence of an elite of educated and dedicated individuals that could serve as the nation's vanguard. What he seemed to favor—and this may show the influence of British Fabians—was the constitutionally legitimated rule of the most educated and virtuous people of the nation. He warned that the power or weakness of a nation did not derive from the size of its population—ancient Athens was a small entity, and the imperial nations of the contemporary world were considerably smaller than many of the nations they subjected—but that "power and glory is in the number of educated men with noble characters and productive minds" (al-Sayyid 1965, 76). This, of course, echoed Plato's views in the *Republic*, which Lutfi studied closely, and also reflected the spread of meritocratic thinking with the rise of the bureaucratic state in Europe in the nineteenth century and its export into the colonized world. It also accorded with an upper class's flattering view of its role in society.

Lutfi promoted the idea of an independent Egyptian nation, organized according to the principles of liberalism, governed democratically, and linked educationally and culturally to Europe. He was a gifted and intelligent writer, and his ideas gained wide currency among the Egyptian upper classes and large portions of the new intelligentsia.

The Appeal of Egyptian Nationalism

As with early Arab nationalism (see chapter 2), the psychological appeal of Egyptian nationalism as a source of relief from acute social and psychological strain was not great. Moreover, the class this conservative nationalist ideology appealed to, the Egyptian landowning and merchant upper class, like its sister class in Syria, did not suffer much from such strain. Ideology to them was more a direct expression of their material and political interests in the Marxist sense than a source of escape from psychological stress in the sense that Fromm, Geertz, Isaacs, or other Strain Theory protagonists might understand it.

Nevertheless, the ideology was not without its psychological appeal. This was especially true in the sphere of identity formulation where Egyptian nationalism could offer an alternative source of identity as Egypt turned away from its Arab and Islamic environments and oriented itself toward the West. It drew on elements of Egyptian history and facts of Egyptian political, social, economic, and cultural life to offer an Egyptian identity distinct from wider religious or cultural identities. This approach was attractive to those Muslim Egyptians who felt increasingly uncomfortable within their traditional religious-based identity patterns and those Copts and other minority members who sought to break out of the confines of their communal identities. Egyptianism, however, had little of the potential for deep spiritual intensity that Arabism or Islamism had because the latter two appealed indirectly or directly to Islamic symbols that, after all, had shaped Egyptian social consciousness over thirteen centuries.

In the sphere of moral guidance, Egyptian nationalism offered a liberal moral creed that raised more moral questions than it answered. For an individual facing conflicting moral imperatives and myriad urban temptations, Egyptian nationalism offered the disquieting freedom to choose freely among them. As moral confusion grew increasingly intense, the liberalism of Egyptian nationalism would become increasingly intolerable. While revolutionary Arab nationalism succeeded in eliminating the burden of liberalism from the political sphere, it did not do away with it in the moral sphere. Islamism finally managed to relieve the individual of the burden of liberalism both in the political and moral spheres.

In the intellectual sphere, Egyptian nationalism fared little better, for it did not claim to provide a comprehensive explanation of social reality as did Marxism, revolutionary Arab nationalism, and, to some extent, Islam. Its basic attitude toward grand social and historicist theories was one of skepticism. What it did provide was an explanation of society as a system of rights and duties in which individuals associated and competed freely for the promotion of their individual and common interests. For the confused individual, Egyptian nationalism had little to offer in convenient ideological simplifications of complex social realities. It left the task of understanding society up to individuals through the use of their own faculties and experience. This was a heavy intellectual load that could not be borne easily as the social and cultural environment became more and more baffling. Arab socialism and Islam both relieved this intellectual burden by providing dogmatic versions of reality.

Finally, in the category of aggression release, the farthest Egyptian nationalism got toward helping vent popular aggression was in opposing the British, especially in 1919. But even in doing so, the nationalist leaders posited only limited opposition. They encouraged no deep hostility or enmity toward Britain and the West on cultural or moral grounds. Their opposition was almost exclusively political and, as such, quite sterile and psychologically unrewarding. They opposed British domination—and even that not all of the time—but proposed to build Egypt along British lines and with British help and friendship. In short, they did not depict an enemy despicable enough to serve as a useful target of frustration and aggression.

Liberal Egyptian nationalism was not equipped to serve very effectively as a source of relief from acute social psychological strain. If

Egyptian nationalism had that liability, then how was it able to gain the widespread appeal that it did? The answer to this question lies in examining the groups to which this ideology appealed and the time period in which it was popular. It consistently appealed to the landed and merchant upper class, and it was popular in the early decades of the twentieth century when the processes of urbanization, modernization, and Westernization had not yet transformed the Egyptian social landscape to the extent they would in later decades.

Members of the land owning and merchant upper class were, as is common for that class, in a rather secure frame of mind. As members of traditionally prominent families who enjoyed positions of power in society, these people were not going through acute identity, moral, or intellectual crises. They knew who they were and understood their place and role in society. Consequently, also, they did not suffer from high levels of frustration that would require some channel of aggressive release. All in all, this was not a particularly "ideological" class in the sense that, unlike the middle-class groups that formed the recruiting pool for the highly ideological Marxist, Arab nationalist, and Islamic movements of the 1950s and 1960s, this comfortable upper class was fairly well adjusted to its political, social, and cultural position. Properly speaking, this upper class related to Egyptian nationalism more as a set of tenets and beliefs consciously adopted than an ideological system of doctrines and dogmas emotionally embraced.

In the wider population, the need for ideological relief from psychological strain had not yet reached the high levels it would achieve in the decades after World War II. The processes of development had not yet transformed Arab society to the extent they would in a few decades. Signs of anomie and social psychological strain were beginning to emerge but had not yet reached a critical pitch. Furthermore, cultural Westernization was still confined to a small portion of the population; it had not yet broken into the mass of the society as it would in later decades. Although the seeds of change had already been sown, the institutions of a traditional society still organized and regulated the lives of the majority.

Nevertheless, the content of Egyptian nationalism did reflect the interests of the dominant upper class. An emphasis on Egyptian nationalism in contrast to Arab or Islamic nationalism and an orientation toward the Mediterranean and Europe reflected this class's Western orientation both in their material interests and their political alliances. Laissez faire economics favored their capitalist business interests, and liberal politics protected them as a class from domination by the Khedive or the British colonial power. Their secularism reflected their competition for power with the traditional *ulama* class as well as the multisectarian makeup of the class itself, which was only partially Sunni.

The Social Dynamics of Egyptian Nationalism

The upper class, composed of the land owning and merchant bourgeoisie, provided the most important audience for Egyptian nationalism. From the late nineteenth century, this increasingly assertive class was engaged in a struggle for power with the monarchy and the *ulama* and, after 1882, with the British as well. As in Europe, the Egyptian "third estate" gravitated to the idea of republican nationalism as a means of translating its economic power into legitimate political power. Owning much of the land and resources of the country, this class naturally felt a right to share in the governance of the country. For the upper class, therefore, the idea of secular parliamentarian Egyptian nationalism accorded well with their political interests. As mentioned, nationalism would justify weakening the British; parliamentarianism would justify weakening the king; and secularism would help weaken the *ulama*.

It is important to note, however, when discussing the class basis for Egyptian nationalism, that the movement also enjoyed the support of a large portion of the new professional middle class. This group, composed of journalists, bureaucrats, officers, teachers, and university students, had not yet achieved the size and ambition that would make it part of a politically independent middle class after World War II. Nevertheless, it sought a political voice and role for itself even if in the shadow of the upper class. The interest of this rising intelligentsia in Egyptian nationalism derived from the fact that Egyptian nationalism seemed to follow logically from the secularist Western political outlook that they had imbibed in private and public nonreligious schools and come to admire. Because Egypt was a political community with a long history and clear boundaries, it surely deserved independent statehood. In addition, from their perspective, republicanism would challenge the dominance of the king, and nationalism would challenge the power of the colonial powers, all of which would allow them a larger role in the political system through the avenues of a national parliament, a free press, a meritocratic bureaucracy, and so on. In terms of political identity, encouraging the idea of Egyptian nationalism provided this new secular intelligentsia with an alternative to the traditional heavily Islamic social identity with which they no longer felt comfortable.

From the perspective of minorities, Egyptian nationalism served as an agent for the integration of many non-Sunni and non-Arab elements into the Egyptian power structure. It emphasized characteristics common to all Egyptians and avoided definitions of nationalism based on language (as in Arab nationalism) or religion (as in Islamic nationalism). This was of critical significance to large sections of the upper bourgeoisie and intelligentsia who were either non-Muslim (Lebanese and Syrian Christians) or non-Arab (Greeks, Armenians, and European Jews). Egyptian nationalism was, thus, in large measure, a vehicle for these members of minority groups, who had already achieved considerable economic and cultural prominence, to gain political power as well.

A look at the role of generations in the rise and decline of Egyptian nationalism is also fruitful. As an inherently anti–status quo group, youth is almost always on the side of challengers to established authority. And, to be sure, the young generation of the 1910s and 1920s enthusiastically supported the upper class and intelligentsia against the king and the British. Predictably, though, they also supported the Arab nationalist middle class against the upper class in the 1950s and the radical Islamic lower middle class against the middle class in the 1970s. To talk of generations, however, is not simply to talk of the rebellious posture of almost all youth movements in crowded societies, for the political, social, and cultural environment in which each generation matures also affects its political outlook. The generation that came to political maturity before World War I had not been exposed much to Arabism, for the eastern Arab provinces were still under Ottoman control, and Egypt's political and economic circumstances differed markedly from theirs. With the collapse of the Ottoman empire, however, the extension of the British and French mandates over eastern Arab lands, and the growth of Zionist activity in Palestine, a new generation of Egyptians came to maturity with a consciousness of a set of common concerns and conditions that created a bond between them and other Arabs in the East. The shared experience of Western colonialism and the common opposition to Zionist encroachment on Arab-Muslim land served as a basis for a broadening of political and social horizons beyond Egypt proper. This variation in generational experience sheds light on the decline of Egyptian nationalism and the rise of both pan-Arab and pan-Islamic movements.

The Legacy of Egyptian Nationalism

The period in which Egyptian nationalism dominated Egyptian politics provided one of the rare examples of constitutional parliamentary government in the Arab world. Given Egypt's centrality in the Arab world, this experiment left an important imprint throughout the region, even though it was eventually overtaken by more authoritarian forms. It provided an example, of sorts, of democratic elections, multiparty politics, the parliamentary process, power sharing, and the rule of law. Although such examples could be observed in the West, the Egyptian experiment proved that constitutional parliamentary politics were relevant and workable in the Arab and Islamic worlds. Similarly, the Egyptian experiment had an important role in spreading the general philosophy of liberalism that accompanied constitutional government. Throughout those years, a vigorous Egyptian intelligentsia adopted and disseminated a long list of liberal principles that would henceforth become part of the intellectual baggage of the Arab educated class. What is important about the role of these Egyptians is not that they made any original contributions to liberal democratic thought but that they Arabized it in tone and nuance to render it more digestible in the Arab world.

The weakness of Egyptian liberalism was that it ended up associating liberalism and democratic politics too closely with the upper class. Henceforth, the concept of a parliament would be synonymous with a club for the privileged classes in which the middle or lower classes could presumably have no role. Although this may have been a reasonable description of parliaments in turn-of-the-century Europe or inter-war Egypt, it is scarcely accurate as a description of contemporary parliaments almost all of which represent preponderantly middle-class interests. Furthermore, the inability of the liberal nationalist governments to respond to the accelerating developmental needs of the population gained parliamentary government a reputation for corrupt inefficiency. What perhaps hurt Egyptian nationalism most, however, was that no able successor to Kamil and Zaghlul was found to carry the system through the turbulent years of World War II and the loss of Palestine. Although a Nehru could have held the system together, men of lesser caliber were doomed to failure.

Lebanese Nationalism

Perhaps of all the ideologies in the Arab world, the ideology of Lebanese nationalism had the most difficult task. All societies are governed by a combination of consensus and coercion. In most of the Arab states, what was lost in consensus could be made up in coercion. In modern Lebanon, however, the balance of confessional communities preempted the possibility of coercion and staked everything on the promise of consensus. Because dictatorship was impossible, dialogue was necessary. If that dialogue broke down and consensus disappeared, anarchy, not autocracy, would ensue. Indeed, the collapse of the Lebanese political system in 1975 is not very different from the collapse of the political systems of Egypt, Syria, Iraq, and other Arab countries in the forties and fifties; the difference is that whereas authoritarian regimes could emerge there to manage political affairs even in the absence of consensus, the same could not happen in Lebanon. Lebanon, as it had been constituted since 1920, could only be governed through consensus; and until a new consensus was arrived at, the turmoil would continue.

Indeed, the appointed task of any ideology of Lebanese nationalism was a formidable one. That ideology would have to provide a basis for consensus for a new state, composed of several Christian and Muslim religious communities, at a time of great social and economic change, and in one of the most militarily turbulent regions in the world. It is not surprising that the efforts to create and maintain consensus broke down. Nevertheless, Lebanese nationalism, such as it is, succeeded in maintaining an open democratic political system for many years after most of the other political systems of the Arab world had collapsed and reemerged as military or one-party dictatorships.

The History of Lebanese Nationalism

The emergence of a political framework for a Lebanese identity can be traced back to the sixteenth century when a Druze emir, Fakhr al-Din II, united Mount Lebanon and significant portions of the coastal and inner plains under his control. The emirate was perpetuated by a succession of Druze Maʿanid emirs and then revived at the end of the seventeenth century by a dynasty of Sunni-turned-Maronite Shihabi emirs until its dismantlement in 1840. The Ottomans recognized the special privileges of this emirate and the Maronite, Druze, and other smaller communities that lived within its boundaries shared a political and economic existence separate from that of the Syrian hinterland and the Ottoman-administered coastal areas. The relative stability and prosperity of the Shihab emirate (1697–1840) attracted increasing numbers of Christians who moved from the north to take advantage of economic opportunities on the estates of Druze feudal landlords (Hourani 1970, 63).

In the early decades of the nineteenth century, the ambitious Shihab emir, Bashir II, tried to expand his power and curtail feudal prerogatives partially through an alliance with the new Christian middle class and smallholder peasantry that had prospered in the manufacture and commerce of silk (Salibi 1971, 77). This particularly aggravated Druze feudal lords who perceived Bashir's policies as encouraging a creeping Christian Maronite domination of their traditional patrimony on that portion of the mountain that had been officially recognized since the thirteenth century. Emir Bashir's downfall came about in 1840 after the forced retreat from Syria of Muhammad Ali's Egyptian army on whose alliance Bashir had relied. In 1841, Druze and Christian feudal lords, with support from the Ottomans and the British, dismantled the emirate and ushered in a turbulent two decades of sectarian division and tension under the double *qaʾimmaqamiyyah* system, which carved the emirate into two areas of Druze and Maronite control. This system collapsed in 1860 in the wake of violent clashes between Christians

and Druzes in which the latter got the upper hand and left an estimated ten thousand dead and one hundred thousand homeless (Zamir
1985, 8). Attacks on Christians also erupted simultaneously in Damascus. The tragic events of 1860 gave new credence to demands for an
autonomous Maronite entity that the Maronite church had been calling for since the collapse of the emirate in 1840.

The interconfessional strife of 1860 attracted European attention.
French troops landed in the Christian port town of Jounieh, and an
international commission was set up in Beirut to devise a solution to
the Lebanese problem. The result was the Règlement Organique of
1861, which established Mount Lebanon plus the coastal strips between Sidon and Beirut and between Beirut and Tripoli (excluding
the large Sunni cities) as an autonomous Ottoman sanjak ruled by a
non-Lebanese Christian Ottoman governor. The special status of this
autonomous province, *mutasarrifiyyah,* was to be guaranteed by the
European members of the commission. France, a traditional patron of
the Catholic Maronites, took the lead in negotiating the Règlement. It
regarded the new Lebanese province as a safe haven for Christians of
the East as well as a base for the extension of its influence into other
areas of the declining Ottoman empire.

With the mutasarrifiyyah, Lebanese nationalism acquired its first
concrete legal referent. To be Lebanese was to be a citizen of the Lebanese mutasarrifiyyah. Furthermore, the economic prosperity of the
province and its educational and cultural advancement owing to the
enlightened rule of a succession of governors and the vigorous activity of Western mission schools and colleges made the Lebanese
sanjak one of the foremost Ottoman provinces and inculcated in its
citizens a sense of pride and distinction. The Lebanese mutasarrifiyyah had its own administration, a French-trained militia, and an
advisory Administrative Council made up of twelve members elected
by the shaykhs of the various villages and representing all the sects of
the mountain. Furthermore, the inhabitants enjoyed tax privileges
and exemption from military service.

Despite the obvious advantages offered by the Règlement, the new
system came in for considerable criticism from the Maronite church
and some other Maronite circles who had already begun to read
much more into the idea of Lebanese nationalism. They complained

that the new system fell far short of true autonomy and that the boundaries of the mutasarrifiyyah were much narrower than the "natural and historic" boundaries of Lebanon as it had emerged since the sixteenth century. Some among them also complained that the decision not to allow a Shihabi Maronite as governor compromised Maronite authority over what many among them essentially considered a Maronite and Christian homeland. Nevertheless, the mutasarrifiyyah proved to be a relative success and the experience of pluralism and confessional bargaining would serve as the political cornerstone for the Greater Lebanon that was established in 1920.

As the turn of the twentieth century approached, dissatisfaction with the Lebanese province's narrow boundaries intensified. In 1860–61, the Europeans had favored a small Lebanon to ensure an overwhelming Christian majority and avoid the possibility of confessional strife; for their part, the Ottomans had been intent on limiting the province's expanse to lose as little tax revenue as possible (Zamir 1985, 12). As a result, the mutasarrifiyyah was narrower than the traditional boundaries of the emirate had been and, according to many Lebanese activists of the time, rendered Lebanon a small and vulnerable entity. A movement began to emerge within the province and in the emigrant community for the establishment of a larger state. The movement marshaled several arguments to its purpose. The historical argument was that Lebanon had traditional political boundaries that had been unjustly compromised in the Règlement Organique. The geographic argument was that Lebanon was a *natural* entity bounded by the Anti-Lebanon mountain range in the east, the Nahr al-Kabir in the north, the Litani River in the south, and the Mediterranean in the west. The economic argument was, perhaps, the most compelling, for it pointed out that the rugged and densely populated Lebanese mountain was isolated from the arable lands of the Biqaᶜ and Akkar regions and from the natural trading ports of the coast, especially Beirut. This had already led to large-scale emigration and economic stagnation and threatened more dire consequences in the future. The economic argument was advanced most forcefully by prominent Christian businesspeople who saw the province's economic limitations most clearly.

These demands for a larger Lebanon were, perhaps, best expressed by Bulus Nujaim, a Maronite lawyer who enjoyed close connections with both the political elite of the mutasarrifiyyah and the French government. In a book entitled *La question du Liban,* published in 1908 in Paris, under a pseudonym (M. Jouplain), Nujaim recounted the historical, natural, and economic arguments for the establishment of a *Grand Liban* and called on France, as the traditional protector of the Christians of Lebanon, to shoulder the responsibility for establishing that Greater Lebanon. As Meir Zamir points out, "Nujaim's formulation was to become the basis for Lebanese Christian arguments in favor of a Greater Lebanon" (Zamir 1985, 15). This Lebanese cause was taken up in the first two decades of the twentieth century by various Lebanese societies and committees both in Lebanon and among the diaspora community in Egypt, France, the United States, and South America. Among these were *al-Nahda al-Lubnaniyyah* (The Lebanese Awakening), the Alliance Libanaise, and the Comité Libanais of Paris. The latter was the most influential. It included Shukri Ghanem, K. T. Khairallah, and George Samné, who together also founded the Comité Central Syrien, which established close ties with France and played a central role in swinging French government and public opinion behind the idea of a Grand Liban in the crucial years after World War I (Zamir 1985, 23).

As the tragic events of 1860 formed the backdrop for the establishment of the mutasarrifiyyah in 1861, so the painful events of World War I formed the background for the establishment of Grand Liban in 1920. Many Maronites welcomed the outbreak of the war because they expected an Allied victory and occupation by France. Turkish suspicions of Christian sympathies and fear of a European landing in Lebanon with Christian collusion led Jamal Pasha to send his troops into Lebanon in violation of the Règlement Organique. By the summer of 1915, the Administrative Council had been dissolved, the Christian Ottoman governor had resigned, and a Muslim governor had been appointed in his place. Nothing remained of the Règlement Organique, and Mount Lebanon became an ordinary Ottoman province. The Turkish authorities also took over control of monasteries and other institutions under European control, attempted to oust the influential Maronite patriarch Huwayyik, and arrested or deported numerous other clergy. Most serious, however, was a devastating famine that killed approximately one-fifth of the population of the mountain. The famine, blamed by the local inhabitants on the Turkish authorities, seemed to prove the economic argument for the need for a Greater Lebanon, and provided enormous momentum for the achievement of that goal.

Although it was British troops that first occupied Lebanon during the war, it was France that, in accordance with the Anglo-French Sykes-Picot agreement of May 1916, was left in control of the area at the end of the war. The San Remo Conference in April 1920 granted official European recognition of a French mandate over Syria and Lebanon. In the two years leading up to the announcement by French High Commissioner General Gouraud of the establishment of Grand Liban on September 1, 1920, several political currents competed to influence the outcome of the French decision. On the one hand, the Maronite church with the overwhelming support of the Maronite and Greek Catholic communities and the Christians of the Diaspora demanded the establishment of a Greater Lebanon. On the other hand, King Faysal's Arab government in Damascus, with the overwhelming support of Sunnis, strongly opposed the project. In the middle were the Greek Orthodox, Druze, and Shiᶜa communities of the proposed Lebanon who were internally split on the issue although the Greek Orthodox tended to sympathize with the Maronites while the Druze and Shiᶜa tended more often toward Faysal's position.

The French themselves were undecided. Some among them hoped to gain stable French influence over all of Syria by appeasing Faysal and, thus, foregoing the Greater Lebanon idea in favor of a federation of Syria and a small Lebanon. Others believed that agreement with Faysal was impossible and sought to establish Greater Lebanon as a means of defeating him and weakening the Arab nationalist movement in general. Those who genuinely sympathized with the Maronites and the Christians were also divided. A majority accepted the Maronite church's arguments for the establishment of a Grand Liban while a minority believed that annexing largely Muslim areas to the predominantly Christian Mount Lebanon would only increase the insecurity of Lebanon's Christians. In the end, as it became clear that a deal with Faysal was impossible and as they were prodded by effective Lebanese lobbying efforts in Paris, the French government opted for the establishment of Greater Lebanon. The new boundaries of Lebanon added the plains of the Biqaᶜ and Akkar and the coastal cities of Tripoli, Beirut, Sidon, and Tripoli to the mountain.

Although the establishment of Greater Lebanon represented the triumph of Maronite Lebanese nationalist aspirations, in its consequences, it posed serious challenges to the Maronite nationalist idea. Ever since the early nineteenth century, the main outlines of nationalism among the Maronites had been quite simple and clear. They believed in their right as a national and religious community to a viable and secure homeland. Their strivings throughout the nineteenth century all tended in this direction. The movement was led by the church and, after the dismantling of the feudal system in 1840, gained the increasing support of an independent Maronite peasantry and middle-class. The emirate under Bashir II (1788–1840) and the mutasarrifiyyah both reflected the orientations of this Maronite nationalism because both comprised sizable Maronite majorities and were politically dominated by the Maronite community. With the establishment of Greater Lebanon, however, the old formulas would no longer work. In the new Lebanon, the Maronites were no longer the majority (58 percent in the mutasarrifiyyah, according to the 1911 census) but represented only the largest minority (32 percent according to the 1921 census). Even all the Christian communities taken together represented only a slight majority (55 percent) over the Muslim minority.

The thought of Maronite clerical and lay writers dating back to the late eighteenth century about a Maronite or even a Christian homeland no longer rang true in a state in which non-Christians made up almost half of the population. The arguments of Bulus Nujaim, although convincing in the prewar period, no longer addressed the challenges facing the new Lebanese state. Most importantly, how would the allegiance of the vast Muslim minority to the new Lebanese state be secured? This problem gave rise to a new current of thought within the Christian community, which sought to redefine Lebanese nationalism along all-inclusive secular and pluralist lines. Inspired by Egyptian nationalist formulations invoking Egypt's Pharaonic past and Mediterranean location, a group of Lebanese nationalist thinkers, led by Michel Chiha, a writer and banker, developed an ideology of Lebanese nationalism based on Lebanon's ancient Phoenician and

Mediterranean heritage and drawing on Lebanon's tradition of ethnic and confessional pluralism and coexistence. Lebanon was no longer exclusively a Christian homeland but a refuge for all minorities escaping persecution and authoritarian government in the region. It could no longer orient itself solely toward France and the West but must think of itself as somehow between East and West—a bridge and a meeting place of Western Christendom and Eastern Islam.

In contrast, other thinkers and leaders, such as George Samné and Emile Eddé, clung to the idea of a Christian Lebanon and concluded that the regions of the new Lebanon with a large Muslim majority had to be given up. If that were not possible, a close attachment to France had to be maintained to ensure the survival of a Christian Lebanese state despite the existence of a large and restless Muslim minority. These two strands of political thought were expressed in the political rivalry of Emile Eddé's National bloc and Bishara al-Khoury's Constitutional bloc. In the end, as French power collapsed in 1940 and Britain emerged with the upper hand in the region, Emile Eddé's pro-French policy lost its credibility and Bishara al-Khoury emerged with British support as the predominant Maronite leader. He fashioned a compromise, known subsequently as the National Pact, with his Sunni counterpart, Riad al-Solh, in which the Maronites would forsake French protection, the Sunnis would accept Lebanon's status as a sovereign and independent state, and power would be shared among the Maronites and the Sunnis and the other smaller communities. Lebanon was granted its independence by the British in 1943, and Bishara al-Khoury and Riad al-Solh became the first president and prime minister of the new republic. The secularist, pluralist, and neutralist vision of Lebanon had come out on top and served to define the framework of Lebanese politics in the three decades following independence before the collapse of the political system in 1975.

The Ideology of Lebanese Nationalism: The Nationalist Philosophy of Michel Chiha

A banker by profession, Michel Chiha, a Catholic Christian of Iraqi origin, played a central role in articulating the idea of a Lebanese nation. He wrote extensively on the subject, was a chief architect of the constitution of 1926, and had a broad influence on thinkers and politicians in the interwar and independence periods. In 1934, he founded the *Le Jour* newspaper, which served as a platform for his views and for the views of a number of his close relatives and friends. Many of them such as Bishara al-Khoury, Henri Pharaon, Salim and Philippe Takla, Habib Abi Chahla, and Charles Helou, would come to dominate the politics of the Lebanese state in its first decades of independence. Chiha's thought was also promoted and developed in the *Cénacle Libanais* (est. 1946), a grouping of young intellectuals led by Michel Asmar, who organized weekly lectures and discussion sessions among members of the intellectual, political, and economic elite.

Chiha based his Lebanese nationalism on the premise that the Lebanese nation had its roots in the dawn of recorded history in the community of traders and seafarers that came to inhabit the Lebanese shores of the eastern Mediterranean. This community had its ancient apex in the rise of Phoenicia as a leading commercial nation of the Mediterranean world, an imperial power rivaling Rome, and a cultural capital that gave the world its first alphabet. The glory of ancient Phoenicia served as the historical focal point for Lebanese nationalism and a symbol of its unity. In the words of the Lebanese poet, Charles Corm, who along with Saʿid ʿAql sought to express Chiha's nationalism in verse,

> If I remind my people of our Phoenician ancestors
> It is because we were at the beginning of history,
> Before becoming Muslims or Christians,
> But one people united in the same glory.
>
> (Corm 1964, 53)

Lebanon's long history, it was argued, was characterized by a continuous agitation of emigration, immigration, and conquest; emigration, because Lebanon was a small land and its active population always sought out the far corners of the globe; immigration, because Lebanon was a "refuge of the oppressed and banished" from all ages and empires; and conquest, because Lebanon was strategically located at the intersection of Asia, Africa, and Europe and straddled the passageway between East and West. In addition, Lebanon was in the Holy Land from which sprang the world's great religions and, hence, was also a spiritual center.

Throughout this great flux, the Lebanese nation maintained its distinctive identity by virtue of the particular factors of geography and climate that, for Chiha, constituted the primary determinants of national identity. Lebanon was not the nation of a particular race, for Chiha admitted that emigration and immigration had rendered Lebanese ethnography most indistinct; nor of a particular language, for over the centuries Lebanese had spoken several languages and usually spoke more than one language at any given time; but of a particular way of life, a particular history, and a particular relationship to the environment and the world.

Essentially, Lebanon was a Mediterranean nation. Its geography oriented it squarely toward that sea and its history had inextricably interwoven its destiny there. By virtue of the distinct climate and ecology of the Mediterranean, Lebanon had evolved differently from the nations of the steppe and the desert to its east and differently also from the nations of the cold climate and dark forests of northern Europe. It was an eastern Mediterranean nation that bore the closest similarity to the Egyptian, Syrian, and Greek nations that shared similar geography and history. More than any of these other nations, however, it served to link the civilizations of the various continents.

Of the many waves of conquest to which Lebanon was subjected, Chiha treated the Islamic and Crusader conquests with especial care. The Islamic conquest introduced a vast influx of Arabs and directly linked Lebanon to Arab and Islamic culture and civilization and to the fortunes of the Arab world. It also introduced religion rather than ethnicity or nationhood as the basis of political organization (Chiha 1949, 39). The Crusader conquests and Frankish rule, which lasted almost two centuries, also linked Lebanon racially and culturally with Europe at the beginning of the latter's long progress toward the Renaissance (Chiha 1949, 39). Lebanon, therefore, was of both East and West and was the capital of their interaction as civilizations, cultures, and religious and linguistic worlds. Indeed, Chiha often insisted that the Islamic world was itself, properly speaking, part of the Western world. He decried the artificial opposition posited between Europe and the Arab-Islamic world. The latter inhabited the entire southern littoral of the Mediterranean and, therefore, should consider itself closer to Mediterranean and European cultures than to the distant cultures of Asia and the Indian Ocean (Chiha 1950, 36). By claiming that Christianity and Islam were parts of the same Western civilization, he hoped to encourage Lebanese Muslim acceptance of political and cultural affiliation with Europe and to dampen general Arab hostility to the West of which Lebanon would necessarily be partially a victim. A meeting place of East and West, Lebanon could survive only if that meeting were relatively peaceful.

"Arab civilization," Chiha insisted, "was one of our mother civilizations" (Chiha 1962, 176). But its influence was not alone. It followed Greek, Roman, and Byzantine civilizations and "was followed by the civilizations of the Middle Ages, the Renaissance, and the civilization of Europe in modern times; all these have left their mark on our laws, rites, traditions, and our means of expression and living" (ibid.). Moreover, Arab civilization did not manifest itself similarly in different places. "Arab civilization is *our* civilization to a large extent. But life in Beirut, even in Damascus, differs from that in Riyadh, or in Jeddah, or in Sanʿa, Yemen" (ibid.).

Following this line of reasoning, he argued against Arab nationalism and Arab unity. He criticized those who promoted a nationalism based on an entire race or religiocultural group. This type of "gigantic" nationalism, maintained Chiha, was artificial and beyond the grasp of the individual (Chiha 1962, 165). True nationalism, he said, was based on loyalty to the people and fatherland that one knew and loved intimately. For him, Arab and Islamic nationalisms were misguided, dangerous, and doomed to failure. Furthermore, he felt that Lebanon and other countries of the Arabic-speaking world all had peculiar modes of political organization, ways of life, and interests. "Arab society on the shores of the Mediterranean does not evolve socially, intellectually and politically as it does on the shores of the Persian Gulf or in Hadramawt on the Indian Ocean" (Chiha 1962, 133). Furthermore, he argued, the history of the Umayyads, Abbasids, and Fatimids showed that attempts to bring different regions under central control only produced "a series of tragedies" (ibid.). He urged the Arabs to acknowledge their differences and to abandon the quest for unity in favor of cooperation and coordination based on the reality of a mixed bag of common and conflicting interests. Within the Arab world, Chiha was proud of the role Lebanon had played and would continue to play in Arab politics, economics, and culture.

Although part of the Orient, Lebanon's existence depended on a strong relationship with Europe and close friendship with it. Without Europe, Lebanon would not only be unable to survive politically as a small nation among larger ones but its very raison d'être as a meeting place of East and West and a link between Christendom and the Islamic world would be lost. Cut off from Europe, Lebanon would cease to be itself. In general, he felt secure in the belief that Europe had a natural interest in Lebanon. Because of Lebanon's strategic location at the intersection of three continents and between East and West, he surmised that "no world power could disinterest itself from our fate" (Chiha 1949, 11). Furthermore, "The high spiritual authorities [of Europe] . . . could not ignore us. They could not ignore our proximity to the Holy Lands. . . . We are bathed here in ancient history, in the history of religions, in divine history" (Chiha 1949, 52). The Great Powers of the world "cannot disinterest themselves from our fate, from the spiritual patrimony which we represent, without failing in their moral duty and their political ambitions" (Chiha 1949, 61).

Chiha interpreted the rise of Europe to world prominence in the centuries after the Renaissance favorably and saw in it good things for Lebanon. The division and warfare that devastated Europe in the twentieth century, however, caused him much concern. A divided Europe could not take its world predominance for granted. In a number of articles written toward the end of World War II, he urged the Europeans, especially the French and the British, to unite (Chiha 1950, 202). Unity would keep Europe strong, he argued, and a strong Europe was in Lebanon's interest. "We here in Lebanon are by choice and necessity the friends of the masters of the world; but in the interest of this Orient to which we belong, we are not disposed to resign ourselves to the decline of Europe" (ibid.). Indeed, Chiha criticized the British for promoting Arab unity when instead they should have been promoting European unity, for he insisted that there was more real diversity in the Arab world than there was in Europe.

In internal political affairs, Chiha advocated a liberal democratic political system based on the sharing of power among the principal confessional groups. He made no apologies for his advocacy of the institutionalization of confessionalism but insisted instead that

confessionalism in Lebanon, is the guarantee of equitable political and social representation for the associated minorities . . . a force for order and peace. . . . In spite of many errors and abuses, it is confessionalism that has taught tolerance to the Lebanese. . . . It is by no means prejudice that has created it but the necessity for recognizing parochialisms that cover as broad a range as do those among political parties. With time, these differences may blur and slowly disappear. For now, the purpose of Lebanon's existence lies in the confessionalism that characterizes it and manifests itself first in the arrangement of legislative power. (Chiha 1966, 303–6)

Chiha understood that Lebanon was a delicate and precarious political entity. According to him, however, this was not only the result of its multiconfessional makeup but also because Lebanon had always been subject to immigration and emigration and because Lebanon lay in a particularly volatile region of the Middle East. Furthermore, Lebanon was surrounded by neighbors who were jealous of its harmony and prosperity. For him, Lebanon's fragility stemmed from all these causes. And, in order to avoid a political or social collapse, Lebanon must take care to evolve slowly and gradually. "We must prefer slow profound evolution to revolution." Above all, he insisted, "Lebanon is not a country of coups d'état" (Chiha 1949, 64–65).

In the interest of gradual change, Chiha maintained that Lebanon should be constituted as a parliamentary democracy in which the various communities could preserve their own traditions and at the same time interact peacefully and productively together (Chiha 1949, 66). Great care should be taken in the formulation of laws to make sure that the interests or sensibilities of no community were compromised (Chiha 1949, 67). Surrounded by jealous neighbors, any Lebanese government should ensure that its population enjoyed ample liberties and privileges to dissuade any Lebanese from being "seduced" by neighboring countries (Chiha 1949, 68). In linguistic matters, Chiha defended polyglotism, arguing that Lebanese were accustomed to it and that their interests in the world required it (Chiha 1949, 55–56). In the economic sphere, Chiha advocated a free economy based largely on private initiative and open to the trade and commerce of the world. Lebanon had been this way since the time of the Phoenicians, he argued, and still needed to be so. A closed Lebanon would be weak and poor. The Lebanese people needed to roam the world free in order to ensure their prosperity and realize their mission in life.

Chiha insisted time and again that Lebanon was a special nation and, therefore, must be understood in special categories. If Lebanon did not exist so "marvelously," he mused, it would surely "be considered by the philosophers and pure reason to be an impossibility" (Chiha 1949, 51). But Lebanon did exist, he proclaimed, and its past and future had to be considered with more than the usual delicacy and insight. Employing one of his favorite analogies, Chiha posited that Lebanon, in political and institutional makeup, was most like Switzerland. "Lebanon is basically a beautiful and noble experiment in peaceful cohabitation of religions, of traditions, of races. It is a natural experiment, which history offers as a still more decisive demonstration than that of Switzerland in the heart of Europe" (Chiha 1966, 250).

Chiha developed a mental picture of Lebanon, rooted in ancient history, situated between the civilizations of Christendom and Islam, and characterized by confessional pluralism, polyglotism, democracy, and a laissez-faire economy. His thought dominated that of almost all later Lebanese nationalists and became part and parcel of Lebanese state ideology through the text of the constitution of 1926 of which he was the principle author, the National Pact of 1943 negotiated by his brother-in-law and the country's first president, Bishara al-Khoury, and the writings of a large group of his followers.

His thought, however, failed to reach effectively beyond the upper-class, merchant elite circles in which it was developed. It served as a valid framework for intellectual discourse but failed to develop any strong mass-based, ideological following. His political thought was effective as a means of compromise and consensus-building among established elites, but weak as a tool of popular mobilization in an era of growing mass politics. While Chiha's thought dominated the state and Beirut's economic elites, the rest of the population fell increasingly vulnerable either to the more militant Lebanese nationalism of the Phalange (Kataʾib) party or the radical Syrian nationalism of the Syrian Social Nationalist party, the Arab nationalism of the Baʿth and Abd al-Nasir, and the pseudosocialism of the Progressive

Socialist party, the Communist party, the Organization of Communist Labor, and other groups.

Although Chiha's version of Lebanese nationalism served to provide the ideological or intellectual foundations for more than three decades of peace, prosperity, and democratic liberalism (1943–75), his thought failed to stem the tide of competing leftist, Arab nationalist, even Palestinian nationalist ideologies nor to prevent the rise of a more militant and less-tolerant strand of Lebanese nationalism in the Kataʾib party. Tensions between all these ideologies contributed to the collapse of the political order in 1975.

The Lebanese war represented the triumph of the ideologies of militarism, and parochialism over Chiha's vision of pluralism, tolerance, and moderation. Throughout the war, militant versions of Lebanese nationalism, Arab nationalism, Palestinian nationalism, and, later, Islamic nationalism were honed and sharpened. In the end, however, no alternative was found to Chiha's multiconfessional liberal state: the Document of National Reconciliation negotiated and signed in Taif, Saudi Arabia, in 1989, which brought an end to the war, represented a ceremonious return to the National Pact of 1943 and the constitution of 1926, albeit with important but not systemic modifications. Whereas in other Arab states the breakdown of liberal nationalism led quickly to the consolidation of authoritarian one-party states, the breakdown of liberal nationalism in Lebanon led to anarchy and civil war, the only road of retreat from which was back along the path of liberal nationalism.

The Appeal of Lebanese Nationalism

It is clear that Lebanese nationalism was not an extensive ideology comparable with those of Marxism, Baʿthism, or Islam. It was a limited body of political ideas directed toward explicating the history of Lebanon and describing the place of the Lebanese citizen within that historical process. Nevertheless, it did claim to provide a sense of identity and community to individuals and give them a sense of place and purpose. As such, one may assess the viability of Lebanese nationalism within the psychological categories described in chapter 1.

From the perspective of identity, for the Maronites, the Lebanese identity was almost coterminous with their sectarian communal identities as their presence was quite definitely concentrated in Mount Lebanon. For them, therefore, a romanticized Lebanese identity took nothing away from their communal identity and only enriched it. For the Melchite (Greek Orthodox and Greek Catholic) Christians, however, who were dispersed throughout the towns of Lebanon and Syria, Lebanese nationalism cut across their communal identities. On the one hand, for those with family and other connections in Syria, Lebanese nationalism seemed a painful and illogical abrogation. On the other hand, Lebanese nationalism did provide Melchites in Lebanon with the opportunity to be part of a state in which other Christians, namely, the Maronites, played a leading role. This, of course, held a certain attraction for these communities that had previously been living under Islamic Ottoman rule. The Greek Catholics were particularly willing to go along with the political project of their fellow Maronite Catholics, whereas the Greek Orthodox were more wary of Catholic domination. The Druze and the Shiʿa shared the ambivalence of the Greek Orthodox toward Lebanese nationalism. On the one hand, it cut them off from other members of their communities in Syria; on the other hand, it offered them an alternative to Sunni domination. Unlike the Greek Orthodox, however, the Druzes and Shiʿa were hard pressed to accept fully a social and political identity that was articulated and championed primarily by Christians.

The Sunnis, of course, found little that was appealing in the idea of an independent Lebanon. It strongly cut across their communal identity and reduced them from the status of a dominant self-confident majority to an insecure minority. It cut them off from the Sunni hinterland in Syria and from other Sunni societies around the Arab world. Furthermore, they were not thrilled by the thesis that Lebanon was a refuge for the persecuted and the oppressed because they were the ones that were supposed to have carried out that persecution and oppression.

Only for the Maronites, Greek Catholics, and, eventually, many of the Greek Orthodox has Lebanese nationalism over the years provided a strong and sustaining sense of personality and identity. Although nearly all Druze, Shiʿa, and Sunni Lebanese in the 1990s, identify themselves quite plainly as Lebanese, Lebanese nationalism itself, as presented by Chiha and his followers, has not been enthusiastically embraced, and Lebanese nationalism has remained an unsatisfactory source of identity. Partly for this reason, sectarian identities remained central in Lebanon and helped unravel the Lebanese polity.

As a source of moral guidance, like Egyptian nationalism, Lebanese nationalism had a liberal outlook that provided more questions than answers at the moral level. It did not even have Egyptian nationalism's serious emphasis on ethics and good citizenship that Lutfi al-Sayyid wrote tirelessly about. Instead, it opted for a romanticization of the Phoenician and Mediterranean idea, which was of very little actual substance. In the intellectual sphere as well, Lebanese nationalism did not provide much framework within which to understand the modern social environment. While Arab nationalism invoked socialism, Islamists invoked Islam, and the Egyptian nationalists invoked a considerable tradition of Western natural law theory, liberalism, and the like, Lebanese nationalists insisted that Lebanon was sui generis and could be appreciated only in its own particular but undefined categories. In the category of aggression-release, Lebanese nationalism was a very unsatisfactory ideology. It professed kinship and friendship to both East and West. It provided no clear or present enemy. Thus, it provided no avenue for the displacement of aggression. This may help explain how such high levels of aggression came to be invested in and against rival sectarian communities. Lacking enemies without, the Lebanese turned to finding enemies within. With no one to hate collectively, they set about hating each other. Therefore, Lebanese nationalism, like Egyptian nationalism, could not function very well as a psychologically sustaining ideology for the majority of the Lebanese population. Not surprisingly, it gave way in various periods to other more effective ideologies.

The Social Dynamics of Lebanese Nationalism

In the rise and decline of Lebanese nationalism from the various sociological perspectives outlined in chapter 1, the perspectives of sectarian and class competition are especially relevant. From the perspective of sectarian competition, of course, the idea of an independent Lebanon emerged first among Maronites as a secure homeland for them and other Christians in the engulfing sea of Islam. It began essentially as the defensive reaction of an insecure minority. It gained adherents among the other Christian communities on similar grounds, as a secure land where Christians could live in freedom and dignity. Even among Druze and Shiʿa, this idea of Lebanon as a haven for persecuted religious minorities had some appeal. As discussed, only the Sunnis could not find this idea of "Lebanon as a haven for the oppressed" appealing because they were the ones who had allegedly carried out the oppression.

The perspective of class reveals other angles. As Salibi has argued (Salibi 1971), Lebanese nationalism received a great boost from among the Christian middle class that emerged after the dismantlement of the feudal system in 1840 and grew steadily throughout the nineteenth and twentieth centuries. This new middle class, increasingly centered in Beirut, no longer part of a feudal system and acquiring new material interests and intellectual outlooks, naturally sought some political entity and identity to call its own. It valued Lebanese autonomy and independence as a safeguard against political domination and a defense against economic control from the power centers first of Istanbul and then of Damascus. It appreciated a liberal polity and a laissez-faire economy as a means to its continued prosperity. Chiha's Phoenicianism, moreover, was a flattering identity. It glorified the Lebanese commercial middle classes by comparing them with the Phoenician traders of ancient times; it explained the condition of expatriate Lebanese in terms of the daring adventurism of the Phoenicians; it compared the advanced educational position of modern Lebanon with the central role of Phoenicia in developing and spreading the alphabet.

With reference to the role of crises in triggering particular ideological responses, the rise of Lebanese nationalism and the establishment of Greater Lebanon cannot be understood apart from the sectarian clashes of 1860 and the great famine of World War I. Similarly, the opposition to Lebanese nationalism was punctuated by several clashes, most notably the destruction of Faysal's Arab kingdom by the French in 1920 and the defeat of the Great Revolt, which began in 1925 in Syria and spread to many parts of Lebanon before its defeat by the French in 1927. Interestingly, the brief conflict of 1958 represented the last large-scale manifestation of resistance to the idea of an independent Lebanon because the Lebanese protagonists in the war that erupted in 1975 (excluding Palestinian and other foreign actors) all accepted the idea of an independent Lebanon even though they differed on the political and economic makeup of the Lebanese state and its military and foreign policies. Indeed, Lebanon's recent history has been shaped by crisis despite the stretches of peaceful and prosperous coexistence in between. As Arend Lijphart and other theorists of politics in plural societies point out, however, frequent crises are typical of multiconfessional and multiethnic societies, especially as they go through the turbulent process of modernization.

The variable of intergenerational opposition that proved useful in analyzing Arab nationalism and shed light on the rise of Communist and Islamic movements does not appear to be a very useful analytical tool in explaining the rise of Lebanese nationalism because it is greatly overshadowed and nearly cancelled out by the sectarian and class variables and by the traumatic crises through which Lebanon has passed since the mid-nineteenth century.

The Legacy of Lebanese Nationalism

On the bright side, Lebanese nationalism has succeeded in imbuing Lebanese political culture with the principles of liberalism, constitutional democracy, and power sharing. Although the democratic political system that was designed in 1926 and achieved independence in 1943 nearly collapsed in 1975, almost all parties to the conflict remained strongly committed, at least in principle, to a revived liberal democratic system—albeit reformed. Throughout all the discussions and negotiations about the reform of the Lebanese political system leading up to the Taif Agreement of 1989, the liberal democratic model was always the framework of debate. The only important exceptions to this were the radical Islamic groups, such as Hizballah, that emerged in Lebanon after the Iranian Revolution of 1979. These groups, however, many of whom called for the establishment of an Islamic state, still represented only minority views even within their own communities. The endurance of the idea of liberal democracy in Lebanon is not only important for Lebanon but also for the wider Arab world for whom Lebanon served as the disturbing counterexample to repressive authoritarianism for several decades.

On the negative side, however, the thought of Lebanese nationalism did not take the task of state building seriously. It regarded nationalism as a largely romantic and poetic affair having to do with historical and emotional issues and left aside a careful analysis of political and governmental affairs. Even in its political themes, those of power sharing, the articulators of Lebanese nationalism were more concerned with sharing power than with creating it. The main challenge of government in developing countries is to create enough political power to manage change and keep politics under control at a time of great social, economic, and cultural upheaval. Through the examples of strong one-party rule presented by European fascism and Soviet communism, the Arab nationalists had an answer to the problems of creating and consolidating political power. The Lebanese nationalists, like the Egyptian liberal nationalists who were their contemporaries, did not. The Lebanese state did not grow in power at a rate sufficient to keep up with galloping social and economic developments. In this sense, the Lebanese nationalists have left a legacy that is weak in addressing myriad social and political problems—problems that require active intervention by the government.

Furthermore, the architects of Lebanese nationalism did not adequately appreciate the complexities and pitfalls of politics in multiconfessional societies. They relied on the practice of traditional inter-elite bargaining that developed in the Lebanese mountain first within the emirate and then within the mutasarrifiyyah without elaborating a more comprehensive and flexible framework that could accommodate the rapid social and demographic flux that would necessarily accompany modernization. First, the traditional elites on whom this bargaining relied gradually lost their hold over an increasingly urbanized and politicized population. The modern political parties that emerged to capitalize on the increasing politicization of the populace were left out of the consensus-oriented political system dominated by the traditional elites and developed conflictual political styles destructive to consensual politics. Second, the balance of sectarian power that had been struck in 1943 was gradually undermined by diverging birth rates and emigration patterns among the various communities. Gradual allowances were not made for these demographic shifts. The result was an accumulation of grievances and a massive eruption in the 1970s.

Finally, the legacy that Lebanon's experience, in general, has left around the Arab world is a heightening of intersectarian tensions and a mistrust of open liberal political systems. The breakdown of peaceful sectarian coexistence in Lebanon coincided roughly with heightened conflict between Sunnis and Alawis in Syria, between Sunnis and Shiʿa in Iraq, and between Muslims and Copts in Egypt. Furthermore, the liberal political system was blamed by many around the Arab world as responsible for allowing the anarchy and political corruption that led to the destruction of the Lebanese polity and Lebanese society. Unfortunately, the collapse of Lebanon in 1975 seemed to reinforce a view, common in the tradition of Arab-Islamic political culture, that tyranny is preferable to anarchy. It is yet to be seen whether Lebanon's post-Taif order can prove that a golden mean between the two extremes is possible in the Arab World.

Syrian Nationalism

The movement of Syrian nationalism is inseparable from the political party that most forcefully proposed and promoted it, the Syrian Social Nationalist party (SSNP). The party was founded by Antun Saʿadeh, a Lebanese Greek Orthodox Christian, in the mid-1930s and had a seminal influence on a broad spectrum of intellectuals of the time. It also served as a model of sorts for the growth of other parties such as the Lebanese Kataʾib party and the Baʿth. Saʿadeh himself was an individual of exceptional "conviction, vigilance, strength of character, and charisma" (Khadduri 1970, 190). He dominated the party and cut an imposing figure on the political stage. In addition, as Daniel Pipes correctly emphasizes, his party "introduced a panoply of new ideas to the Middle East. These include the ideological party, complete political secularism, fascistic notions of leadership, and a dedication to pull down borders between states" (Pipes 1988, 320). Under various guises, most of these notions found their way into the body of radical Arab nationalism. The general notion of a Greater Syria, however, comprising present-day Syria, Lebanon, Palestine, and Jordan, predates the formation of the SSNP. It had its origins in French policy in the wake of World War I and was given a new lease on life after the eclipse of the SSNP by the Syrian wing of the Ba'th party, which made this notion of a Greater Syria a cornerstone of its foreign policy toward Lebanon, Jordan, and the Palestinians.

The History of the Idea of Syrian Nationalism

The name "Syria" appears in ancient Greco-Roman texts and was used throughout subsequent centuries to describe the territories of Damascus and the surrounding areas. The exact domain of the region described as Syria varied from period to period. The geographic notion of Syria, however, only began to acquire political significance with the arrival of Western ideas of territorial nationalism in the nineteenth century. The spirit of Islam and the ethos of the Arab tribes that spread it did not set much store in attachment to a particular piece of land or *patria;* loyalty was to the tribe or the Community of the Faithful (the *umma*). As ideas of Western territorial nationalism encouraged Egyptian nationalism in Egypt and Lebanese nationalism among the Maronites of Lebanon, however, they also gave rise to notions of Syrian nationalism among the Greek Orthodox and Greek Catholic Christians of the coastal and inner towns of Syria. The political significance of the name "Syria" was given an official push "after the Vilayet of Damascus was renamed the Vilayet of Syria in 1864, borrowing the name from European and Christian Arabic usage. To the Christians of the country, more particularly the Melchites (i.e., Greek Orthodox and Greek Catholics), the name had a special emotional appeal, because it denoted their historical diocese of Antioch" (Salibi 1988, 132).

In political terms, also, the idea of a Syrian nation was attractive to the Melchites who were scattered throughout geographical Syria. Lebanese nationalism would split their communities between Syria and Lebanon and bring those in Lebanon under the domination of the Maronites. Melchite sympathies for Syrian nationalism were echoed by some Druze and Protestant converts of the American Protestant missions because it provided them with an alternative to Maronite domination in an independent Lebanon and the domination of Sunni Muslims in a larger Islamic state. In addition, some Western-influenced Muslims also saw it as a natural expression of local patriotism similar to the patriotism that fueled Egyptian nationalism.

Despite the sympathetic attitude of members of several communities, the idea of Syrian nationalism did not have a strong and vociferous constituency similar to that of the Maronites for Lebanese nationalism. Unlike the Maronites, the Melchites of Lebanon and Syria were dispersed and had neither the cohesion nor the will to challenge the Ottoman status quo. Furthermore, Russia, which was the foremost patron of the Greek Orthodox community and would have had to play a central role in such a nationalist movement, was ambivalent about promoting Syrian nationalism because of the links between the idea of Syrian nationalism and French policy in the region. Beginning in the late nineteenth century, the French foreign office promoted Syrian as well as Lebanese nationalism as a means of separating these territories from other Arab and Muslim territories and carving out a sphere of French influence there. Russia was clearly opposed to such French ambitions.

Indeed, the theoretical framework for Syrian nationalism was first explored by French or French-educated writers. Bulus Nujaim, for example, the French-educated Lebanese author of *La question du Liban,* 1902, argued that Lebanon could only have a safe existence within the framework of a larger Syria. All of Syria, he insisted, should one day be autonomous and free. Two other Lebanese Christians, Shukri Ghanem and George Samné, with encouragement from the French government, expounded from Paris the idea of an independent Syria described as a secular and decentralized state. Like Nujaim, they saw Lebanon as enjoying a secure place only within an independent Syria (Hourani 1970, 286). They spoke of a common Syrian nationality based on shared elements of culture, language, and heritage.

The idea of a Syrian nation, however, found a fuller elaboration in the work of Henri Lammens (d. 1937). Lammens, a Jesuit priest of Flemish origin and a professor of Oriental Studies at the Jesuit Saint Joseph University in Beirut, published in 1921 an influential—if not entirely accurate—study of Syria entitled *La Syrie: Precis historique.* The book had an explicit political message and was written with the encouragement of the French government. The latter needed a cover for its policy of separating Lebanon and Syria from other Arab and Muslim lands and also needed an ideology to counter the rising tide of Arab nationalism that was supported openly by the British and more subtly by the American mission schools in the area.

In his interpretive account of Syrian history, Father Lammens argued that the Syrians existed historically as a people long before the advent of the Arabs and Islam. Syria, he wrote, was defined by the geographic barriers of the Taurus mountains to the north, the desert to the east and south, and the Mediterranean Sea to the west. The Syrians had deep roots in antiquity and played a leading role in Greco-Roman civilization. They were intellectually creative people with natural love of freedom. The great divide in Lammens's version of Syrian history lay in the seventh century with the conquest of Syria by the tribes of Arabia under the banner of Islam. Lammens regarded the Arab tribes as harsh and uncivilized and disparaged Islam as a dark and oppressive religion. Except for a brief period of enlightened Syrian-Umayyad rule, Lammens regarded Islamic history as just one long period of occupation that resulted in the repression and emasculation of the Syrian nation. Lammens called for a rebirth of the Syrian nation and the establishment of an independent and sovereign Syrian state. This reborn Syrian nation would naturally turn its back on the desert and reorient itself toward the civilizations of the Mediterranean and Europe.

Of course, in accordance with French policy toward the Lebanese Maronites, Lebanon (or in Lammens' phrase, *l'asile du Liban,* the Lebanese "refuge") would enjoy a privileged and separate existence alongside this reborn Syria. Lammens's writings and his authority as a professor at the Saint Joseph University in Beirut gave him great influence over Western-educated Lebanese and Syrian intellectuals. His views became the common currency of the Lebanese and early Syrian nationalists of the day. As Kamal Salibi notes, "to the Syrian nationalists wherever they happened to be, and also to the Christian Lebanists in Lebanon, the *La Syrie* of Father Lammens became a standard work of reference, as it was, naturally, to the French High Commission in Beirut, for whose policies the book provided intellectual cover" (Salibi 1988, 135).

In any case, the idea of Syrian nationalism never really got off the ground in this period as a majority of the Christians of Lebanon lined up behind the Maronite idea of Lebanese nationalism while many of the Christians of Syria went along with rising Sunni demands for Arab nationalism. The situation did not improve after World War I as Syrian nationalism was associated more than ever with French policy, which had proven deeply hostile to the demands of the Arab nationalists. The movement of Syrian nationalism, however, was recast and revived through the influence of Antun Saʿadeh and his Syrian Social Nationalist party.

The Syrian Social Nationalist Party: The Power of Proto-Fascist Ultranationalist Party Politics

Antun Saʿadeh was born to a Lebanese Greek Orthodox family in Shuwayr, Lebanon, in 1904. His father, Khalil Saʿadeh, a prominent physician with a passion for political issues, lived in Egypt for a few years before moving to São Paolo where his son joined him in 1920. Together, they published *al-majallah,* a journal for the predominantly Christian expatriate community, which promoted ideas of Syrian independence and political secularism. Antun Saʿadeh's coming of age in Brazil of the 1920s had a decisive effect on the formation of his political views. First, while Arab and Lebanese nationalism were emerging as the main expressions of nationalist sentiment in Syria and Lebanon to the disadvantage of Syrian nationalism, Saʿadeh developed a concept of Syrian nationalism based on a "Syrian" identity that had been popular among Syrian and Lebanese Melchites of his parents' generation but was being eclipsed at home by Lebanese and Arab identities. This notion of a "Syrian" identity, however, which had gained prominence during the late nineteenth century, had been preserved intact in the Syrian and Lebanese expatriate communities of South America. Furthermore, as Thomas Philipp shows, the idea of a separate "Syrian" identity had also grown among the important Levantine community in Egypt whose separate "Syrianness" became more conspicuous with the rise of Egyptian nationalism (Philipp 1985, 114). In other words, Saʿadeh's choice of "Syria" as the focus of his nationalistic and patriotic yearnings very much reflects the mood and identity patterns of Lebanese and Syrian expatriate communities both in Egypt and in America to which his father and himself were exposed.

In terms of content, Saʿadeh was impressed by the fascism that was growing in Europe and being imitated in the Latin countries of America. He understood its ability to mobilize mass support and create a powerful state. Indeed, Saʿadeh would establish his Syrian Social

Nationalist Party along fascist lines. As Pipes noted, "Party rituals imitated the fascists in many details, from the Hitler-like salute and the anthem set to 'Deutschland, Deutschland Über Alles,' to the party's symbol, a curved swastika called 'the red hurricane'" (Pipes 1988, 304). Sa'adeh learned German and was heavily influenced by German writings on nationalism, racism, and fascism.

Armed with his patriotism and ambition, Antun Sa'adeh arrived in Beirut in 1929 and took a position teaching German at the American University of Beirut. From there, he had ready access to students and other intellectuals of the country and wasted no time in trying to organize a Syrian nationalist movement. In 1934, he founded the Syrian Social Nationalist party with a small and secretive band of followers (Zuwiyya-Yamak 1966, 34). As mentioned, the SSNP was fashioned along fascist lines with Sa'adeh as its supreme leader. Its objectives were the unification and liberation of Syria and the establishment of a strong and secular state. It was ready to use any and all means at its disposal to achieve those objectives. Within months, the ranks of the party swelled with new branches sprouting in the towns and cities of Lebanon and Syria. It proved especially popular among the Greek Orthodox community as well as among students and intellectuals who appreciated the movement's secularism and its modern attitude toward state and society. By the late 1930s, the SSNP was the most powerful organized party in the political arena.

Indeed, the party's strength and rapid growth were astonishing. Apparently, it filled a gap in an increasingly volatile political environment that none of the liberal nationalist movements had succeeded in filling. It showed the power of party organization and the appeal of totalitarian ideologies. Its success hastened the formation of rival political parties impressed with its success but apprehensive about its political message. The establishment of the Kata'ib party, the Ba'th, and Akram Hurani's Arab Socialist party can all be traced partially to the reaction against the rapid growth of the SSNP.

The SSNP's early success, however, cannot be understood in isolation from popular attitudes toward Germany and the rising fascist powers of Europe. As Bassam Tibi has pointed out, the interwar period in Syria and some other parts of the Arab world was characterized by a marked Germanophilia. France and Britain had reneged on their wartime promises to the Arabs and now presided over an unpopular colonial administration stretching from Iraq to Palestine. Germany was regarded as the only serious challenger to French and British power—a theme which German agents tirelessly promoted. Furthermore, a frustrated colonial population was attracted to the machismo and defiance expressed in the fascism developed in Italy, Germany, and Franco's Spain. Saʿadeh's SSNP was the principal expression in the Arab world of this fascist impulse and the promise held out for Arab peoples by Germany and the other antiliberal regimes. A pseudofascist nationalist organization in Egypt, *Misr al-Fatat* (Young Egypt), did not gain the power or prominence of the SSNP.

In any case, after its founding in 1934, the party and its leaders were continuously in trouble with the mandate authorities. In 1935, the French discovered the existence of the party and sent Saʿadeh and several of his lieutenants to jail. Released after six months, Saʿadeh was jailed again in what became a regular pattern of SSNP defiance of government authority. On a tour of Italy, Germany, and Brazil in 1939 to gather support for his cause, Saʿadeh was stranded in South America when World War II broke out. He could not return to Lebanon or Syria because the French clamped down on the SSNP, suspecting it of complicity with Axis powers. The party, however, was allowed to resume its activities in 1944 in the wake of Lebanese independence; because Saʿadeh was still in South America, one of his lieutenants assumed chairmanship of the party's organization. To accommodate itself to the popular enthusiasm for Lebanese independence, the SSNP renamed itself the Social party and, in Saʿadeh's absence, charted a new course respectful of Lebanese sovereignty and focusing mainly on domestic Lebanese issues.

Saʿadeh, however, returned to Lebanon in 1947 and quickly set out to purge the party of its conciliatory leadership and to reestablish the themes of Syrian nationalism and Syrian unity. His hostility to the Lebanese state inevitably led to clashes with the government and, after a failed coup attempt, to his capture and execution in July 1949. After Saʿadeh's death, party headquarters were moved to Damascus where a more sympathetic government prevailed. But in Syria, the

SSNP came into direct competition with the Ba‘th. The founders of the Ba‘th, Michel Aflaq and Salah al-Din al-Bitar, had long discussions with Sa‘adeh before founding the Ba‘th, reportedly suggesting that Sa‘adeh rename the SSNP the Arab Social Nationalist party (Pipes 1988, 312). Akram Hurani, founder of the Arab Socialist party that had eventually merged with the Ba‘th in 1953, had been a member of the SSNP for several years before founding his own organization. But now, the SSNP and the Ba‘th were in open competition, advocating contradictory Syrian and Arab nationalist ideologies. The showdown came in 1955 when the SSNP attempted a coup against the Ba‘th-dominated government. During the attempt, a SSNP member shot and killed Lieutenant Colonel ‘Adnan Maliki, one of the most powerful Ba‘thist officers in the army. The Ba‘th struck back by purging SSNP members from the government and the army, outlawing the party, and driving its leaders from Syria. The SSNP was dealt a further blow by a brutal attack on SSNP ideology written by Sati‘ al-Husri, the foremost theoretician of Arab nationalism, who had previously dealt respectfully with Sa‘adeh and his ideology.

Defeated in Syria, the SSNP regained breathing space in Lebanon by supporting President Chamoun's government against his Arab nationalist opponents in 1958. The SSNP soon ran afoul of the Lebanese authorities, however, as a result of another failed coup attempt in Lebanon in December 1961. This defeat, and the collapse of the UAR in September 1961 set the stage for a rapprochement between the SSNP and the Ba‘th party. Persecuted in Lebanon, the SSNP needed to regain some refuge in Syria; meanwhile, some Syrian members and officers of the Ba‘th party who had suffered under the Nasir unity experiment and who had become disillusioned with the goal of immediate pan-Arab unity had begun to see some merit in the SSNP slogan of pan-Syrian unity. It echoed irredentist Ba‘thist slogans but put Syria comfortably at the center of a Greater Syrian state instead of at the sidelines of an Egyptian-dominated pan-Arab state. This new regionalism within the Syrian wing of the Ba‘th party contributed to the split within party ranks that culminated in the 1966 putsch against the old guard of the party. As the Syrian Ba‘th in effect adopted the Greater Syria foreign policy objectives of the SSNP, the SSNP began to sound more like the Ba‘th. It abandoned fascist principles and adopted instead the rhetoric and slogans of the Left. Furthermore, it fell in line with Arab nationalist slogans by declaring that the unification of Greater Syria could be regarded as just a step toward the establishment of a larger Arab state. The transformation was rapid and thorough.

When the Lebanese war broke out, the SSNP was lined up alongside other leftist Arabist parties and enjoyed very close relations with the Syrian government. Indeed, the SSNP and the Syrian Ba'th had become nearly indistinguishable, as members of the former party joined the latter and served in the Syrian government. Throughout the Lebanese war, the SSNP proved an effective and well-disciplined militia almost entirely under Syrian control with a deserved reputation for daring action. Although there were a number of schismatic attempts to free the party from direct Syrian government influence, under the leadership of 'Isam al-Mahayri, the party's first Syrian-born and Muslim leader who succeeded to power in 1984, the SSNP came to lie more than ever under Syrian control.

The Ideology of Syrian Social Nationalism

Sa'adeh's thought had its roots in the racial and totalitarian nationalist theories popularized by the rise of European fascism in the inter-war period. Fascistic elements were "clearly expressed in Sa'adeh's exalted status, the party's organization, and its ideology, including the stress on bloodlines and mystical nationalism" (Pipes 1988, 304). Sa'adeh admitted that his thought resembled that of the Italian and German fascists but insisted that his nationalist philosophy, Social Nationalism, was original and a product of the history and intelligence of the Syrian nation to which he belonged (Sa'adeh 1959, 32). Indeed, Sa'adeh's social nationalism should not be misread as Hitler's national socialism, for the Arabic equivalents of social and socialist have entirely different roots (social, *ijtima'i;* socialist, *ishtiraki*). Furthermore, Sa'adeh's understanding of Syrian history and the Syrian nation is not altogether dissimilar to the ideas put forward by Father Lammens. Here, however, little evidence links Sa'adeh's ideas about Syria to those of Lammens, for Sa'adeh had formulated his concepts of Syrian nationalism abroad and was influenced much more by German writings than those of French authors. Nevertheless, there is no doubt that the propinquity of their views about Syrian nationhood gave Saʿadeh a head start in promoting his Syrian nationalist movement in Lebanon and Syria.

The "origin of nations," argued Saʿadeh in his book by the same name, is based on "a shared life over generations within a territorial boundary" (Saʿadeh 1938, 169). He, thus, credited material over linguistic and cultural factors with the leading role in shaping the boundaries and characteristics of nations. Natural barriers, he argued, defined the limits of a society's reach, and vegetation, climate, and topography determined its means of livelihood and way of life. In basing his nationalism on territorial and material principles, Saʿadeh, of course, was at odds with most of the Arab nationalists of his day who based Arab nationalism on principles of common language and history. In defining the territorial limits of Syria, however, Saʿadeh was not altogether consistent. Until his return from exile in 1947, he had considered Syria to comprise roughly the territories of Lebanon, Syria, Jordan, and Palestine. After 1947, however, he added Iraq, part of Iran west of the Zagros mountains, and Cyprus to his concept of Syrian boundaries. Syria was now declared to comprise the entire Fertile Crescent with Cyprus "as its star." His change of heart about the boundaries of natural Syria may reflect the fact that Arab nationalism had convincingly shown the links between Syrians and other Arabs, especially in Iraq. His claim to Cyprus was based on the historical footnote that Cyprus had occasionally fallen under Syrian Arab control; although somewhat outdated, the claim helped distinguish his territorial claims from those of the Arab nationalists of Syria.

According to Saʿadeh, the Syrian nation had been formed in the early periods of history by the influence of the Syrian environment on the mix of "Canaanite, Chaldean, Aramean, Assyrian, Ammurian, Hittite, Metannite and Akkadian" peoples that came to populate the land (SSNP 1955b, 22). Out of this variety of populations evolved a particular Syrian racial type shaped by the Syrian environment and the racial inheritance of all the various contributing racial groups. The Syrians, therefore, had a distinct physiological constitution. As Saʿadeh argued, "although the Syrians do not have one racial source, they share one set of racial characteristics—the result of their unique blend—that distinguishes them from other peoples in the world"

(Saʿadeh 1959, 65). The Syrian racial blend, Saʿadeh insisted, was both distinctive and distinguished. It was a particular blend that brought together the best strains from a set of less-sophisticated racial groups and elevated and refined them over the centuries.

The Syrian nation, according to Saʿadeh, was established long before the spread of Christianity and Islam. Therefore, its identity existed before those religious identities and was more important than them. Even the great wave of Arab immigration into Syria in the seventh century did not alter the Syrian character, for Syria was not Arabized; rather, the Arab immigrants were Syrianized. That the Syrians adopted Arabic did not affect their nationality either, for they had adopted and abandoned many other languages in the past. He did not think highly of the Arabs as a race. He regarded them strictly as the Bedouin desert dwellers of the Arab peninsula and denied that the Syrians, the Egyptians, or other Arabic-speaking nations were, properly speaking, Arab. The word Arab, he pointed out, was derived from the word for desert, ʿurba; the Arab race, he maintained, exhibited the deep physiological and psychological influence of that harsh and primitive environment. Syrians, however, were a sedentary nation of the Fertile Crescent. His emphasis on the distinction between Syria and Arabia was as strong as his hostility to the independence of Lebanon from Syria. He insisted that the isolation of Lebanon was artificial and based on religious differences that should not and could not form the basis of any nationalism (SSNP 1955b, 81). Religion had a universal outlook, he argued, whereas nationalism demanded a well-defined attachment to a limited social unit (Saʿadeh 1938, 174).

In the political sphere, Saʿadeh bemoaned the condition of Syria. It was weak and divided, and its social fabric was being torn apart by centrifugal forces of sectarian chauvinism. He saw the Christians of Lebanon tending toward Phoenicianism and the Muslims tending toward Arabism. He regarded both as misguided myths contributing to the demise of the Syrian nation. What Syria needed, he insisted, was a national revival galvanized by a renewed awareness of the reality and history of the Syrian nation and led by the Syrian Social Nationalist party.

The SSNP was the vanguard of the Syrian nation and must act on behalf of the entire nation. Saʿadeh considered the contemporary population of Syria to represent the Syrian nation only in potentiality. The people of Syria were too riven with misguided sectarian, ideological, and political differences to rise up spontaneously as one nation. Therefore, the party itself, unified as it was in organization and ideological outlook, represented the Syrian nation and state in nucleus. Its members represented future citizens of the Syrian nation, and its political organization represented the future Syrian state (Saᶜadeh 1959, 18). In no uncertain terms, the immediate aim of the party was to overthrow the various existing regimes that ruled over a divided Syria and to establish a strong and unified government in their place. Through the establishment of this state, under the absolute control of the vanguard SSNP and its leader, Syria would find the means for its rebirth as a powerful and creative nation deserving of its own place in the sun alongside other great nations.

Because governments were not expected to hand over power willingly, the SSNP was well aware that it would have to accomplish its aims by violent means. This result was not regretted, for Saᶜadeh glorified violence and insisted that the aggressive and martial instincts of humans were their highest resource that had to be enthusiastically cultivated. Darwin had revealed that species progressed through competition; nations also, argued Saᶜadeh, would only progress through struggle and conflict.

As mentioned earlier, the party itself was organized along fascist lines. Saᶜadeh was called simply *al-zaᶜim*, the leader. Allegiance was sworn to him personally, and all party laws and policies were decided by him and executed on his authority. In a sense, he was the party. Furthermore, party initiates could not withdraw from the party once they had become members. By taking the oath of allegiance to Saᶜadeh and the party, they in effect had given up their autonomous will and even their individuality. They were expected to become Syrian Social Nationalists in every aspect of their inner and outer lives. Moreover, as part of their oath, they had to swear to make Syrian Social Nationalism not only their way of life but also that of their families. The credo of the party was embraced with the same zeal and all-consuming devotion usually reserved for religious movements.

Saᶜadeh based his "social" nationalism on the simple premise that humans are social not individualistic beings. People were born into society and achieved their fullest potentiality by abandoning their individuality and becoming one with that society (Zuwiyya-Yamak 1966, 101). The original and most complete social unit was the nation—a group of people who shared a long history of living together in a common well-defined natural environment. Individuals could achieve their highest potential only by realizing their belonging to their nation and subordinating all aspects of their lives to it. Individuals were to dissolve into the nation and to derive all their spirit and consciousness from it. The eighth principle of the SSNP's charter stated that "the interest of Syria is above all interests" (SSNP 1955b, 47); this was not a dry political statement but extended beyond politics to economics, ethics, aesthetics, and even religion. The interest of the nation, as decided, of course, by the party and its leader, determined all choices. There was no room for individual free will or private preference. The national cause was a total cause, and the Syrian Social Nationalist movement was unabashedly totalitarian.

In the realm of religion, worship of the deity was to be replaced by worship of the nation and its state. Indeed, Saʿadeh considered his ideology a new religion, and himself, its prophet."The world has witnessed the descent of religions from heaven down to earth," he proclaimed, "but today it witnesses the rise of a new religion from earth to heaven" (Saʿadeh 1959, 109). Traditional religions, he complained, had a theocentric vision and enslaved humankind to an unseen being created from ignorance and superstition; his new religion, however, had a sociocentric vision, it liberated humankind. Indeed, Saʿadeh argued, the spiritual unity of society could not be achieved through the traditional religions, for they sowed only superstition and discord. Spiritual unity could only be achieved through the dominance of one outlook on life, one set of values, one metaphysics, one spirituality—that of Social Nationalism (Saʿadeh 1959, 108). Indeed, for members, being a Syrian Social Nationalist was a religious experience. Initiation was compared to the act of baptism, and devotion to the party often withstood the ultimate test of sacrificing one's life for the cause.

Saʿadeh also tried to provide his ideology with a new metaphysics, as if, confident of having deflated the old religions, he now sought to take on modern philosophy. He coined a new word, *mad-hiyyah*—a concatenation of the Arabic words for material and spiritual—to denote a new metaphysics in which the truth in all human affairs was to be found in a balanced harmony between the material and spiritual realms (Zuwiyya-Yamak 1966, 104). He denied any necessary conflict between these two realms and claimed that his philosophy was superior to those of capitalism, communism, fascism, and National Socialism. The harmony he posited between the material and spiritual worlds provided the philosophical underpinnings for his glorification of power and his belief that might makes right. Influenced by Darwinism, Saʿadeh proclaimed that in the natural and violent contest of nations, power was the only common currency; therefore, the martial virtues were the most necessary and valuable for any nation.

The main principles of reform advocated by the party centered around the eradication of sectarianism. Saʿadeh called for the separation of religion from the state, the prevention of men of religion from participating in any political or judicial affairs, and the eradication of all social barriers between different religious sects (SSNP 1955b, 53–63). He considered that sectarianism was Syria's most serious problem and made his party's first aim to eliminate it and replace sectarian differences with a common belief and allegiance to the principles of social nationalism. This militantly secular stance was perhaps the most popular element in Saʿadeh's ideology. It appealed widely to an intelligentsia who were anxious to reduce the influence of religion and religious men in society, and appealed also to members of minority religious groups, such as the Greek Orthodox and Greek Catholics, who saw secularism as the only means of breaking out of their communal confinement.

In economic matters, Saʿadeh called for the elimination of "feudalism" and the development of a national industrial-based economy controlled but not owned by the state (Saʿadeh 1959, 119). All decisions of production would be made in the national interest and distribution would be arranged so that all had what they needed while the productive were justly rewarded (Saʿadeh 1959, 124). This position echoed the general economic principles of European fascism. Saʿadeh also opposed Communism or any independent trade union activity because he maintained that such activity divided the nation and hindered its progress. Most important of all, the state was to establish a strong army to protect the sovereignty of the Syrian nation from all threats and provide Syrians with a source of pride and discipline.

Piecing together ideas and theories borrowed from European fascism and adjusting them to apply to Syria and the condition of Syrian society, Saʿadeh was able to present a fairly coherent ideological worldview of a Syrian nation, suffering division and repression, on the verge of unity and rebirth. What is most remarkable about the movement, however, is perhaps not the content of the ideology itself but rather the forcefulness with which it was presented and promoted. Saʿadeh's great charisma and conviction had a lot to do with this, as did the efficient organization of the party and the zeal of its members.

The Appeal of Syrian Social Nationalism

Syrian Social Nationalism had a much greater appeal as a means for relieving psychological strain than, say, Egyptian or early Arab nationalism. It provided a complete, dogmatic version of social and political realities and urged acceptance of this dogma on the pure authority of the leader. Furthermore, through its philosophy and party practices, it encouraged individuals to abandon their individuality and immerse themselves in the life and thought of the party. By joining such an engrossing party, individuals could escape any personal crises by simply escaping their responsibilities and anxieties as individuals. The SSNP did not simply offer answers to political questions; it did not just offer a new way of life, but a new life altogether. In this sense, Syrian Social Nationalism had a much deeper impact on individuals and their psychological orientations than did other ideologies of the interwar period.

Syrian Social Nationalism, from the perspective of psychological strain in the category of identity confusion, provided a strong social identity to alienated individuals by providing a concrete and powerful image of the Syrian nation, its history, present and future. The process of acquiring this new identity was reinforced by party practices that forced initiates to abandon any assumptions of free will and comply with the authority of the party. By losing their freedom as individuals, persons became, in effect, part of a larger social entity; hence, they could derive their own sense of identity from their absorption into that larger entity. The need for a firm sense of identity was further satisfied through the person of the leader himself. The leader was portrayed as a figure of mythical proportions who symbolized the spirit of the Syrian nation and the spirit of each member of that nation. He was the nation, and identification with the nation meant identification with him. In a sense, all members adopted the identity of the leader.

In the moral sphere, by shedding individuality and free will, initiates to the SSNP also escaped moral responsibility and the problem of moral choice. They were in submission to the party and its leader. They did what they were told to do and claimed no moral independence. Whatever moral choice was left to them was heavily influenced by the extensive indoctrination and guidance they received from the party. In other words, in most cases they exercised no choice; in situations in which they had to, moral choices were guided for them by the principles and teachings of the party.

In the intellectual realm, Saʿadeh claimed to provide a comprehensive philosophy of history and social evolution. Rudimentary as his theories were, there was enough there to construct a skeletal worldview that was strongly reinforced by the organs and institutions of the party. History was the story of nations evolving; the Syrian nation, suppressed by foreign powers and reactionary classes, was on the verge of self-realization in a strong secular national state. Individuals had no separate existence from the nation but were secondary and subject to it.

In the category of aggression release, the SSNP unreservedly glorified the aggressive instincts and the martial spirit. Aggression was at the heart of the Darwinian evolution of humans; aggression was also the engine of the progress of nations. The venting of aggression, the use of force, and hatred of the adversary, were all central categories in the practice of Syrian Social Nationalism. Aggression toward the enemy was simply the outward expression of patriotism.

Indeed, from the perspective of social psychology, Syrian Social Nationalism was one of the most psychologically satisfying ideologies that developed in the modern Arab world. The reason for this is partially that the ideas themselves, with their emphasis on the abandonment of individual free will, provided an escape from all issues of personal crisis. But more critically, the personality of Saʿadeh himself and the efficient authoritarianism of the party could actually carry out that program of domination of the individual. No other ideological movement in the Arab world, not even the radical Arab Nationalists or the Islamists, attempted such a thoroughgoing domination of the individual.

The Social Dynamics of Syrian Social Nationalism

The membership of the Syrian Social Nationalist party was young, fairly well-educated, and drawn disproportionately from the Greek Orthodox community and other minority communities. Its members were generally of urban or semi-urban middle-class backgrounds. The appeal of a fascist nationalism to such groups can be examined within the sociological categories described in chapter 1. The issue of sectarianism was central to SSNP ideology. From the perspective of minority groups, the SSNP drew its main following from the Greek Orthodox and Greek Catholic communities of Lebanon and Syria. As mentioned earlier, these communities, dispersed as they were throughout Syria and Lebanon, partially resisted the idea of Lebanese nationalism, which would cut their communities in half and put their members in Lebanon under Maronite domination; however, they also feared being subsumed in a larger Arab or Islamic political unit that would inevitably be dominated by Sunnis. The establishment of a Syrian state would be more suitable to their communal interests. Some Druzes and Protestants shared their concerns about isolation in Lebanon and domination by Maronites or Sunnis. This is not to say that membership of the movement was strictly confined to these communities, for many Sunnis were attracted to its pan-Syrian outlook while many Maronites found the secularism and pseudoscientific outlook of the party quite appealing.

From the perspective of class and class interests, it is noteworthy that the SSNP sought to take over control of the central economy and large enterprises; yet it sought to protect the privileges of small businesspeople and small landholders. Understandably this appealed most to elements of the rising middle class. This petty bourgeois element valued private property but, at the same time, felt threatened and overwhelmed by the power of big capital in an uncontrolled capitalist system.

From the perspective of generational opposition, the SSNP was very consciously a youth movement. It accepted no members over the age of forty, and recruited heavily from people in their early twenties. As in the fascist movements of Europe, it saw in youth the energy and malleability necessary for forging a strong ideological movement.

In the end, it was a combination of sectarian and class opposition expressed in several crises with the government that ended the SSNP's activity. Sectarian and religious leaders were alarmed at the thoroughgoing secularism of the SSNP, whereas the upper class feared the consequences of the success of such a totalitarian party. Had the SSNP succeeded in striking an alliance with members of the upper class, as the fascists did in Italy and Germany, perhaps they could have been provided with a better platform from which to woo the middle class and bolster their power. Nevertheless, unlike in Italy and Germany, sectarian cleavages may still have been too much for the SSNP to fully overcome.

The Legacy of Syrian Social Nationalism

The SSNP was the first modern political party in the Arab world to mobilize mass support successfully in a sustained and effective manner. Saʿadeh and his followers showed what could be done with organization, ideology, and charisma. Because of its early successes, the SSNP became a focus of political attention and a model of sorts for other political activists. As such, it had a considerable influence on the development of other political parties and the formulation of other political ideologies. As mentioned earlier, the birth of the Lebanese Kataʾib party and the Arab Baʿth party can both be linked more or less directly to the success of the SSNP.

In ideological content, the SSNP's greatest legacy is, perhaps, in the reinforcement of the idea of secularism in politics. The liberal nationalist movements in Egypt, Lebanon, and Syria before the arrival of the SSNP all had a decidedly secular flavor, but none raised the issue of secular politics as explicitly and forcefully as the SSNP. The SSNP showed that thoroughgoing secularism could be an immensely popular theme. Not only was it the only way to appeal to the important religious minority communities that were just beginning to become integrated into mainstream political life, but it was also a theme around which a rising Western-educated generation, unhappy with the influence the traditional religious classes had in politics and society, could rally. The political successes that the SSNP had with the theme of secularism did not go unnoticed; this secularism became one of the pillars of the new Arab nationalist ideology that was formulated by the Baʿth and adopted in large part by Nasir and the entire Arab nationalist generation of the 1950s and 1960s.

The SSNP, however, was first and foremost a nationalist party. Its entire ideology revolved around the idea of the nation as did its propaganda. In this sense, it was the first political party to commit so much energy and to pin such high ambitions on the nationalist ideal. Of course, there were other nationalist parties before the SSNP, but none even came close to the intensity and purity with which it presented the idea. Again, as with the theme of secularism, Saʿadeh had hit upon a theme that his party proved to be an explosively popular one. The early successes of his radical Syrian nationalism gave a boost both to Lebanese nationalism and Arab nationalism in that it reaffirmed the viability of the nationalist idea. Most importantly, it convinced an important wing of the Arab nationalist movement to develop a more radical and purist version of Arab nationalism. Indeed, the Arab nationalism developed by Michel Aflaq and the Baʿth had abandoned the moderation of the early Arab nationalists and adopted the enthusiastic, almost mystical, approach to nationalism first popularized by the SSNP. The shift in the direction of Arab nationalism can also be partially explained by the introduction of German ideas of nationalism into the region, a task also largely carried out by the SSNP. Saʿadeh, as discussed, was greatly influenced by German thought and shaped his ideology along the lines of German, as well as Italian, fascism. And although German writings were not unknown, indeed Satiʿ al-Husri and Michel Aflaq both had direct exposure to them, few of the political activists of the interwar period had the background that Saʿadeh did. Whereas Western education in the Middle East of the time typically came in the form of British, French, or American schooling, Saʿadeh's education was primarily German. And because of historical differences, German notions and emotions of nationalism were profoundly different than those associated with French, British, or American nationalism. German nationalism was much more enthusiastic and mystical and unlike other nationalisms, its emphasis was on resistance to foreign domination and the establishment of national unity. German nationalism, after all, developed in the wake of Napoleon's conquest of Germany and culminated in the unification of the myriad kingdoms and principalities of Germany under one state. Although Husri successfully imported much of the theory of German nationalism, Saʿadeh was the first to evoke fully the passion and drama of this form of nationalism in the Arab world, and he met with great success. The Baʿth and Nasir would follow in his footsteps. The fact that Britain and France had become enemies in the eyes of Arab nationalists because of their role in the defeat of the Arab government in Damascus and the establishment of the mandate system cast Germany in a favorable light and helped ease the transition toward Germanic expressions of nationalism.

With the Germanic spirit of nationalism came a number of related elements that differed markedly from the liberalism and constitutionalism of British, French, or American nationalism. Even though Germany itself was defeated in World War II and Nazi ideology discredited, many elements of German nationalism had already been imported by Husri and then the SSNP and adopted by the Baʿth, the ANM, and others. I refer here to such elements of German nationalism popularized by the SSNP as the rejection of artificial state boundaries, an emphasis on militarism, and the legitimation of an authoritarian, or even totalitarian, state. Adopted also from the German model was a new concept of the political party and its role: in place of the loosely organized parties of the British and French models was to develop the one, strictly organized, monolithic political party. This party was to act as the vanguard of the nation and seize power through force, if necessary. The multiparty system was to be abolished and in its place a robust one-party system established. The German example also carried with it a new understanding of the use of rhetoric in politics. In place of the fairly mundane debating that took place in democratic parliaments and spilled over into election campaigns, the German and Italian fascists showed the power of grandiose poetic or mythological rhetoric organized around a studied propaganda campaign. Unfortunately, this, too, found its way, partially through the SSNP, into the Arab nationalist mainstream.

Of course, the SSNP cannot be considered solely responsible for the shifts in Arab nationalism or the influx of German ideas to supplant French and British ones, yet their influence at this early stage should not be underestimated. They helped set the stage for a radical, secular, authoritarian, irredentist form of Arab nationalism that seized center stage in Arab politics for several decades.

CHAPTER SIX

The Future of Ideology
in the Arab World

In this examination of ideology in the Arab world, I have described the main movements within a general age of ideology that began after the collapse of the Ottoman empire, gained momentum after the loss of Palestine in 1948, and began a gradual decline in the 1970s. This age of ideology is traced to a period of rapid social, economic, political, and cultural change that leaves people in considerable psychological strain and, thus, open to ideological formulations of reality. This period since World War I can be divided into three fairly distinct phases. The first extends between the collapse of the Ottoman empire and the loss of Palestine. It is dominated by various liberal nationalist ideologies such as Egyptian nationalism and conservative Arab nationalism. The second extends between the defeats of 1948 and 1967 and is dominated by radical Arab nationalism. The third began in the late 1960s and is dominated by Islamic fundamentalist ideologies.

These phases correspond to changes at various levels. From the perspective of class, the first phase represented the consolidation of a local upper-class elite after the Ottoman collapse; the second phase represented the breakthrough of a new middle-class to power; the third phase has a less-clear class referent but to some degree represents attempts of middle- and lower-middle-class out-groups to secure a place for themselves in the political arena. These classes use ideologies as battering rams to discredit other classes, as a cover to legitimize their own rise to power, and as a means for making sense out of the new social, political, and economic environment into which they are moving.

From the perspective of intergenerational competition, there is a fairly regular rhythm of ideological change that corresponds to the formation of new generation groups and their challenge to old generation groups. The timing of these generational upheavals seems to be following roughly a twenty-five-year schedule: phase 1, circa 1920–circa 1945; phase 2, circa 1945–circa 1970; phase 3, circa 1970–? The exact timing of these general class and generational shifts is often determined by particular, less-predictable, historical events such as the Arab Revolt of 1916, the dismemberment of Syria in 1920, the loss of Palestine in 1948, the Suez War of 1956, the Six-Day War of 1967, and the October War of 1973. Such events help trigger ideological shifts and class and generational shifts.

The dynamics of interethnic and interconfessional competition is also an important variable. Most importantly, confessional and ethnic minorities entered the central arena of power along with the new middle class in the 1950s. This partially explains the popularity of secular Arab nationalism and ethnically neutral Communism during that period. A return to religious, confessional, and ethnic politics in the 1970s and 1980s, however, indicates that the integrationist attempts of the 1950s and 1960s have not been completely successful.

The Failure of Ideology

To be sure, ideologies in the Arab world performed several useful tasks. Most importantly, they played the central role in mobilizing large sections of the population and overthrowing the traditional regimes of the interwar period; subsequently, they served to organize and maintain the power of the new regimes. Furthermore, in the socioeconomic and cultural spheres, as Kemal Karpat observed and as noted here earlier, many of these ideological movements provided the ideational and political framework within which new ideas about society, economy, polity, modernity, and religion entered the Arab world. In that sense, they served as conduits for the transformation and modernization of consciousness in the Arab world. Critically reviewing the foregoing chapters from the perspective of contemporary

Arab political life, however, one is driven to the conclusion that after more than seven decades of ideological activity, political culture in the Arab world is still in great disarray. There is no clear definition of political community, no agreed basis of political legitimacy, no intelligible understanding of political rights and duties, no stable framework for political interaction, and no widely recognized agenda of political goals. This is a failure of ideology in as much as ideology explicitly attempts to resolve and provide a foundation for these issues. These problem areas in Arab political culture have been left as a legacy of Arab ideologies in the twentieth century.

The Crisis of Legitimacy

One of the principal functions of any ideology once its proponents have succeeded in seizing power is to legitimize their rule and to legitimize the new political order that they have established. By defining the ethical and ideational framework within which a society, or an important part thereof, conceptualizes politics, ideology can provide the fundamental basis of legitimacy for a political regime. As Apter noted, ideology provides "those transcendental ends that define the state as a moral entity" (Apter 1963, 267). In new states, such as those in the Arab world, this legitimizing function of ideology would be especially useful in providing a measure of stability to the political order. On the whole, however, the ideological movements that developed in the Arab world were not effective in providing the legitimacy necessary for the stabilization of Arab political systems. The problem was manifested in two areas: the legitimization of new political boundaries and the legitimization of new political systems. Both are essential for stable politics, and both remain in considerable crisis.

The problem of political boundaries is a nationalist issue and began with the collapse of the Ottoman empire and the carving up of the Ottomans' eastern Arab provinces into separate states by European powers. It gave rise to the first conservative wave of Arab nationalism, which focused on the reunification of Syria. Although it grew out of a natural hostility toward foreign domination (first Turkish and then French) and the fragmentation of the Arab provinces, which, under Ottoman rule, had been closely intertwined with one another, and although it was still narrower in scope and lower in intensity than the radical Arab nationalism that would follow it in the 1950s, this early Arab nationalism, in practical political terms, set the pattern in Arab ideological thinking of challenging the legitimacy of state boundaries. Although this made sense in Syria to some degree, the passion for challenging the legitimacy of state boundaries eventually spread to Iraq, Egypt, Yemen, and the *maghrib* states, most of which had been fairly distinct political units for many years. It eventually posed a challenge to the legitimacy of the political boundaries of all the Arab states and remains to this day a source of illegitimacy and, hence, of instability and political praetorianism throughout the Arab world.

The problem was particularly acute for self-proclaimed Arab nationalist regimes such as those of the Ba'th in Syria and Iraq and the Arab nationalist movement in Yemen, for the very Arab nationalist ideology with which they seized power and which they used to legitimize their rule challenged the legitimacy of the state that they claimed a right to govern. In other words, their ideology asserted that they were a legitimate government in an illegitimate state. This, of course, is a contradiction. It has contributed to a lingering crisis of legitimacy in the Arab nationalist states that has helped make them among the most repressive in the region and the world.

Beyond the problem of the legitimacy of political boundaries is the problem of the legitimacy of political systems within those boundaries. Here the problem comes more from the competition of different ideologies than from the internal contradictions of Arab nationalism in a fragmented state system. In short, ideologies in the Arab world have proposed three different standards for judging the legitimacy of political regimes. The first is the standard of constitutional democracy derived from British and French models and dominant in the interwar period. The second is the standard of the one-party authoritarian system inspired by the German and Soviet models and dominant in the fifties and sixties. The third is the Islamic standard that gained renewed prominence after the bankruptcy of Arab nationalism in the late 1960s and the triumph of the Islamic Revolution in Iran in 1979. The competition between these three profoundly dissimilar political philosophies has left Arab political systems with no stable basis for measuring political legitimacy. This, of course, contributes to political instability and the need for governments to rely on coercion to maintain themselves.

The Crisis of Community

Although the crisis of legitimacy as described above relates quite specifically to the legitimacy of particular political boundaries and political regimes, the crisis of community refers to a more subjective and psychological variable, namely, that of communal identity. All the nationalist movements that arose in this century had as one of their principal aims supplanting the confessional identities that had been the basis of political life within the Ottoman state with all-inclusive and secular national identities. This objective was true of Egyptian, Syrian, Lebanese, and Arab nationalism. The Marxist movements as well aimed to overcome these confessional identities by appealing to class identities. Some of these ideological movements, most notably Egyptian and Lebanese nationalism and the Marxist movements, also tried to supplant ethnic and racial identities. Although some of these confessional and ethnic identities were temporarily submerged during periods of particular ideological excitement, no melting pot process has taken place to fuse robust corporate identities out of this social psychological mosaic. Instead, centrifugal subnational identities have experienced a dangerous revival. Arab-Kurdish tensions flared into war in Iraq, Alawi-Sunni strain fomented open rebellion in Syria, Christian-Muslim stress led to civil war in Lebanon, and Muslim-Coptic distrust led to recurring unrest in Egypt. In Iraq and Syria one also sees an increasingly acute reliance on members of the family or tribe in the business of government; this indicates that the circle of trust, which defines one's communal identity in practical terms, has grown very narrow. A minimum of trust and common identity is necessary, however, for stable political life.

The task for ideology in this sphere is to provide an identity structure attractive and durable enough to outrank other identities, if not supplant them completely. Here the Arab nationalists were, in a sense, the most successful. They were able to articulate from the Islamic past and from facts of common language, culture, and history an Arab identity that has left its mark on a whole generation of Arabs. Other regional and class identities were less successful. The problem with Arab nationalism, however, was that it put forward a communal—and, after all, political—identity that was at odds with the political reality of the Arab world. The community that was emphasized by Arab nationalist ideology was directly contradicted by the fragmentation of the Arab state system and the often hostile interaction of those states. Instead of being reinforced by experience, the Arab national identity was undermined by it and declined as a viable source of communal identity. A communal identity, after all, must be a practical and reliable thing. It is a tool for social interaction, and, if it fails, it is discarded for another. From the perspective of practical politics in the modern world, the most stable arrangement is that in which a group's communal identity more or less coincides with its actual political boundaries; expressed in other words, the most successful and stable modern political entity is the nation-state. In the Arab world, there are nations smaller than the existing states and some larger, but none that accurately fit the political status quo.

The Crisis of the Political Process

Politics may be described as a process through which important decisions affecting a large collectivity are made. In a society of any significant size, this process would necessarily have to be complex to accommodate all the various forces and interests present within the society. A process that ignored a large group of forces and interests would lead the society into a form of political dysfunction and crisis that could be prevented from erupting into outright political instability only through the increased use of coercion. The processes of modernization introduce increasing complexity into the web of social forces and interests that need to be taken into account; consequently, the political process that seeks to dominate that society would also have to be increasingly complex. In developing societies, part of the role of ideology is to provide a framework for such a political process. In essence, an ideology tries to put forward a new set of rules of the political game after older traditional rules have been discredited. Inasmuch as the new rules are widely accepted, they will contribute to the smooth conduct of politics; inasmuch as they are not, politics will become an unmediated conflict in which force plays the central role.

The Arab world of the Ottoman period had developed over the centuries fairly comprehensive and widely accepted rules that helped regulate the normal process of political decision making. This obviated the government's need to rely on the naked use of force in its everyday dealings. In the decades following the collapse of the Ottoman state, however, two developments undermined the proper functioning of such rules. First, the socioeconomic and political environment of the Arab world was transformed beyond the point at which the old rules of the game could still apply; second, the set of rules themselves was directly challenged by other sets of political rules introduced by new ideologies.

The problem in the 1990s is that whereas the old rules of the game have been more or less discredited, no new rules have been able to gain a stable ascendancy. Part of this is owing to the fact that ideological movements in the Arab world have put forward competing sets of rules summarized in the three ideology types of liberal constitutionalism, secular one-party authoritarianism, and religious fundamentalist totalitarianism. None of these ideology types has succeeded in completely eradicating the others and providing a comprehensive framework within which political life is conducted. Instead, the three ideology types often coexist uncomfortably in the same polity, contributing to high levels of disarray and instability within the system. With no widespread agreement about the basis of political life and the modalities of political interaction, political life is disorganized, volatile, and highly conflictual and requires a significant dose of government coercion to keep under control.

The problem of chaos and unregulated competition in Arab politics, however, is not due solely to the unresolved competition of different ideological frameworks. It can also be traced to the fairly recent emergence of the contemporary political units of the area and the rapid social and economic developments with which they are still contending. In the end, although ideologies try to take a shortcut toward developing new political rules of the game, a fine-tuned set of political rules requires time to develop. In other words, many of the polities of the Arab world are just still too young to enjoy the simple stability of that maturity.

The Crisis of Political Development

In successful political development, the political system changes in such a way as to maintain or reestablish political order and stability over a society transformed by the various components of modernization. This process involves a great increase in the political system's capacity in two categories: managing demands and providing socioeconomic and political goods. The first involves inputs; the second, outputs. In the first, the state acts as a receptor and organizer; in the second, it is a producer and distributor. In the interwar period, the Arab upper classes that had established their dominance over Arab political life forced on the state structures of the time an expansion of their capacity to handle diverse political demands. These demands were the various demands of members of the main upper-class families and were institutionally expressed in the parliamentarian systems favored by this class. In essence, this upper class succeeded in temporarily institutionalizing a mode of power-sharing and demand-inclusion not previously seen in the area. While the state's capacity to accommodate and manage diverse demands grew, there was little comparable growth in its capacity to produce and distribute socioeconomic and political goods. This is largely the result of the fact that the main demands of the upper classes revolved around issues of political participation rather than the provision of particular goods. Members of the upper classes were well off. They provided for themselves through private means. They did not look to the state to produce goods for them but on the contrary, they sought to have a hand in controlling the state to ensure that it stayed out of their business and generally promoted a political framework favorable to their private interests.

Two events transformed the political developmental challenges facing the Arab state. The first was the entrance of the new middle class to the center of political life; the second was the loss of Palestine. Unlike the upper class, the new middle class was a needy class in material terms. Beyond demands of political participation, this class needed the state to help produce jobs, housing, social security programs, roads, schools, and so on, for it. It looked to the state as a source of welfare and wealth rather than as a threat to be controlled. Thus, the need for the state to increase its capacity to produce and distribute socioeconomic and political goods rose dramatically. In addition, the loss of Palestine created an immediate demand for a dramatic increase in the military capacities of most Arab states, especially those neighboring the new Israel. This too, of course, augmented the need for the state to increase its output capacity.

The socialist radical Arab nationalism that rose to prominence in the wake of these two events responded well to the need for the state to increase its productive capacities. New regimes arose in Egypt, Syria, Iraq and elsewhere that seized the principal assets of the upper classes and foreign interests, struck militarily lucrative alliances with foreign powers (mainly the Soviet Union), and established large public sectors that benefited large segments of the population. Indeed, the Arab nationalist regimes have been quite effective in this aspect of statebuilding.

The lingering political developmental crisis, however, is that in enhancing the output capacity of the state the ruling groups of these regimes dramatically restricted the channels of acceptable inputs to the system. In other words, to enhance production and distribution, they sacrificed participation. Indeed, the ideologies that vied for attention in the 1950s and 1960s were unanimous in disparaging the democratic models of the interwar years and favored authoritarian models of the Marxist, German, or Islamic fundamentalist type. As some Arab societies move ahead on the road of social and economic development, however, and the politically central middle class grows less economically desperate and more politically aware, the political demands of that class will probably shift from the provision of particular socioeconomic goods to the right of political participation. A rise in such demands took place in South America, Eastern Europe, and Asia throughout the late 1970s and 1980s, and signs of it appeared sporadically in Egypt, Jordan, Kuwait, and other Arab countries in the 1970s and 1980s. Eventually, it is likely to emerge with more force in the Arab world. The impending crisis in this sphere is that the dominant ideologies in the post-World War II Arab world show a strong commitment to authoritarianism and sanction extensive use of force by the state in suppressing dissent, whether on class, nationalistic, or religious grounds. This ideological orientation bodes ill for the process of accommodating rising demands for participation that seem to be part of the Arab world's future.

The Crisis of Political Thought

A normal ingredient of life in a stable political system is a measure of political dialogue and reflection. This helps identify dangerous problem areas, suggest remedies, and enhance the sense of political community within a society. But to maintain its coherence and have an impact on society, this process must exist within some generally accepted framework of ideas and values; otherwise, it will lose its audience and lose its own focus. Whereas philosophers in their studies can afford to grapple with basic principles, political and social commentators, in order to be productive and effective, must operate within a fairly well-defined ideological framework. However, as the disagreement on fundamentals increased in the Arab world after the collapse of Arab nationalism and the challenge of Islamic fundamentalism, Arab intellectuals have increasingly lost sight of the general framework within which to think, to write, and to interact with society; as a result, an expanding vacuum has emerged in Arab intellectual circles. It is as if, no longer agreed on a ship's desired final destination, the ship's navigators and cartographers have simply given up charting the vessel's course. This crisis of political thought is one of the most serious political developments of recent years. There are, of course, other important reasons for its emergence at this time.

First, ideological options have been nearly exhausted. Most intellectuals like ready-made fixes, and ideologies provide exactly that. Yet the Arab world has already tried many ideologies of varied description, such as regional nationalism, Arab nationalism, Marxism, fascism, and Islam. None has been able to offer a fully satisfactory and effective set of political ideas and institutions. As Juan Linz has argued (1976), there is a point at which the ideological arena of a society can become overcrowded. At that point, there are no ideologies left to try; all are tainted with age and failure. Left with the task of constructing a political consciousness derived not from facile ideological formulas but from the complex and disappointing realities of contemporary Arab political life, many intellectuals find the task too complex and too daunting. Gone are the possibilities for simple abstractions that reduced the Arab condition to a few ready principles, and gone is the youthful optimism that held that if only a few things were put right, an Arab utopia would come about.

Second, the regimes themselves that have emerged to govern Arab societies are, of course, highly repressive. They borrow principles of autocracy either from the Marxist Left or the nationalist Right or from the practice of autocracy embedded in Arab-Islamic history. Moreover, the new regimes are keenly aware of the power of the pen because many of them were swept into power on waves of ideological upheaval. Consequently, they take especial care to control political thought and stifle political expression.

Third, in the 1970s, the Arab world lost the intellectual participation of two of its most able members—Egypt and Lebanon. Lebanon collapsed as a state and succumbed to internal war in 1975, and Egypt was cut off from the rest of the Arab world after the Camp David Accords of 1978. Egypt had provided a critical mass of thinking and reflection from a rich tradition of political and religious thought; Lebanon had provided an open forum for trends of political thought to be aired and to compete with one another. Both countries helped to tie the Arab world together and to allow Arab intellectuals to interact with one another—Egypt by virtue of its size and traditional cultural centrality and Lebanon by virtue of its open universities, its free press, its teeming political landscape, and its liberal political system. As Egypt and Lebanon left the Arab arena, Arab political thinkers grew more isolated from one another and more constrained within their own state boundaries; it made their intellectual task much more difficult, and the task of their governments to control them much easier. Exiled to Paris or other foreign capitals, they could survive, but they became too cut off from their natural cultural and political environment to remain constructively engaged in it.

Fourth, the oil boom of the early 1970s had its own dramatic effects. It provided a great reserve of money to help buy off writers and thinkers with whom the oil states did not agree. Furthermore, it introduced the great allure of materialism and encouraged a great number of promising social and political thinkers to go into the far more profitable professions of business, engineering, and other sciences that the oil boom had produced a great need for. The relative social and economic status of the social thinker plummeted.

Taken together, these factors have contributed to a serious intellectual crisis in the Arab world. There is very little consensus about the language of informed political discourse, the context of social thought, or the role of the intellectual. With the loss of Lebanon and the isolation of Egypt, a number of state-sponsored universities and cultural institutes emerged to fill the widening intellectual gap with magazines, journals, and books that projected a bland conservative outlook serving more to deflect rather than encourage critical social and political thought.

The Future of Ideology in the Arab Middle East

Although the competition of ideologies in the Arab world has left many areas of political culture and political thought in considerable crisis, this, ironically, has scant bearing on the future of ideology in the Arab world. Because the spread of ideology is not a result of rational choice, so its continuation or decline also is not particularly a matter of rational choice.

The future of ideology in the Arab world, from the perspective of Strain Theory, can be linked generally to the high level of strain and stress experienced at the individual level. We posited in chapter 1 that the emergence of an age of ideology in the Arab world was related to the escalation of material and cultural change and the consequent intensification of individual psychological strain. Similarly, a slowing down of the rate of material and cultural change could reduce psychological strain and then contribute to an ebb in ideological thinking. As Johnson argued, "If ideology builds up like an oyster's secretion around strain, then anything that reduces strain will tend to limit the spread of ideology" (Johnson 1968, 83).

Indeed, a quick assessment would reveal that the rate of significant material and cultural change is slower now than it was in the decades around World War II. In other words, for example, the environment of 1960 differed more radically from that of 1910 than that of 2010 is likely to differ from that of 1960. In the first period, several fundamental changes took place: in politics, a multinational empire was replaced by a subnational state system and the institutions of a traditional government were replaced by those of a large modern bureaucratic state; in economics, a largely agricultural economy was replaced by a quasi-industrial state-dominated economy; in the cultural sphere, Westernization and secularism were introduced; in sociological terms, a large middle class replaced the small upper class in the central positions of power. If the history of previously developed societies is any measure, these four fundamental transformations are likely to remain in place indefinitely as pillars of the modern social system. Indeed, there have been few social, economic, or cultural changes in the Arab Middle East of this magnitude since the socializing decrees of the 1960s that changed the locus of economic and political power in Egypt, Syria, and Iraq. These societies, in other words, seem on the road not to fundamental change, but to development along the path they are already on. If such is the case, psychological strain is likely to decrease as individual and environment achieve a gradually closer integration. In this case we can expect to see a general ebb in ideological thinking and a rise in pragmatic attitudes as may already be noticed from the mid-1970s onward.

From the particular perspective of class, the middle class used the ideology of revolutionary Arab nationalism in the 1950s both as a means to overthrow the ruling upper class and to explain the complex and new social environment in which it found itself. As time passed, however, because this class now enjoyed actual political dominance, it was no longer acutely in need of a powerful ideology from which to derive its authority. It could now largely rely on the conventional levers of political power and coercion and the general sense of legitimacy that accumulates around any status quo that manages to endure for a significant time. Furthermore, as this class remained in its new social position for some time, it grew familiar with that position in real terms and no longer needed the explanatory and mediating assistance of ideology as much. This partially explains the drift of the Arab middle class away from ideological thinking throughout the 1970s and 1980s. Now comfortable and relatively at peace with their environment and social position, members of this class no longer had an acute need for ideology. The same, of course, is not true of all classes. Members of the newly urbanized lower middle class in Egypt, for example, feel much the same political frustration and social confusion today that the new middle class felt in the 1940s. They currently need ideology as a source of political power and as a vehicle for interpreting their new experience in the world. They have turned to fundamentalist Islam as such an ideology. In any case, from the perspective of class, one can expect a continued drift away from ideology among the dominant middle class although other classes, especially newly mobilized or newly urbanized ones, may still be attracted to ideologies as means to gain more political power and as a framework within which to understand new social and political environments.

From the angle of interethnic or interconfessional competition, one still finds a dynamic role for ideology in the countries of the Fertile Crescent. In Syria, sectarian tensions are helping to maintain strong support for an Islamic movement as they are also doing in Iraq among the Shiʿa and in Lebanon among the Shiʿa and some Sunnis. In Syria and Iraq, sectarian tensions are also helping to maintain support for Arab nationalism as a defensive ideology among the Alawi and Sunni minority ruling elites. As sects are still battling to work out their positions in the political system, they will probably continue to have recourse to ideologies to lend them more power in that political struggle. A resolution of those sectarian tensions would eventually contribute to a receding of ideological dynamism from that sphere.

From the perspective of generational opposition, two factors must be taken into consideration. First, if a political regime can successfully socialize the young, then ideological challenges generated by generational opposition may be minimized. Second, as Mannheim noted, if the pace of material and cultural change is high, then new generations will need new ideological worldviews to cope with the rapidly emerging conditions; if it is low, then older worldviews will be adequate. Given the general low level of top-down socialization in the Arab Middle East and the still relatively high rate of change and high level of socioeconomic and cultural stress (although less than previous decades), youth is likely to remain an active source of ideological rejection of the status quo in the foreseeable future. In the rhythm of generational change in the Arab world one can detect, as mentioned, a twenty-five-year cycle. Extrapolating from this, one may expect an eclipse of the Islamist phase that began circa 1970 sometime in the late 1990s to be followed by an antithetical ideological phase.

From the perspective of crises, inasmuch as serious crises will continue to beset the Arab Middle East, new ideological dynamism may be expected to emerge. The crises of the last seventy years have mostly been political and military. States collapsed and new ones emerged; foreign occupiers came and went; wars were fought between Israel and the Arab states. Beginning with the issue of regime or state stability, few of the Arab states seem immune to serious unrest. Lebanon collapsed in 1975 while Syria, Iraq, and Egypt all faced serious internal challenges in the late 1970s and early 1980s. The possibility of regime collapse will likely remain significant in such countries as Syria, Iraq, and Algeria although a more remote concern in such countries as Egypt, Morocco, or Saudi Arabia. Any regime change, or serious regime crisis, will likely be accompanied by intense ideological effervescence as occurred with the overthrow of the Shah's regime in Iran. Moving on to external crises, wars can be determining events in adjusting or reversing the course of ideological development. The wars with Israel of 1948, 1967, and 1973 all served as watersheds in the development of Arab ideological trends. Consequently, any military conflict with Israel will likely have a direct effect on the ideological climate of the Arab world. An Arab defeat, such as those of 1948 and 1967, will encourage radical revolutionary ideologies, whereas any victory, even if limited, such as that of 1973, will likely encourage moderate conservative ideologies. Of course, the effects of such crises in ideological terms will very much depend on the ability of elites to formulate compelling responses to those crises.

The causes for continued ideological effervescence seem mixed. Continued sectarian competition and generational opposition will likely militate toward continued ideological dynamism fueled by occasional crises to which the region is still quite vulnerable, whereas from the perspective of class, which may be the most important perspective, the dominant middle class seems to have passed its ideological phase. At most, the appetite for ideological thinking in the near future will be limited to generational, sectarian, and class out groups who are likely only to define the outer margins of politics rather than determine its core which is dominated by a fairly homogeneous and integrated middle class.

Even if a considerable appetite for ideological thinking were to continue for the reasons listed, another factor may be very relevant in determining the translation of that appetite for ideological thinking into actual ideological movements, and that is the extent to which the established ideological field has enough space to allow the emergence of a new ideological movement. In the article mentioned previously, Juan Linz argued that the "anti" character of fascist movements in the interwar period—"anti-parliamentarian, anti-liberal, anti-communist . . . anti-proletarian . . . anti-capitalist, anti-bourgeois . . . anti-clerical . . . even anti-conservative"—was symptomatic of the overcrowding of the ideological arena in Europe by that time (Linz 1976, 12). Most ideological positions had already been staked out by one group or another over the past century. What was left to these hypernationalist movements was a position that simply defined itself negatively vis à vis these ideologies. This, for Linz, in a sense, represented the closing stages of ideological dynamism in the West and foreshadowed the "end of ideology" and the rise of nonideological politics after World War II.

Interestingly, the Islamic movement of the 1970s and 1980s has many of the "anti" characteristics of the European hypernationalism of the interwar period. It is anti-Western, anti-capitalist, anti-Communist, anti-secular, anti-Christian, anti-liberal, anti-conservative (it advocates a program of radical change), and, in several important ways, anti-modern and anti-traditional at the same time. What is more, the Islamic movement often defines itself in these oppositional terms. It makes clear what it is against and thereby attracts dissatisfied social groups from a wide spectrum, but it is unclear about what it proposes beyond the application of the Shariᶜa and respect for Islamic law and practices, which leaves much unanswered in the complex political and social agenda of modern times. If the recent Islamic movement is indeed an "anti" movement with important similarities to the interwar hypernationalism of Europe, then, perhaps, it is signaling the exhaustion of ideological alternatives in Middle Eastern Arab society.

If such is the case, then even if a considerable appetite for ideology exists in the foreseeable future, it may have a difficult time finding a satisfactory ideological expression that has not already been tried and compromised in the region's past. Since World War I, Middle Eastern Arab society has courted ideologies from the far left to the far right: the Maoist Marxism of the New Left, the mainstream Marxism of the Communist parties, the socialist nationalism of the revolutionary pan-Arabists, the liberal nationalism of the conservative nationalists, the activist Islamism of the Muslim Brotherhood, and the radical Islamism of the new fundamentalists of the 1970s and 1980s. Ideologies do not exist in a void; how many new ideologies can be brought forward without running into undisguisable repetition? Indeed, from this perspective, as Linz argued, even if ideological appetites remain significantly high, the overcrowding of the ideological arena will make it more difficult than before for these appetites to find expression in believable and attractive political ideological movements. If this analysis is correct, it may help explain the partial decline of ideological politics in the 1970s and 1980s and may indicate that the current wave of Islamic radicalism does not represent the beginning of a new phase of ideological effervescence but the last throes of an Arab age of ideology that is gradually coming to an end, and which may give way to a period of more widely pragmatic politics in the not-too-distant future.

Works Cited

Index

Works Cited

Abdel-Malek, Anouar. 1968. *Egypt: Military Society.* New York: Vintage.

————, ed. (1970) 1983. *Contemporary Arab Political Thought.* London: Zed

Abu Jaber, Kamel. 1966. *The Arab Baʿth Socialist Party: History, Ideology, and Organization.* Syracuse: Syracuse Univ. Press.

Abu-Manneh, Butrus. 1980. "The Christians Between Ottomanism and Syrian Nationalism: The Ideas of Butrus al-Bustani." *The International Journal for Middle Eastern Studies* 11, no. 33:287–304.

Abduh, Muhammad. 1956. *Risalat al-tawhid* (The epistle of unification), edited by Rashid Rida. Cairo: N.p.

Adams, Charles. 1983. "Mawdudi and the Islamic State." In *Voices of Resurgent Islam,* edited by John Esposito, 99–133. Oxford: Oxford Univ. Press.

al-Afghani, Jamal al-Din and Muhammad Abduh. 1958. *Al-ʿurwah al-wuthqa wa al-thawrah al-tahririyyah al-kubrah* (The strong knot and the great revolution of liberation). 2d ed. Cairo: Dar al-ʿArab.

Aflaq, Michel. 1958. *Maʿrakat al-masir al-wahid* (Struggle toward a single end). Beirut: Dar al-Adab.

————. 1959. *Fi sabil al-baʿth* (Towa Arab renaissance). Beirut: Dar al-Taliʿah.

————. 1971. *Nuqtat al-bidayah* (The starting point). Beirut: al-Muʾassassah al-ʿArabiyyah lid-Dirasat wan-Nashr.

Agwani, M.S. 1969. *Communism in the Arab East.* New York: Asia Publishing

Ahmed, J.M. 1960. *The Intellectual Origins of Egyptian Nationalism.* London: Oxford Univ. Press.

Ajami, Fouad. 1979. "The End of Pan-Arabism." *Foreign Affairs.* 57, no. 2: 355–73.

————. 1981. *The Arab Predicament.* Cambridge: Cambridge Univ. Press.

————. 1986. *The Vanished Imam: Musa al-Sadr and the Shiʿa of Lebanon.* Ithaca, N.Y.: Cornell Univ. Press.

————. 1987. "The Arab Road." in *Pan-Arabism and Arab Nationalism, The Continuing Debate,* edited by Tawfiq Farah, 115–32. Boulder, Colo.: Westview.

Amin, Samir. 1978. *The Arab Nation.* London: Zed.

Amuzegar, Jahangir. 1974. "Ideology and Economic Growth in the Middle East." *Middle East Journal* 28, no. 1:1–9.

Antonius, George. 1946. *The Arab Awakening*. New York: Putnam.

Apter, David E. 1963. "Political Religion in the New Nations." In *Old Societies and New States: The Quest for Modernity in Asia and Africa,* edited by Clifford Greetz, 57–104. New York: Free Press.

———. ed. 1964. *Ideology and Discontent*. New York: Free Press.

Arjomand, Said Amir, ed. 1984. *From Nationalism to Revolutionary Islam*. Albany: State Univ. of New York Press.

ʿAql, Saʿid. 1944. *Qadmus*. Beirut: Dar al-Fikr.

al-Azm, Sadeq Jalal. 1968. *Al-naqd al-dhati baʿd al-hazima* (Self-criticism after the defeat). Beirut: Dar al-Taliʿa.

———. 1969. *Naqd al-fikr al-dini* (A critique of religious thinking). Beirut: Dar al-Taliʿa.

———. 1970. *Dirasat yasariyya hawl al-qadiyya al-filistiniyya* (Leftist studies on the Palestine question). Beirut: Dar al-Taliʿa.

Bakdash, Khaled. 1944. *Al-Hizb al-shuyuʿi fi al-nidal li-ajl al-istiqlal wa al-siyada al-wataniyya* (The Communist party in the struggle for independence and national sovereignty). Damascus: Dar al-Taqaddum.

al-Banna, Hassan. n.d. *Majmuʿat rasaʾil al-imam al-shahid* (The collected letters of the martyred Imam). Cairo: Dar al-Qurʾan al-Karim.

Barnard, F. M., ed. and trans. 1969. *J.G. Herder on Social and Political Culture*. Cambridge: Cambridge Univ. Press.

Batatu, Hanna. 1978. *The Old Social Classes and Revolutionary Movements of Iraq*. Princeton, N.J.: Princeton Univ. Press.

———. 1981a. "Iraq's Underground Shiʿa Movements: Characteristics, Causes and Prospects." *Middle East Journal* 35, no. 3:578–94.

———. 1981b. "Some Observations on the Social Roots of Syria's Ruling Military Group and the Causes for its Dominance." *Middle East Journal* 35, no. 3:331–44.

———. 1982. "Syria's Muslim Brethren." *MERIP Reports* 12, no. 9:12–23.

al-Bazzazz, ʿAbd al-Rahman. 1954. "Islam and Arab Nationalism." Translated by Sylvia Haim in *Die Welt des Islams* 3:201–18.

———. 1964. *Hadhihi qawmiyyatuna* (This is our nationalism). 2d. ed. Cairo: n.p.

Bell, Daniel. 1960. *The End of Ideology: The Exhaustion of Political Ideas in the Fifties*. Glencoe, Ill.: Free Press.

Bennett, Tony, et al., eds. 1981. *Culture, Ideology, and Social Process: A Reader*. London: Open University.

Bill, James. 1972. "Class Analysis and the Dialectics of Modernization in the Middle East." *International Journal for Middle Eastern Studies* 3, no. 4:417–34.

Binder, Leonard. 1964. *The Ideological Revolution in the Middle East*. New York: Wiley.

———. 1978. *In a Moment of Enthusiasm: Political Power and the Second Stratum in Egypt*. Chicago: Univ. of Chicago Press.

Botman, Selma. 1984. "Oppositional Politics in Egypt: The Communist Movement,1936–1954." Ph.D. diss., Harvard Univ., Cambridge, Mass.

———. 1986. "The Egyptian Communists and the Free Officers: 1950–54." *Middle Eastern Studies* 22, no. 3:350–66.

Bracher, Karl Dietrich. *The Age of Ideologies,* translated by Ewald Osers. New York: St. Martin's.

Carre, Olivier, and Gerard Michaud. 1983. *Les Frères Musulmans, Egypt et Syrie.* Paris: Editions Gallimard/Julliard.

Chiha, Michel. 1949. *Liban Daujord'hui.* Beirut: Editions du Trident.

———. 1950. *Essais.* Beirut: Editions du Trident.

———. 1962. *Lubnan fi shakhsiyyatihi wa hudurihi* (Lebanon: Its personality and present), translated into Arabic by Fuad Kanᶜan. Beirut: Manshurat al-Nadwah al-Lubnaniyyah.

———. 1966. *Politique Interieure.* Beirut: Editions du Trident.

Cleveland, William. 1971. *The Making of an Arab Nationalist: Ottomanism and Arabism in the Life and Thought of Satiᶜ al-Husri.* Princeton, N.J.: Princeton Univ. Press.

Commins, David. 1986. "Religious Reformers and Arabists in Damascus, 1885–1914." *International Journal for Middle Eastern Studies* 18, no. 4:405–25.

Corm, Charles. 1964. *La Montagne Inspiree.* Beirut: La Revue Phenicienne.

Coury, Ralph. 1982. "Who Invented Egyptian Arab Nationalism?" P.1, 2 *International Journal for Middle Eastern Studies* 14, nos. 3, 4:249–81, 459–79.

Dakroub, Mohammad. 1974. *Juzur al-sindiyana al-hamraʾ: hikayat nushuʾ al hizb al-shuyuᶜi al-lubnani, 1924–1931* (The story of the growth of the Lebanese Communist party, 1924–1931). Beirut: Dar al-Farabi.

Darwazah, al-Hakam and Hamid Jabburi. 1960. *Maᶜ al-qawmiyya al-ᶜarabiyya* (With Arab nationalism). 4th ed. Beirut: N.p.

Davis, Eric. 1984. "Ideology, Social Class and Islamic Radicalism." In *From Nationalism to Revolutionary Islam,* edited by Said Amir Arjomand, 134–57. Albany: State Univ. of New York Press.

Dawn, C. Ernest. 1973. *From Ottomanism to Arabism: Essays on the Origins of Arab Nationalism.* Urbana: Illinois Univ. Press.

Dekmejian, Hrair. 1971. *Egypt Under Nasser.* Albany: State Univ. of New York Press.

———. 1985. *Islam in Revolution.* Syracuse, N.Y.: Syracuse Univ. Press.

Dessouki, Ali E. Hillal, ed. 1982. *Islamic Resurgence in the Arab World.* New York: Praeger.

Entelis, John. 1973. "Belief-System and Ideology Formation in the Lebanese Kataʾib Party." *International Journal for Middle Eastern Studies* 4, no. 2:148–62.

Erikson, Erik. 1968. *Identity, Youth, and Crisis.* New York: Norton.

Esposito, John, ed. 1983. *Voices of Resurgent Islam.* London: Oxford Univ. Press.

Farah, Tawfic, ed. 1987. *Pan-Arabism and Arab Nationalism, the Continuing Debate.* Boulder, Colo.: Westview.

Fichte, Johann Gottlieb. 1922. *Addresses to the German Nation,* translated by R. F. Jones and G. H. Turnbull. Chicago: Open Court.

Fischer, Michael. 1982. "Islam and the Revolt of the Petit Bourgeoisie." *Daedalus* 111, no. 1:101–26.

Freud, Sigmund. 1973. *Civilization and its Discontents,* translated by J. Strachey. New York: Norton.

Fromm, Erich. 1941. *Escape from Freedom.* New York: Rinehart.

Geertz, Clifford, ed. 1963. *Old Societies and New States: The Quest for Modernity in Asia and Africa.* New York: Free Press.

———. 1964. "Ideology as a Cultural System." In *Ideology and Discontent,* edited by David Apter. New York: Free Press.

Gellner, Ernest. 1981. *Muslim Society.* Cambridge: Cambridge Univ. Press.

———. 1983. *Nations and Nationalism.* Ithaca, N.Y.: Cornell Univ. Press.

———. 1987. *Culture, Identity, and Politics.* Cambridge: Cambridge Univ. Press.

al-Ghazali, Muhammad. 1980. *Al-daʿwah al-islamiyyah tastaqbil qarnaha al-khamis ʿashar* (The Islamic call enters on its fifteenth century). Cairo: N.p.

Gibb, H. A. R. 1947. *Modern Trends in Islam.* Chicago, Ill.: Univ. of Chicago Press.

Gibb, H. A. R., and H. Bowen. 1950, 1957. *Islamic Society and the West: A Study of the Impact of Western Civilization on Moslem Culture in the Near East.* 2 vols. Oxford: Oxford Univ. Press.

Gould, Julius. 1964. "Ideology." In *A Dictionary of the Social Sciences,* edited by Julius Gould and William Kolb, 315–17. New York: Free Press.

Greil, Arthur. 1977. "The Modernization of Consciousness and the Appeal of Fascism." *Comparative Political Studies* 10, no. 2:213–38.

von Grunenbaum, Gustav. 1962. *Modern Islam, The Search for Cultural Identity.* Berkeley and Los Angeles: Univ. of California Press.

Haddad, Yvonne. 1982. *Contemporary Islam and the Challenge of History.* Albany, N.Y.: State Univ. of New York Press.

———. 1983. "Sayyid Qutb: Ideologue of Islamic Revival." In *Voices of Resurgent Islam,* edited by John Esposito, 67–99. Oxford: Oxford Univ. Press.

———. 1986. "Muslim Revivalist Thought in the Arab World: An Overview." *Muslim World* 76, nos. 3, 4:143–67.

Haim, Sylvia. 1955. "Islam and the Theory of Arab Nationalism." *Die Welt des Islams* 4, nos. 2, 3:124–49.

———. 1964. *Arab Nationalism: An Anthology.* Berkeley and Los Angeles: Univ. of California Press.

Halpern, Manfred. 1959. "Middle Eastern Armies as the Vanguard and Chief Political Instrument of the New Middle Class." Santa Monica: Rand Corporation.

———. 1963. *The Politics of Social Change in the Middle East and North Africa.* Princeton, N.J.: Princeton Univ. Press.

Harik, Iliya. 1972. "The Ethnic Revolution and Political Integration in the Middle East." *International Journal for Middle Eastern Studies* 3, no. 3:303–23.

Hawwa, Saʿid. 1971. *Jund allah* (The soldiers of God). N.p.

Hayes, Carlton. 1960. *Nationalism: a Religion.* New York: Macmillan.

Heberle, Rudolf. 1951. "The Problem of Political Generations." *In Social Movements: An Introduction to Political Sociology,* 118–28. New York: Appleton Century-Crofts.

Helou, Farjallah. 1974. *Kitabat mukhtara* (Selected writings). Beirut: Dar al-Farabi.

Herf, Jeffrey. 1984. *Revolutionary Modernism.* Cambridge: Cambridge Univ. Press.

Hinnebusch, Raymond. 1982. "The Islamic Movement in Syria: Sectarian Conflict and Urban Rebellion in an Authoritarian-Populist Regime." In *Islamic Resurgence in the Arab World,* edited by Ali Dessouki, 138–70. New York: Praeger.

———. 1988. "Islamic Revivalism in the Arab East: Syria." In *The Politics of Islamic Revivalism,* edited by Shireen Hunter, 39–56. Bloomington: Indiana Univ. Press.

Hoffer, Eric. 1951. *The True Believer.* New York: Harper and Row.

Hourani, Albert. 1970. *Arabic Thought in the Liberal Age, 1798–1939.* Oxford: Oxford Univ. Press.

Hudaybi, Hasan Isma⁢ᶜil al-. N.d. *Du⁣ᶜat . . . la qudat* (Proselytizers . . . not judges). Cairo: Dar al-Tibaᶜah wa al-Nashr al-Islamiyyah.

Hudson, Michael. 1968. *The Precarious Republic.* New York: Random House.

———. 1979. *Arab Politics: The Search for Legitimacy.* New Haven, Conn.: Yale Univ. Press.

Hunter, Shireen, ed. 1988. *The Politics of Islamic Revivalism, Diversity and Unity.* Bloomington: Indiana Univ. Press.

al-Husri, Satiᶜ. 1944. *Araᵓ wa ahadith fil-wataniyyah wal-qawmiyyah* (Opinions and conversations on patriotism and nationalism). Baghdad: Muhammad Naji al-Khudari, Publisher.

———. 1951a. *Araᵓ wa ahadith fil-qawmiyyah al-ᶜarabiyyah* (Opinions and Conversations on Arab nationalism). Egypt: al-Iᶜtimad.

———. 1951b. *Muhadarat fi nushuᵓ al-fikra al-qawmiyyah* (Lectures on the origins of the nationalist idea). Beirut: Dar al-ᶜIlm lil-Malayin.

———. 1952. *Alᶜurubah bayn duᶜatiha wa muᶜaridiha* (Arabism between its proponents and opponents). Beirut: Dar al-ᶜIlm lil-Malayin.

———. 1958. *Al-urubah awwalan* (Arabism first). Beirut: Dar al-ᶜIlm lil-Malayin.

———. 1956. *Difaᶜan ᶜan al-ᶜurubah* (In defense of Arabism). Beirut: Dar al-ᶜIlm lil-Malayin.

———. 1974. *Abhath mukhtarah fil-qawmiyyah al-ᶜarabiyyah* (Selected essays on Arab nationalism), 1923–1963, pt. 1. Beirut: Dar al-Quds.

Hussein, Mahmoud. 1973. *Class Conflict in Egypt 1945–1970.* New York: Monthly Review.

Ibrahim, Saad Eddin. 1980. "Anatomy of Egypt's Militant Islamic Groups." *International Journal of Middle Eastern Studies* 12, no. 4:423–53.

Isaacs, Harold R. 1975. *Idols of the Tribe: Group Identity and Political Change.* New York: Harper and Row.

Ismael, Tareq, and Jacqueline Ismael. 1985. *Government and Politics in Islam.* New York: St. Martin's.

Ismael, Tareq. 1976. *The Arab Left.* Syracuse, N.Y.: Syracuse Univ. Press.

Issawi, Charles. 1982. *An Economic History of the Middle East and North Africa.* New York: Columbia Univ. Press.

Johnson, Harry. 1968. "Ideology and the Social System." In *The International Encyclopedia of the Social Sciences,* edited by David Sills, 76–85. New York: Macmillan, Free Press.

al-Jundi, Anwar. 1981. *Al-qarn al khamis ᶜashar al-hijri* (The fifteenth century A. H.). Beirut: al-Maktabah al-ᶜAsriyyah.

al-Jundi, Sami. 1969. *Al-baᶜth* (The Baᶜth). Beirut: Dar an-Nahar lil-Nashr.

Karpat, Kemal, ed. 1982. *Political and Social Thought in the Contemporary Middle East.* 2d ed. New York: Praeger.

Kazziha, Walid. 1975. *Revolutionary Transformation in the Arab World: Habash and His Comrades, from Nationalism to Marxism.* New York: St. Martin's.

Kaylani, Nabil. 1972. "The rise of the Syrian Baᶜth, 1940–1958: Political Success and Party Failure." *International Journal for Middle Eastern Studies.* 3, no. 1:3–23.

Keddie, Nikki. 1983. *An Islamic Response to Imperialism: The Political and Religious Writings of Sayyid Jamal ad-Din al-Afghani.* Berkeley and Los Angeles: Univ. of California Press.

Kedouri, Elie. 1966. *Afghani and ᶜAbduh: An Essay on Religious Unbelief and*

Political Activism in Modern Islam. London: Frank Cass.

———. 1992. *Politics in the Middle East.* New York: Oxford Univ. Press.

Kerr, Malcolm. 1966. *Islamic Reform: The Political and Legal Theories of Muhammad Abduh and Rashid Rida.* Berkeley and Los Angeles: Univ. of California Press.

———. (1965) 1971. *The Arab Cold War, Gamal ʿAbd al-Nasir and His Rivals, 1958–70.* 3d ed. London: Oxford Univ. Press.

Khadduri, Majid. 1970. *Political Trends in the Arab World.* Baltimore, Md.: Johns Hopkins Univ. Press.

Khalidi, Rashid. 1977. "Arab Nationalism in Syria: The Formative Years, 1908–1914." In *Nationalism in a Non-national State: The Dissolution of the Ottoman Empire,* edited by W. Haddad and W. Ochsenwald, 207–37. Columbus: Ohio State Univ. Press.

———. 1984. "The Social Factors in the Rise of the Arab Movement in Syria." In *From Nationalism to Revolutionary Islam,* edited by Said Amir Arjomand, 53–70. Albany: State Univ. of New York Press.

Khoury, Philip. 1981. "Factionalism among Syrian Nationalists During the French Mandate." *The International Journal for Middle Eastern Studies* 13, no. 4:441–69.

———. 1983. *Urban Notables and Arab Nationalism: The Politics of Damascus 1860–1922.* Cambridge: Cambridge Univ. Press.

———. 1987. *Syria and the French Mandate: The Politics of Arab Nationalism, 1920–1945.* Princeton, N.J.: Princeton Univ. Press.

Khoury, Sami. N.d. *Al-rad ʿala satiʿ al-husri* (The reply to Satiʿ al-Husri). Beirut: N.p.

Knutson, Jeanne N. 1972. *The Human Basis of the Polity: A Psychological Study of Political Man.* Chicago: Atherton.

Kohn, Hans. 1944. *The Idea of Nationalism.* New York: Collier.

Kornhauser, William. 1959. *The Politics of Mass Society.* Glencoe, Ill.: Free Press.

Lammens, Henri. 1921. *La Syrie.* Beirut: Catholic Press.

Lane, Robert. 1962. *Political Ideology.* New York: Free Press.

———. 1972a. "Patterns of Political Belief." in *Handbook of Political Psychology,* edited by Jeanne Knutson. San Francisco, Calif.: Jossey-Bass.

———. 1972b. *Political Man.* New York: Free Press.

Laqueur, Walter. 1961. *Communism and Nationalism in the Middle East.* London: Routledge and Kegan Paul.

Laroui, Abdallah. 1976. *The Crisis of the Arab Intellectual.* Berkeley and Los Angeles: Univ. of California Press.

———. 1977. *L'idealogie Arabe Contemporaine.* Paris: Edition Revue.

Leiden, Carl, ed. 1966. *The Conflict of Traditionalism and Modernism in the Muslim Middle East.* Austin, Tex.: Univ. of Texas Press.

Lerner, Daniel. 1958. *The Passing Of Traditional Society: Modernization In The Middle East.* Glencoe, Ill.: Free Press.

Lewis, Bernard. 1954. "Communism and Islam," *International Affairs* (London) 30, no. 1:1–12.

———. 1965. *The Middle East and the West.* 2d ed. Bloomington: Indiana Univ. Press.

———. 1968. *The Emergence of Modern Turkey.* London: Oxford Univ. Press.

Linz, Juan. 1976. "Some Notes Toward a Comparative Study of Fascism in Sociological Historical Perspective." In *Fascism: a Reader's Guide,* edited by

Walter Laqueur, 3–124. Berkeley and Los Angeles: Univ. of California Press.

Lockman, Zachary. 1988. "The Social Roots of Nationalism: Workers and the National Movement in Egypt, 1908–19." *Middle Eastern Studies*. 24, no. 4:445–59.

Lockman, Zachary, and Joel Beinin. 1987. *Workers on the Nile: Nationalism, Communism, Islam, and the Egyptian Working Class, 1882–1954*. Princeton, N.J.: Princeton Univ. Press.

Mallat, Chibli. 1988. "Islamic Revivalism in the Arab East: Iraq." In *The Politics of Islamic Revivalism*, edited by Shireen Hunter, 71–87. Bloomington: Indiana Univ. Press.

Mannheim, Karl. 1952. "The Problem of Generations." In *Essays on the Sociology of Knowledge*, 276–321. London: Routledge and Kegan Paul.

———. (1936) 1968. *Ideology and Utopia: An Introduction to the Sociology of Knowledge*, translated by Lois Wirth and Edward Shils. New York: Harcourt, Brace, and World.

Maudoodi, Sayyid Abul Aᵓla. 1963. *A Short History of the Revivalist Movement in Islam*, translated by al-Ashᶜari. Lahore, Pakistan: Islamic Publications.

McLellan, David. 1986. *Ideology*. Minneapolis: Univ. of Minnesota Press.

Mitchell, Richard. 1969. *The Society of the Muslim Brothers*. London: Oxford Univ. Press.

Murqus, Elias. 1964. *Tarikh al-ahzab al-shuyuᶜiyya fi al-watan al-arabi* (The history of the Communist parties in the Arab homeland). Beirut: Dar al-Taliᶜa.

———. n.d. *Naqd al-fikr al-qawmi* (A critique of nationalist thought). Beirut: Dar al-Taliᶜa.

Nasser, Gamal Abdul. 1970. *Falsafat al-thawrah wal-mithaq* (The philosophy of the revolution and the national charter). Beirut: Dar al-Qalam wa Dar al-Maᶜrifah.

Nietzsche, Friedrich. 1961. *Zarathustra*, translated by R. J. Hollingdale. New York: Penguin.

Nuseibeh, Hazem Zaki. 1956. *The Ideas of Arab Nationalism*. Ithaca, N.Y.: Cornell Univ. Press.

Odeh, B.J. 1985. *Lebanon: Dynamics of a Conflict*. London: Zed.

Owen, Roger. 1981. *The Middle East in the World Economy*. London: Methuen.

Philipp, Thomas. 1985. *The Syrians in Egypt, 1725–1975*. Stuttgart: Franz Steiner Verlag.

Pipes, Daniel. 1988. "Radical Politics and the Syrian Social Nationalist Party." *International Journal for Middle Eastern Studies* 20, no. 3:303–24.

Plumb, J. H. 1970. *The Death of the Past*. Boston: Houghton Mifflin.

Popular Democratic Front for the Liberation of Palestine. 1970. *Harakat al-muqawama al-filistiniyya fi waqiᶜiha al-rahin, dirasa naqdiyya* (The Palestinian Resistance movement in its current state, a critical study). Beirut: Dar al-Taliᶜa.

Popular Front for the Liberation of Palestine. 1970. *ᶜAla tariq al-thawra al-filistiniyya* (On the path of the Palestinian revolution). Beirut: Dar al-Taliᶜa.

Qutb, Sayyid. 1964. *Maᶜalim fi al-tariq* (Milestones on the road). Cairo: N.p.

———. n.d. (1965a). *Hadha al-din* (This religion). 2d ed. Cairo: Dar al-Qalam.

———. n.d. (1965b). *Al-salam al-ᶜalami wa al-islam* (World peace and Islam). Cairo: Dar al-Kitab al-ᶜArabi.

Razzaz, Munif al-. 1967. *Al-tajrubah al-murrah* (The bitter experience). Beirut: Dar Ghandour.

Reid, Donald. 1974. "The Syrian Christians and Early Socialism in the Arab World." *International Journal for Middle Eastern Studies.* 5, no. 2:177–93.

Renan, Ernest. 1882. *Qu'est-ce qu'une Nation?* Paris: Ancienne Maison Michel Levy Freres.

Rintala, Marvin. 1968. "Political Generations." In *The International Encyclopedia of Social Sciences,* edited by David Sills, 92–95. New York: Macmillan, Free Press.

Rodinson, Maxime. 1974. *Islam and Capitalism.* London.

———. 1981. *Marxism and the Muslim World,* translated by Jean Matthews. New York: Monthly Review.

Saʿadeh, Antun. 1938. *Nushuʾ al-umam* (The origin of nations), vol. 1. Beirut: Matbaʿat al-Ittihad.

———. 1959. *Al-muhadarat al-ʿashr.* (The ten lectures) Beirut: Matbaʿat Feghali.

al-Sadr, Musa. 1979. *Al-islam: ʿaqidah rasikhah wa manhaj hayat* (Islam: A solid creed and a way of life). Beirut: Dar al-Taʿaruf.

———. 1982. *Al-islam khayaruna litaghyir al-waqiʿ al-mutakhallif* (Islam is our choice for changing the backward situation). Beirut: Dar al-Taʿaruf.

Safran, Nadav. 1961. *Egypt in Search of Community.* Cambridge, Mass.: Harvard Univ. Press.

Sahliyeh, Emile. 1988. "Islamic Revivalism in the Arab East: The West Bank and Gaza." In *The Politics of Islamic Revivalism,* edited by Shireen Hunter, 88–100. Bloomington: Indiana Univ. Press.

Salibi, Kamal. 1971. "The Lebanese Identity."*Journal of Contemporary History* 6, no. 1:76–86.

———. 1988. *A House of Many Mansions: The History of Lebanon Revisited* London: Tauris.

Samarbakhsh, A. G. 1978. *Socialisme en Irak et en Syrie.* Paris: Editions Anthropos.

al-Sayyid, Ahmad Lutfi. 1937. *Al-muntakhabat* (The selections) vols. 1, 2. Cairo: n.p.

———. 1946. *Safahat matwiyyah min tarikh al-harakah al-istiqlaliyyah fi misr* (Folded pages from the history of the independence movement in Egypt). Cairo: N.p.

———. 1965. *Taʾammulat fi al-falsafah wa al-adab wa al-siyasah wa al-ijtimaʿ* (Reflections on philosophy, literature, politics and society). Egypt: Dar al-Maʿarif.

al-Sayyid-Marsot, Afaf Lutfi. 1977. *Egypt's Liberal Experiment, 1922–36.* Berkeley and Los Angeles: Univ. of California Press.

Seliger, M. 1976. *Ideology and Politics.* New York: Free Press.

Shafer, Boyd C. 1955. *Nationalism: Myth and Reality.* New York: Harcourt, Brace, and World.

———. 1976. *Nationalism: Its Nature and Interpreters.* American Historical Association pamphlet no. 701.

Sharabi, Hisham. 1966. *Nationalism and Revolution in the Arab World.* Princeton, N.J.: Princeton Univ. Press.

Shehadi, Nadim. 1987. "The Idea of Lebanon: Economy and State in the Cénacle Libanais, 1946–54." *Papers on Lebanon.* Oxford: Centre for Lebanese Studies.

Shils, Edward. 1968. "The Concept and Function of Ideology." in *The International Encyclopedia of the Social Sciences.* edited by David Sills, 66–76. New York: Macmillan, Free Press.

Sivan, Emmanuel. 1985. *Radical Islam*. New Haven, Conn.: Yale Univ. Press.

Smith, Wilfred Cantwell. 1957. *Islam in Modern History*. Princeton, N.J.: Princeton Univ. Press.

Stoakes, Frank. 1975. "The Supervigilantes: The Lebanese Kataeb Party as Builder, Surrogate and Defender of the State." *Middle Eastern Studies* 11, no. 3:215–36.

Suleiman, Michael. 1965. *Political Parties in Lebanon*. Ithaca, N.Y.: Cornell Univ. Press.

Syrian Communist Party. 1972. *Qadaya al-khilaf* (The issues in the dispute). Beirut: Dar Ibn Khaldun.

Syrian Social Nationalist Party. 1955a. *Dustur al-hizb* (The constitution of the party).

———. 1955b. *Al-taʿalim al-suriyyah al-qawmiyyah al-ijtimaʿiyyah*. (The Syrian Social Nationalist teachings).

Taheri, Amir. 1987. *Holy Terror: Inside the World of Islamic Terrorism*. Bethesda, Md.: Adler and Adler.

Therborn, Goran. 1980. *The Ideology of Power and the Power of Ideology*. London: Verso.

Tibawi, A. L. 1969. *A Modern History of Syria*. London.

Tibi, Bassam. 1981. *Arab Nationalism: A Critical Enquiry*, edited and translated by Marion Farouk-Slugglett and Peter Sluglett. New York: St. Martin's.

———. 1986a. "The Arabs and the Iranian Revolution." *Arab Studies Quarterly* 1.

———. 1986b. "Islam and Modern European Ideologies." *International Journal for Middle Eastern Studies* 18, no. 1:15–29.

Torrey, Gordon. 1969. "Baʿth Ideology and Practice." *Middle East Journal* 22, no. 4:445–470.

Vatikiotis, P. J. (1969) 1985. *The History of Egypt*. 3d ed. Baltimore, Md.: Johns Hopkins Univ. Press.

Voll, John. 1982. *Islam: Continuity and Change in the Modern World*. Boulder, Colo.: Westview.

Weber, Max. 1958. *The Protestant Ethic and the Spirit of Capitalism*, translated by Talcott Parsons. New York: Charles Scribner's Sons.

Wendell, Charles. 1972. *The Evolution of the Eygtian National Image*. Berkeley and Los Angeles: Univ. of California Press.

World Marxist Review. Toronto: Progress.

Wright, Erik Olin. 1978. *Class, Crisis and State*. London: NLB.

Wright, Robin. 1988. "Islamic Revivalism in the Arab East: Lebanon." In *The Politics of Islamic Revivalism*. edited by Shireen Hunter, 57–70. Bloomington: Indiana Univ. Press.

Yinger, J. Milton. 1973. "Anomie, Alienation, and Political Behavior." In *Handbook of Political Psychology*, edited by Jeanne Knutson, 171–202. San Francisco, Calif.: Jossey-Bass.

Yusuf, Yusuf Salman, (Fahd). 1976. *Kitabat al-rafiq fahd* (The writings of comrade Fahd). Beirut: Dar al-Farabi.

Zakarayyah, Fuad. 1986. *Al-haqiqah wa al-wahm fi al-harakah al-islamiyyah al-muʿasirah* (Truth and illusion in the contemporary Islamic movement). Cairo: Kitab al-Fikr.

Zamir, Meir. 1985. *The Formation of Modern Lebanon*. Ithaca, N.Y.: Cornell Univ. Press.

Zeine, Zeine. (1958) 1973. *The Emergence of the Arab Nation*. New York: Caravan.

Zurayq, Constantine. 1939. *Al-waᶜy al-qawmi* (National awakening). Beirut: Dar al-Makshuf.

———. 1948. *Maᶜnah an-nakbah* (The meaning of the catastrophe). Beirut: Dar al-ᶜIlm lil-Malayin.

———. 1957. *Ay ghad* (Which tomorrow?). Beirut: Dar al-ᶜIlm lil-Malayin.

———. 1959. *Nahnu wa al-tarikh* (We and history). Beirut: Dar al-ᶜIlm lil-Malayin.

Zuwiyya-Yamak, Labib. 1966. *The Syrian Social Nationalist Party: An Ideological Analysis.* Harvard Middle East monograph, no. 14, Cambridge, Mass.

Index

Europe (continued)
   world, 90–91; secularization in, 10–11
Europhilism, 82

Fadlallah, Muhammad Husayn, 116
Fahd. See Yusuf, Yusuf Salman
Fahmi, Abd al-ᶜAziz, 206
Fakhr al-Din II, 220
Famine: in Lebanon, 223–24, 236
Farouk, King, 44, 99
Fascism, 86, 87, 153–54, 243–44, 245,
   252, 258, 269; of Syrian Social Na-
   tionalist Party, 247–53, 250–51, 256
Fatat, al-, 37, 38
Fateh, 48, 189, 193, 201
Fatherland, The (newspaper), 203–4
Fatimids, 229
"Fatwa on the Nusayris [Alawis]"
   (Taymiyya), 111
Faysal, 39, 73, 74, 75, 224, 236
Fertile Crescent, 248, 249
France, 5, 39, 45, 73, 87, 91, 245; and
   Arab nationalism, 32, 75, 78, 191;
   colonialism of, 156, 157, 262; and
   Egypt, 202, 205, 218; and Greater
   Syria, 239–40; and Lebanon, 221,
   223, 224–25, 236; opposition to,
   149, 155, 190; and Syria, 241–42
Franco-Syrian Treaty, 42, 61
Franks, 228
Free Officers, 41, 45, 102, 125, 160
Fuad, King, 32, 97, 99
Fundamentalism, 115; Islamic, 20, 27,
   49, 84, 96–97, 136–38, 139–42, 179,
   200, 260, 266, 268, 269, 273, 275

Gaylani, Rashid Ali, 157
Gaza strip, 47
General Islamic Conference, 40
Generations: ideology and, 24–28
Geography, 54–55
Germany, 58, 154, 245, 268; national-
   ism in, 55, 86, 87, 257–58, 259;
   unity of, 65–66
Ghanem, Shukri, 223, 241
Ghazali, Abu Hamid al-, 96, 117
Giap, General, 189
Gouraud, General, 224
Grand Liban. See Greater Lebanon
Great Britain, 5, 32, 45, 50, 87, 112,
   174, 218, 224, 245; and Arab nation-
   alism, 40, 78, 191; and Arab revolt,
   38, 39; in Egypt, 91, 99–100, 101–2,
   103, 160, 204–5, 206–7; opposition
   to, 149, 155, 190, 214
Greater Lebanon, 39, 223, 224–25
Greater Syria, 41, 239–40

Great Revolt, 40, 236
Greece, 32–33, 117
Greek Catholics, 240, 252
Greek Orthodox, 23, 44, 224, 234, 240,
   252, 255
Greeks, 150, 181
Guerrilla factions, 189–90, 193, 194
Guevara, Che, 189
Gulf states, 130
Gulf War, 114

Habash, George, 23, 47, 48, 188, 189
Habib, Emil, 158
Haddad, Niqula, 148
Haddad, Wadiᶜ, 23, 47
Hafiz, Yasin al-, 187
Hakim, Muhammad Baqir al-, 113
Hama, 90, 109, 110
Hanbal, Ibn, 117, 129
Harakah al-Tashihiyyah, al-, 105
Harakat al-Mahrumin, 115–16
Hasan, 130–31
Hashemite Federation, 47
Hashemites, 161
Hashimi, Mahmud al-, 113
Hawatmeh, Nayef, 23, 48, 187, 189–90
Hawwa, Saᶜid, 111
Haykal, Muhammad, 96
Hazm, Ibn, 117
Helou, Charles, 227
Helou, Farjallah, 152, 157, 165
Herder, Johann G. von, 51
Heroes of the Return, 189
Hindi, Hani al-, 47
Histadrut, 158, 161
History: influence of, 13–15, 58–59;
   and nation, 54–55, 254
Hizb al-Daᶜwah al-Islamiyyah, 112
Hizballah, 90, 116, 136
Hizb al-ᶜUmmali al-ᶜArabi al-Thawri,
   al-, 187
Hizb al-Watani, al-. See National Party
Hizb al-Shaᶜb al-Lubnani, 151
Holy Warriors. See Mujahidun, al-
Holy War organization, 107
Huda, Bint al-, 114, 133
Hudaybi, Hasan al-, 101, 102, 103, 108
Hurani, Akram, 42–43, 44, 244, 246
Husayn, 131, 134
Husayn, King, 168
Husayn, Saddam, 113
Husayn, Sharif, 38
Husayn, Taha, 94
Husayni, Amin al-, 40
Husri, Satiᶜ Khaldun al-, 13, 47, 70,
   246; ideology of, 49–59, 87, 257, 258
Hussein, Mahmoud, 79–80

Ibrahim, Muhsin, 48, 187
Identity, 4, 15, 16, 63, 72, 264–65; aggression and, 20–21; Arab, 34, 56–57, 74, 85; class, 80, 177–78, 180; community, 52–53, 264–65; Islamic, 92, 137; Lebanese, 220, 233–34; national, 114, 123–24, 217; role of, 17–18; Syrian, 249, 253–54; youth and, 24, 25
Ikhwan. See Society of Muslim Brothers
ILO. *See* Islamic Liberation Organization
Imperialism, 147, 155, 160, 167, 174; opposition to, 169, 172, 176, 178, 184–85, 190, 191
Independence, 5, 68, 170, 237; Arab, 39, 68; and Communism, 149, 155; Egyptian, 206–7, 217–18
India, 89, 91, 92
Individuals: morality, 18–20; psychological strain on, 16–17, 118; reform of, 119–20; in society, 15–16, 251
Intellectuals, 148, 151, 195–97, 269–70
Intelligentsia, 38, 216–17, 252
Iran, 115, 116, 172, 248; and Islamic movements, 113, 114; revolution in, 90, 107, 263, 274
Iranian Revolutionary Guards, 116
Iraq, 5, 39, 45, 61, 88, 89, 130, 166, 248, 264, 268, 272, 274; Arab nationalism in, 47, 182, 263; Baʿth in, 43, 44, 137; Communism in, 23, 152–53, 157–58, 162, 164–65, 168–69, 172, 187; Husri in, 50, 58; Islamic movements in, 112–14, 133, 138, 142, 146
Iraqi Revolution, 163–64
Ishtirakiyyah, al-, 148
Iskra, 156
Islam, 21, 28, 54, 89–90; Afghani's views on, 92–93; and Arab nationalism, 34–36, 45, 77, 86, 124; in Egypt, 103–7, 138–42; fundamentalist, 20, 49, 84, 136–38, 179, 200, 260, 266, 268, 269, 273, 275; in Iraq, 112–14; in Lebanon, 114–16; and the Mediterranean, 228–29; nationalism and, 92–93; politics of, 145–46; radical, 22–23; reform of, 93–94, 95–97; role of, 4, 21–22, 137–38, 208, 210–11; and secularization, 11, 143–44; Shiʿa activist, 130–36; social class and, 22–23, 79; Sunni activist, 116–30; in Syria, 109–11
Islamic Front, 90
Islamic Liberation Organization (ILO), 106–7, 129, 140

Islamic Revolution, 107, 116, 263, 274
Ismaʿil, Khedive, 44
Ismaʿiliyya, 98, 122
Israel, 49, 159, 160, 161, 187, 197, 274; and Egypt, 45, 105; and Lebanon, 133, 134; and PLO, 200, 201; and Syria, 111, 168
Istiqlal party, 40, 161, 162, 163

Jabburi, Hamid: *With Arab Nationalism*, 47
Jamaʿah al-Islamiyya, al-, 115
Jamaʿat al-Ikhwan al-Muslimin. See Society of Muslim Brothers
Jamaʿat al-Takfir wu al-Hijra, 106, 107–8, 129, 140
Jamʿiyyat al-Ahrar, 152
Jamʿiyyat Shabab Sayyidna Muhammad, 99
Jarida, al- (newspaper), 207–8
Jazaʾiri, Tahir al-, 35, 36
Jews, 23, 193; Communist, 149, 150, 151, 158, 161, 181
Jibril group, 189
Jihad, 106, 124, 126, 129–30, 140
Jihad in Islam, Islam and Jahiliyya (Maudoodi), 125–26
Jinan, al- (journal), 33
Jordan, 44, 45, 47, 161, 163, 168, 187, 268; and Syria, 109, 248
Jouplain, M. *See* Nujaim, Bulus
Jour, Le (newspaper), 227
Journalism. *See* Press
Jubhah al-Islamiyyah fi Suriyyah, al-, 111
Judicial system, 7. *See also* Legal system
Juniyeh, 221

Kamal, Mustafa, 89, 97, 172
Kamil, Mustapha, 205–6, 207
Karbala, 131, 135
Karpat, Kemal, 71–72
Kataʾib Muhammad, 109, 129
Kataʾib party, 232, 244, 256
Kawakibi, Abd al-Rahman, 35, 45, 148; *Umm al-Qura*, 36
Khairallah, K. T., 38, 223
Khan, Reza, 172
Khatib, Ahmad al-, 47
Khedive, 203, 204, 205
Khomeini, Ayatollah Ruhollah, 112, 113, 132
Khoury, Bishara al-, 226, 227, 232
Khoury, Philip, 76
Khrushchev, Nikita, 161, 172
Kissinger, Henry, 110
Kurds, 23, 88, 181, 168–69, 264

KUTV. *See* Communist University of the Toilers of the East
Kuwait, 114, 188, 268

Labor, 150, 156, 158
Lammens, Henri: *La Syrie: Precis historique*, 241–42
Land tenure, 7–8
Language, 33, 37, 71; and identity, 52, 53; and nation, 54–55, 62; polyglot, 231–32
Laroui, Abdallah: *The Crisis of the Arab Intellectual*, 14–15
League for National Liberation (LNL), 158, 161
League of National Action, 40, 42
Lebanese, 115, 223. *See also* Christians; Maronites
Lebanese Awakening, 223
Lebanese People's party, 151
Lebanese War, 110
Lebanon, 23, 37, 40, 44, 50, 90, 130, 166, 201, 245, 270, 274; Communist party in, 148, 151–52, 156–57, 159, 168; Europe and, 91, 230; French mandate in, 39, 224–25; Islamic movements in, 114–16, 133–36, 137, 138, 142, 143; nationalism in, 34, 219–39, 264; and Syria, 241, 248; Syrian Social Nationalist Party in, 244, 246, 247
Lebanon, Mount, 33, 148, 220, 221, 223–24, 234
Leftist Studies on the Palestinian Issue (Azm), 198
Legal system, 9; in Islamic state, 132–33; reform of, 95, 103, 105
Legitimacy: political, 29, 88, 104–5, 144, 181, 262–64, 272
Lenin, V. I., 20, 179, 189
Liberalism, 208–9; and Egyptian nationalism, 214–15, 218–19; political, 27, 140, 148, 196, 239, 266
Liberty, 66–68
Libya, 89
Literature, 33, 36, 97
LNL. *See* League for National Liberation
Lock, John, 208
Lower class, 32, 109, 111, 139, 180, 191–92, 198
Lutfi al-Sayyid, Ahmad, 94, 96, 202, 206; Egyptian nationalism of, 207–13

Maʾal-qawmiyyah al-ʿArabiyyah (Darwazah and Jabburi), 47
Maʿanids, 220

Mad-hiyyah, 251–52
Madoyan, Artin, 151
Madrasah al-Wataniyyah, al-, 33
Maghrib, 88
Mahayri, ʿIsam al-, 247
Mahmud, Muhammad, 206
Maliki, ʿAdnan, 246
Mamelukes, 202
Maʿna an-Nakbah (Zurayq), 47
Manar, al- (journal), 35, 96
Maoism, 48
Mao Tse Tung, 189
Maronites, 110, 133, 137, 143, 168, 220, 223, 224, 235–36, 255; national identity and, 233–34; nationalism of, 225–26; power of, 221–22
Marx, Karl, 11, 21, 189; on ideology, 1, 2–3, 4, 21–22
Marxism, 28, 48, 72, 80, 89, 112, 155, 181, 264, 268, 269; Aflaq's views on, 68–69, 87; class identity and, 177–78, 180; minorities and, 180, 182–83; and nationalism, 171–72, 173; slogans of, 178–79
Marxism-Leninism, 82, 86, 169, 194
Maudoodi, Abu Aʿla al-, 106, 115, 117; *Jihad in Islam, Islam and Jahiliyya*, 125–26; *The Principles of Islamic Government*, 125–26
MDLN. *See* Mouvement Democratique de Liberation Nationale
Meaning of Catastrophe, The (Zurayq), 47
Mediterranean, 228–29
Melchites, 234, 240, 241
MELN. *See* Mouvement Egyptien de Liberation Nationale
Meritocracy, 212–13
Middle class, 2, 22, 24, 44, 225; Arab nationalism and, 41, 46, 77, 78–81, 83; Communism and, 180, 182; Egyptian nationalism and, 216–17; ideology of, 29, 274–75; Islamic movements and, 23, 108, 139–42, 143; Lebanese, 220, 236; politics of, 200–201, 267–68, 272–73; in Syria, 111, 255
Milestones on the Road (Qutb), 125
Military, 7, 42, 164; defeats, 9–10; in Egypt, 45, 204
Military Academy (Syria), 110
Military rule, 38
Militia, 116, 164
Mill, J. S., 208
Minorities, 23–24, 77, 180–83, 198–99
Misr al-Fatat, 245
Misr Bank group, 45, 167

197–98. *See also* Islamic Revolution
Revolutionary Command Council
  (RCC), 102
Rida, Rashid, 35–36, 40, 45, 91, 94, 96,
  126, 152; influence of, 98, 117
Riots, 101–2
Riyashi, Iskandar, 151
Rosenthal, Joseph, 150
Rural sector, 109, 142, 180
Russia, 32–33, 241. *See also* Soviet
  Union
Russo-Turkish war, 91

Sa‘adeh, Antun, 13, 42, 55, 61, 87,
  239, 245; philosophy of, 250–52,
  255, 258; and Syrian Social National-
  ist Party, 243–44, 247–48, 249–50
Sa‘d al-Din, ‘Adnan, 109, 110
Sadat, Anwar, 90, 200; and Islamic
  movement, 105–6, 107; and Society
  of Muslim Brothers, 101
Sa‘dists, 101
Sadr, Muhammad Baqir al-, 112,
  113–14, 131–33
Sadr, Musa al-, 115–16, 131; ideology
  of, 133–36
Sahafi, al-Ta'ih, al- (journal), 151
SAIRI. *See* Supreme Assembly of the Is-
  lamic Revolution in Iraq
Salafiyyah movement, 96
Salih, Abd al-Qadir, 163
Samné, George, 223, 226, 241
Saudi Arabia, 89–90, 105, 109, 130,
  274
Sayigh, Dawud al-, 165
Schools, 33, 34, 37. *See also* Education
Secret Branch, 100, 103
Secularism, secularization, 4, 7, 9, 114,
  140, 272; and Arab nationalism, 32,
  36, 41, 82, 86, 123, 257; in Egypt,
  96, 103, 128–29; impacts of, 10–15,
  143, 144; opposition to, 131–32; in
  Syria, 111, 252, 256
Self-Criticism after the Defeat (Azm), 196
Sha‘ban, Sa‘id, 115
Shadow of the Qur'an, In the (Qutb), 125
Shamali, Fuad al-, 152
Sha‘rawi, Ali, 206
Shari‘a courts, 103, 105, 107, 132–33
Shawi, Nikola, 152
Shidyaq, Faris al-, 33
Shihab emirate, 220
Shi‘ites, Shi‘a, 23, 44, 77, 91; in Iraq,
  112, 113–14, 142; Islamic activism
  of, 130–36, 142, 143, 146; in
  Lebanon, 115–16, 224, 234, 235
Shils, Edward, 4, 11–12, 20

Shishakli, 108, 160
Shumayyil, Shibli, 148
Siba‘i, Mustafa al-, 108
Sidon, 115
Siriyya, Salih, 106, 107
Six Day War (1967), 6, 28, 49, 104,
  187, 196, 199, 261
Social class. *See* Class; *various divisions*
Socialism, 22, 27, 68, 82, 109, 148,
  149, 151, 162, 171; Arab, 69–70, 81,
  86, 188, 196, 268; and Ba‘th party,
  186–87; under Nasir, 46, 48, 167
Socialist Decreees, 186
Social justice, 148
Society, 13, 73; and individuals, 15–16;
  Islam in, 118, 127–28, 137–38;
  youth in, 24–25
Society for Islamic Culture, 99
Society for Ottoman-Arab Brother-
  hood, 37
Society of Excommunication and Holy
  Flight. *See* Society of Muslims
Society of Liberals, The, 152
Society of Muslim Brothers, 22, 79,
  101, 104, 118, 125, 159; activism of,
  139–41; economy and, 121–22; establishment of, 98–99; mission of,
  119–20, 123, 124; persecution of,
  99–100; politics and, 102–3; radical-
  ism in, 105–7; in Syria, 108–11
Society of Muslims. *See Jama‘at
  al-Takfir wa al-Hijra*
Solh, Riad al-, 226
South America, 223
Soviet Union, 166, 194, 268; alliance
  with, 175–76; and Arab nationalism,
  161, 164, 182; and Nasir, 45, 46; and
  national bourgeoisie, 172–73; sup-
  port by, 159, 160, 165, 168; in World
  War II, 154–55, 157
SSNP. *See* Syrian Social Nationalist
  party
Stalin, Joseph, 153, 161, 172–73
State, 10, 12, 58, 88, 121; building of,
  86–87; Islamic, 132–33; vs. nation,
  51–52
Strain Theory, 16–17, 72
Strikes, 150, 156
*Struggle Between Islam and Capitalism,
  The* (Qutb), 125
Sudan, 90, 146, 160
Suez Canal, 32, 45, 46, 161
Suez Canal Zone, 98–99, 101, 103
Suez War, 261
Sufism, 95, 118, 120
Sulayman, Sa‘d, 160
Sunnis, 23, 44, 82, 86, 114, 137, 185;

Sunnis (*continued*)
Islamic activism of, 116–30, 143; in Lebanon, 115, 133, 143, 224, 226, 234; in politics, 180, 181; in Syria, 110, 111, 142, 146, 255, 264
Supreme Assembly of the Islamic Revolution in Iraq (SAIRI), 113
Sykes-Picot agreement, 39, 224
Syria, 5, 23, 61, 82, 89, 104, 146, 166, 194, 201, 261, 262, 263, 268, 272, 274; Arab nationalism in, 33, 34, 37–41, 47, 58, 182; Baʿth in, 23, 44, 137; Communist party in, 148, 151–52, 156–57, 159, 160–61, 162, 163, 165, 167–68, 172, 173, 187; and Egypt, 6, 32, 43, 85, 163; French mandate in, 39, 224; Husri in, 50, 58; Islamic movements in, 138–39, 142; Muslim Brotherhood in, 108–11; nationalism in, 123, 239–50, 264; upper class in, 72–76
Syrian Communist party. *See* Communist Party of Syria
Syrian-Iraqi unity plan, 47
Syrian Islamic Front, The, 111
Syrian Muslim Brotherhood, 160; actions of, 108–11
Syrian Orthodox church, 32–33
Syrian-Palestinian Congress, 40
Syrian Social Nationalist party (SSNP), 13, 23, 42, 55, 61, 87, 157, 232; and Baʿth, 246–47; formation of, 239, 243–44; ideology of, 247–59; success of, 244–45
Syrie: Precis historique, La (Lammens), 241–42

Tabataba'i, Muhsin al-Hakim al-, 112
Tahtawi, Rifaʿah Rafi ʿal-, 31–32, 90, 203
Taif Agreement, 237
Tajhiz Dimashq school, 42
Takfir. See Jamaʿat al-Takfir wa al-Hijra
Takla, Philippe, 227
Takla, Salim, 227
Talmasani, Umar, 108
Tanzimat period, 32
Tawhid, al-, 115, 129
Taymiyya, Ibn, 96, 117, 129; "Fatwa on the Nusayris [Alawis]," 111
Technical Military Academy, 107
Tibi, Bassam, 59
Trade, 6–7
Tripoli, 143
Tuma, Emil, 158
Tunis, 91
Tunisi, Khayr al-Din al-, 90
Tunisia, 10, 89

Turkey, 41, 91, 172, 223, 262
Turkification, 36, 37, 75
Turkism, 38
Turkomen, 164
Turks, 36, 41, 75
Twelver Shiʿites. *See* Shiʿites, Shiʿa

UAR. *See* United Arab Republic
Ulama, 38, 75, 118, 132, 203
Umayyads, 130, 131, 229
Umm al-Qura (Kawakibi), 36
Unions, 150, 252
United Arab Republic (UAR), 43, 44, 46, 47, 84, 164, 165, 175, 194, 199
United Nations, 159
United States, 32, 33, 39, 191, 197, 223
Units of the Lebanese Resistance (Amal), 116, 136, 201
Unity, 85, 204, 230; Arab, 65–66, 73, 88, 168, 175–76, 194
Upper class, 22, 24, 148, 180, 267; Arab nationalism and, 38, 40–41, 72–76; Egyptian nationalism and, 213, 215–16; ideology of, 29, 82; Islamic movements and, 139, 142, 143; in Syria, 109–10, 111, 255
ʿUqla, ʿAdnan, 109
ʿUrabi Pasha, Ahmad, 204
ʿUrabi Revolt, 206
Urban sector, 10, 23, 25, 44, 109, 180; Islamic movements and, 139–42, 143
ʿUsbat al-ʿAmal al-Qawmi, 40, 42
ʿUsbat al-Tahrir al-Watani, 158, 161

Vasili, Pyotr, 152
Vichy France, 155
Vietnam, 90, 197

Wafd, al-, 45, 101, 150–51, 206–7
Wahhabi movement, 117
Wandering Journalist, The (journal), 151
War, 264, 274; guerrilla, 193, 194; in Lebanon, 233, 247; liberation through, 189–90, 197–98. *See also by name*
War of Attrition, 105
Watan, al- (newspaper), 203–4
Waʿy al-Qawmi, al- (Zurayq), 47
Welfare, 9, 122, 171
West, 118–19, 145. *See also* Europe; *various countries*
West Bank, 161, 163
Westernization, 140, 144, 272
Working class, 180, 191–92, 195
World War I, 2, 8, 38, 73, 76, 206, 223–24

World War II, 5, 40, 245; Communist parties and, 156–57; in Egypt, 99–100, 156; Soviet Union and, 154–55

Yakan, Fathi, 115
Yazbeck, Yusuf Ibrahim, 151, 157
Yazid, 131
Yaziji, Ibrahim al-, 34
Yaziji, Nasif, al-, 33, 34
Yemen, 48–49, 104, 188, 199, 263
Young Egypt, 245
Young Turks, 37, 50
Youth, 76, 140, 196, 256; and Aflaq, 63–65; ideology of, 181–82; and

social system, 24–25, 84; worldview of, 27–28
Youth of Vengeance, 189
Yuhanna, Mikhail, 113
Yusuf, Yusuf Salman ("Fahd"), 152–53

Zaghlul, Sa'd, 150, 172, 206, 207
Zionism, Zionists, 5, 8, 45, 78, 111, 151
Zurayq, Constantine, 46–47, 49, 193, 196; *Meaning of Catastrophe, The*, 47; *National Awakening*, 47

 *Contemporary Issues in the Middle East*

This well-established series continues to focus primarily on twentieth-century developments that have current impact and significance throughout the entire region, from North Africa to the borders of Central Asia.

Recent titles in the series include:

Arab Women in the Field: Studying Your Own Society. Soraya Altorki and Camillia Fawzi El-Solh, eds.

The Communist Movement in Egypt, 1920–1988. Tareq Y. Ismael and Rifa'at El Sa'id

The Crystallization of the Arab State System, 1945–1954. Bruce Maddy-Weitzman

Egypt's Other Wars: Epidemics and the Politics of Public Health. Nancy Elizabeth Gallagher

Extremist Shiites: The Ghulat Sects. Matti Moosa

Family in Contemporary Egypt. Andrea B. Rugh

International Relations of the Contemporary Middle East: A Study in World Politics. Tareq Y. Ismael

The Iranian Revolution and the Islamic Republic. Nikki R. Keddie and Eric Hoogland, eds.

Iraq and Iran: Roots of Conflict. Tareq Y. Ismael

Islam and Politics. Third ed. John L. Esposito

Khul-Khaal: Five Egyptian Women Tell Their Stories. Nayra Atiya

Law of Desire: Temporary Marriage in Shi'i Iran. Shahla Haeri

The Middle East from the Iran-Contra Affair to the Intifada. Robert O. Freedman, ed.

Muslim Hausa Women in Nigeria: Tradition and Change. Barbara J. Callaway

Naguib Mahfouz: From Regional Fame to Global Recognition. Michael Beard and Adnan Haydar, eds.

Oil, Power, and Principle: Iran's Oil Nationalization and Its Aftermath. Mostafa Elm

The Politics of Social Transformation in Afghanistan, Iran, and Pakistan. Myron Weiner and Ali Banuazizi, eds.

Reveal and Conceal: Dress in Contemporary Egypt. Andrea B. Rugh

The Rise of Egyptian Communism, 1939–1970. Selma Botman

The Roots of Separatism in Palestine: British Economic Policy, 1920–1929. Barbara J. Smith

The Rushdie File. Lisa Appignanesi and Sara Maitland, eds.

Speaking Stones: Communiqués from the Intifada Underground. Shaul Mishal and Reuben Aharoni

Toward an Islamic Reformation: Civil Liberties, Human Rights, and International Law. Abdullahi Ahmed An-Na'im

Veils and Words: The Emerging Voices of Iranian Women Writers. Farzaneh Milani

Women Farmers in Africa: Rural Development in Mali and the Sahel. Lucy E. Creevey, ed.

Women in Egyptian Public Life. Earl L. Sullivan

Women in Muslim Family Law. John L. Esposito

Bitter Legacy was composed in 9.5/14 Stone Serif in Quark XPress on a Macintosh by Books International, Norcross, Georgia; printed by sheet-fed offset on 60-pound, acid-free Glatfelter Natural Smooth, and Smyth-sewn and bound over binder's boards in Arrestox B-grade cloth with dust jackets printed in 2 colors and film laminated by Braun-Brumfield, Ann Arbor, Michigan; designed by Kachergis Book Design, Pittsboro, North Carolina; and published by Syracuse University Press, Syracuse, New York 12344-5160.